GAYLORD MG

IT'S OUTTA HERE!

IT'S OUTTA HERE!

The History of the Home Run
from Babe Ruth to Barry Bonds

BILL GUTMAN

TAYLOR TRADE PUBLISHING
Dallas • Lanham • Boulder • New York • Toronto • Oxford

To my longtime good friends

Jan and Tony Pickett

Published by Taylor Trade Publishing
An imprint of The Rowman & Littlefield Publishing Group, Inc.
4501 Forbes Boulevard, Suite 200, Lanham, Maryland 20706

Distributed by NATIONAL BOOK NETWORK

Library of Congress Cataloging-in-Publication Data Available

1-58979-206-8 (cloth : alk. paper)

♾ ™ The paper used in this publication meets the minimum requirements of
American National Standard for Information Sciences—Permanence of Paper for
Printed Library Materials, ANSI/NISO Z39.48-1992.

Manufactured in the United States of America.

Contents

Introduction

It was the third inning of a game between the New York Yankees and Boston Red Sox. Only it didn't take place in 2003 or 2004 when this age-old rivalry had become arguably the most intense in all of sports. This game took place on May 6, 1915, when the struggling Yankees were still sharing the Polo Grounds with the National League New York Giants and the Boston Red Sox were one of the best teams in the American League. The Bosox had won the World Series in 1912 led by their great centerfielder, Tris Speaker, and pitcher, Smokey Joe Wood. In 1914, they had finished second to Philadelphia and now were dead set on reclaiming the top spot.

The Sox still had standouts Speaker and Wood, and other fine players such as pitchers Ernie Shore and Dutch Leonard. Pitching, in fact, was the strong point of the team that year and soon after the season began they felt they had found another star in a twenty-year-old lanky lefthander named George Herman Ruth. Ruth had appeared briefly at the tail end of the 1914 season, winning two of three decisions. Now he was in the rotation and was the Red Sox starter against the Yankees that sixth day in May so many years ago.

In a time long before the advent of the designated hitter in the American League, pitchers had to swing the bat and the young Ruth soon showed he was no shrinking violet at the plate. In the third inning he came to bat for only the eighteenth time in his brief major league career, facing Yankee righthander Jack Warhop. Standing tall in the batter's box, the southpaw swinging Ruth went after the first pitch. At the crack of the bat, the 8,000 or so fans in attendance quickly shifted their eyes out toward the rightfield grandstand and watched the ball sail into the second tier for a home run. It was the first home run of

Ruth's young career and, while he played for the enemy, some of the fans cheered and he trotted around the bases.

The only other notable thing about the game that day was that the Red Sox committed four errors and lost in the thirteenth inning. Typical of pitching back then, Ruth went the distance and was saddled with the defeat. After it ended, however, the sportswriters in attendance couldn't help notice how far the young pitcher had hit the ball. Witness the following account from the legendary Damon Runyan.

"Fanning this Ruth is not as easy as the name and occupation might indicate," Runyan wrote. "In the third inning, Ruth knocked the slant out of one of Jack Warhop's underhanded subterfuges, and put the baseball in the right field stands for a home run. Ruth was discovered by Jack Dunn in a Baltimore school a year ago where he had not attained his left-handed majority, and was adopted and adapted by Jack for use of the Orioles. He is now quite a demon pitcher and demon hitter when he connects."

Runyan, one of the great writers of his day, obviously was beginning to recognize Ruth's talents. Others noted that the homer was just Ruth's fifth hit in eighteen big league at bats, a modest .278 batting average. But pitchers were not supposed to be great hitters, even back then, and more people were interested in the youngster's strong left arm. And, of course, in those days nobody hit a lot of home runs. However, what no one could possibly have realized then was that Ruth's singular blast was like the planting of a first seed. It was the beginning of a great career that would see the player already known as *Babe* join the New York Yankees just five years later, be converted from a pitcher to an outfielder, and proceed not only to break every home run record in existence, but also to herald in a new era in the game, one that has continued right up to the present day.

Thanks to the Babe, and the sluggers who followed, the home run has become the singularly most dramatic, anticipated, and revered moment in the sport. Landmark home runs are remembered with a special kind of awe, relived over and over again. Ruth's 60th, Maris's 61st, McGwire's 70th, Bond's 73rd, Aaron's 715th, Thomson's Shot-Heard-Round-the-World, Mazeroski's World Series Walk-off, Gabby Hartnett's Homer-in-the-Gloamin', Gibson's *I-can't-believe-what-I-just-saw* pinch homer in the World Series, George Brett's *Pine Tar* homer, the Babe calling his shot, and Reggie's three homers on three swings off three different pitchers in the World Series. These are just some of the epic home runs that will live on in memory and eventually in legend. Every big-moment home run is special and has earned an almost sacred place in baseball folklore. A dramatic home run is remembered more than a no-hitter or perfect game, or even a twenty-strikeout performance. It's remembered more than a steal of home, a bases-clearing triple, and any of a number of ultra-exciting baseball plays. The home run remains king—unmatched and unequaled—as baseball's ultimate magic moment.

Many years ago the inimitable Casey Stengel, in speaking about his power-laden New York Yankees, said, "Home run hitters drive Cadillacs!" Back in the 1950s, the Cadillac was the luxury car of choice and, in his own way, Ol'Case knew what he was talking about. Ever since Babe Ruth began belting the ball out of major league parks at a previously unheard of pace, home run hitters have attracted the lion's share of attention and made the most headlines. Moreso, the home run has played a major role in the evolution of baseball since the 1920s. It has led to rule changes and changes in the style of the game. It has altered the makeup of ballparks, brought about the development of new kinds of equipment, and has seen players and teams sometimes go to extreme ends in an attempt to generate more home runs.

It's Outta Here! The History of the Home Run from Babe Ruth to Barry Bonds will examine the entire history of the home run and how it has affected the game of baseball since the beginning and right into the twenty-first century. Starting with the so-called dead ball era when the game was played in a very different way, through the advent of the Babe and the sluggers who followed, making baseball a station-to-station game, then right into the 1960s when speed returned but the home run didn't go away. Finally, it will look at the modern big-money game as contemporary sluggers rewrite the record books under sometimes suspicious circumstances. Though it all, it has been the home run that has symbolized what is both right and wrong with the game.

Not surprisingly, home runs have not been without controversy. When the Babe began belting them in the 1920s, the label of the game changed. The dead ball era became the era of the lively ball. Did the men who ran baseball so long ago make a conscious decision to change the baseball so more and more players could begin following the lead of Ruth and hit the ball a country mile? At the same time, some of the mammoth dimensions of the early ballparks began to shrink. Fences were moved closer to home plate.

Questions about the makeup of the baseball itself would continue, surfacing periodically right to the turn of the twenty-first century. Some say the ball has changed; baseball denies it, but there's no question that the home run has served a purpose in the game and those who oversee the sport always want to create situations where the seats are filled. If the home run and the sluggers who hit them will fill seats, why not make it just a bit easier for them to do their thing? In fact, why not make it easier for everyone to hit home runs?

Even today, when more players than ever are hitting the ball over the fence, there is talk about the ball being juiced. The new, fan-friendly ballparks are definitely smaller and more conducive to home runs. And, finally, in the late 1990s something new entered the equation: the specter that some players were using performance-enhancing drugs such as anabolic steroids to enable them to hit the baseball harder and farther. Once more, baseball had to defend itself against accusations involving the home run. Were the lords of the game turning the other cheek to what is widely perceived of as cheating, allowing the use of potentially dangerous drugs, making it possible for more players to hit more home runs?

All of these factors make the home run so intriguing. More

than fifty years after his death, Babe Ruth remains a larger-than-life figure. People still argue about whether the Babe was a better home run hitter than modern players such as McGwire and now Barry Bonds, who set a new record of 73 in 2001 and threatens not only to surpass the Babe's 714 home runs early in the 2005 season, but also to surpass the all-time mark of 755 set by Hall of Famer Henry Aaron. Because Bonds has hit so many of his home runs late in his career, after the age of thirty-five, some openly question whether he has had the help of illegal substances.

It's Outta Here! will examine all of these elements that have surrounded the home run from the beginning, when young Babe Ruth strode to the plate on that May afternoon in 1915 and slammed the first home run of his great career. The fans cheered for him that day, and they still cheer now whenever one of their favorites hits one high and deep, and into the distant stands. The home run remains king.

1

What's a Home Run? The Dead Ball Era

It's ironic, but the very thing that baseball has denied for nearly 100 years is the tag name of an entire era in the game. The so-called dead ball era comprised the first two decades of the twentieth century, from the time the American League joined with the National League to form what is still the basis for Major League baseball. The game was very different then, though the great players of the time became legends, men like Ty Cobb, Tris Speaker, Napoleon Lajoie, Honus Wagner, Shoeless Joe Jackson, Walter Johnson, Cy Young, Christy Mathewson, and Grover Cleveland Alexander. The great pitchers were winning more than thirty games a year on a regular basis and the best hitters were topping the .400 mark and hitting in the upper reaches of the .300 territory on a regular basis. One thing, however, was conspicuously missing . . . a ton of home runs.

There were a number of good reasons why the home run wasn't an integral part of the early game. In those days they played what is known today as *small ball*. Base hit, stolen base or sacrifice bunt, hit-and-run, squeeze play—anything to get that runner around base by base. Sure, there were doubles and triples, but the game wasn't about big innings. It was more about getting a run or two and letting the pitchers do the rest. In the first twenty years of the past century, the pitchers had a huge advantage. No wonder the good ones wanted to take the mound as often as they could.

For openers, the pitchers were allowed to throw what today are illegal pitches. The spitball was the main offering of a number of top hurlers, and they didn't have to make a secret about throwing it. That wasn't all. Hurlers were also allowed to scuff, cut, discolor, or deface the ball in others ways and no one complained. A scuffed or cut ball moves in ways that a clean, smooth ball will not. That's an aerodynamic fact. In addition, the baseball wasn't thrown out of play as soon as it had a small mark on it. On the contrary, it was left in the game after it was hit, battered, scuffed, or discolored by tobacco and licorice juice. Players would intentionally spit these discoloring substances in their mitts continually during games. Every time they touched the ball, it would be returned to the pitcher a little darker in color and in worse condition than before.

Not only did the ball soften up by being hit repeatedly during the course of a game, shortening the distance it could travel, but it was also more difficult to see. Some of the great hitters of modern times claim they can actually see the rotation of the ball as it approaches home plate, allowing them to identify the pitch early and giving them an advantage. Not so in the dead ball era. Hitters saw pretty much of a mess coming toward them in the form of a baseball. It was as easy to bunt at it, or just try to slap it through or over the infield, as anything else. Striking out wasn't a badge of honor then and virtually no one swung from the heels trying to drive the ball. A player taking three huge swings would undoubtedly be admonished by his manager and might even find himself taking a seat on the bench.

Perhaps the legendary John McGraw, who managed the New York Giants from 1902 to 1932, best epitomized the dead ball era. McGraw played what was often euphemistically called *scientific baseball*. In essence, his teams did everything they could to manufacture runs. Scientific baseball to McGraw also meant getting an edge, putting a runner on base, then advancing him, and preventing the opposition from doing the same thing. As a player in the last decade of the nineteenth century when only a single umpire worked a game, McGraw wouldn't hesitate to grab a baserunner's belt as he rounded third to slow him down or stop him from scoring. He would also instruct his players to sometimes lean over the plate in order to get hit by a pitch. To McGraw, every little trick was a positive, another way to try to win.

As a player, McGraw became especially adept at fouling off pitches while waiting for the right one he could hit fair. To make this point to his players, it's said that McGraw picked up a bat during spring training in 1930, when he was fifty-seven years old, told his pitcher to try to get him out, and then fouled off 26 consecutive pitches. McGraw loved to call the hit-and-run play and wanted players who had the kind of bat control that enabled them to place the ball for a hit. So enamored was McGraw with this type of baseball that it's said he hated the way the game began to evolve in the 1920s once the Babe began hitting homers. Told that the baseball had been made "livelier" in order for more home runs to be hit, McGraw snorted and said: "When you monkey with the ball, you monkey with the game. That's all right, of course, within reason. But you'd better make sure the ball is going to make the kind of game the fans want when you change it."

Those early strategies also played to the prevailing conditions as the ballparks of the day simply weren't conducive to home runs. The outfield fences must have sometimes looked as if they were on a distant planet, especially to hitters, most of whom didn't even think they could hit a ball that far. Some had distant fences that even a Mark McGwire or Barry Bonds would have had difficulty reaching. When Ebbets Field was opened in Brooklyn in 1913, the left-field corner was 419 feet from home plate with the centerfield fence 477 feet away. Shibe Park in Philadelphia opened in 1909 with a 515-foot deep centerfield. The old Polo Grounds had a centerfield clubhouse that was nearly 500 feet from home plate, while Crosley Field in Cincinnati, which opened in 1912, had dimensions of 360 feet down each line and some 420 feet to its center. It was nearly a decade—1921—before any National League player hit an over-the-fence home run at Crosley. Almost all the old parks that remained in existence past 1920 had dimensions that were eventually shortened over the years.

That still wasn't all. During those early years most players swung big, heavy bats with thick handles. These rather large pieces of lumber weren't conducive to generating great bat speed, one of the ingredients the modern slugger uses to hit the ball into the seats. Because of the size and weight of the bats, many players choked up and simply tried to hit the ball through a hole in the infield or crack a line drive into the outfield gaps. Because the outfields in many parks were so deep, any ball that got past the outfielders and continued to roll could set the stage for an inside-the-park home run. Perhaps the statistic that best defines the dead ball era came off the bat of the great Ty Cobb. In 1909, the Georgia Peach led the American League in home runs with nine. Cobb didn't hit a single one of them over a fence. All nine were inside-the-park, helped by Cobb's great speed and willingness to take chances on the basepaths.

The baseball did change in 1910 when a cork center was added for the first time, but that didn't alter the philosophy of pitching, players intentionally discoloring the ball, and keeping the same ball in play no matter how beat up it became in the course of the game. There are, however, a couple of interesting statistics to look at. From 1906 to 1909, the sixteen big league teams averaged 258.5 home runs a year. That's an average of just over 16 home runs per team. Of the 259 home runs hit in 1909, only 109 were hit in the American League. The Chicago White Sox, as a team, hit a grand total of four home runs that year. Four! A year later, with the cork ball, the total increased to 361, then to 514 the next year, but by 1917 the number was back down to 335.

This obviously was not the beginning of a home run barrage. In fact, in 1911 and 1912, big league teams stole more bases per team than ever before, averaging 212 steals in 1911 and 211 per team the following year. And by 1918, albeit a war year, there were only 235 home runs hit in the majors, with 96 being hit in the anemic American League. The next season, 1919, the number jumped back to 447, but that was still eight fewer than the 455 hit back in 1901. So no matter how you cut the pie, the home run wasn't really a big part of major league baseball during the first two decades of the twentieth century. The game was still small ball, and there were no indications that anything would change soon.

That didn't mean that no one hit home runs. In 1901, "Wahoo" Sam Crawford walloped 16 for the Cincinnati Reds to lead the majors. That same year, Nap Lajoie hit 14 to lead the American League in its very first year of existence. Crawford would sign with Detroit of the American League the next season and, while he became a Hall of Fame player, he never hit as many as 16 home runs again, though he wound up the career leader with 312 lifetime triples and won the A.L. homer crown in 1908 with just seven. Not a single National League player would hit as many as 16 home runs for a decade, until Frank "Wildfire" Schulte slammed 21 in 1911, setting a new big league record in the process. During the first decade of the century, the home run leaders in both leagues failed to reach 10 on nine occasions. The league leader with the fewest home runs ever was Tommy Leach of Pittsburgh, who led the National League with just six round trippers in 1902. Then, by the middle of the second decade of the century, two players came along who would actually be remembered for their home runs, the first time in the young game's history that even some slight attention was paid to the four-bagger.

John Franklin Baker played in the big leagues from 1908 to 1933, retiring with a .307 lifetime batting average and a grand total of 96 home runs. A 5'11", 173-pound lefthanded hitter, Baker hit just four homers as a rookie for the Philadelphia A's in 1909 and followed that with a mere two in 1910. But a year later he was said to have learned to pull the ball and jumped out of the pack to lead the league with 11 home runs. In the World Series that year, the A's went up against the New York Giants and, in the second game, Baker hit a game-winning two run homer into the short right field stands at the Polo Grounds off lefty Rube Marquard. A day later, Baker did it again, hitting a ninth-inning home run off the great Christy Mathewson to tie the game, 1-1, allowing the A's to win it in the eleventh. Two home runs in two days was such an unheard of feat in those days that Baker was forever after known as "Home Run" Baker.

Baker's 96 lifetime home runs represent a number today's top sluggers can sometimes surpass in two seasons, yet he was well respected in those early days as a guy you had to pitch to

Baseball's Early Bats

The bats used by most of the players in the first two decades of the game also made it extremely difficult to hit home runs. They were, for the most part, big and heavy with thick handles. "Home Run" Baker used a 52-ounce bat, huge by today's standards. Because of the thick handles, most players "choked up" on the bat, giving them better control for hitting the ball through holes and lining base hits to the outfield. They were so big that they were sometimes called *wagon tongues*, alluding to a long piece of wood used on horse-drawn wagons.

Using these bats, players couldn't generate what hitters today call bat speed. With small, lighter, thin-handled bats, today's top sluggers can take a mighty cut with the bat coming through the zone with tremendous speed. With the old bats, it took strength and timing to hit one out, especially with the way the baseballs were beat up and still kept in games. Babe Ruth used a heavy bat, usually 44 ounces, though he was known to change often and once used one that weighed 54 ounces, showing again that he was a home run hitter extraordinaire.

carefully because he could hit it out. And while his home run total didn't exactly soar, he hit just enough at the right time to earn his nickname. He won his four home run crowns with 9, 10, 11, and 12 dingers, numbers a punch-and-judy hitter can reach easily today. Besides his home runs, Baker was a fine all-around player who once drove in 130 runs in a season and had a lifetime batting average of .307, good enough to get him elected to the Hall of Fame. Baker lived to 1963, more than long enough to see the home run become a paramount part of baseball strategy. Once asked home many home runs he could have hit in a season had he played during the era of the lively ball, Baker answered without hesitation: "I'd say 50 anyway. The year I hit 12 I also hit the right-field fence at Shibe Park 38 times."

The National League's answer to Home Run Baker was a largely forgotten player named Clifford Carlton Cravath, who had a rather short, eleven-year career between 1908 and 1920, yet emerged for a very short time as baseball's all-time home run leader. The righthand hitting Cravath, who was usually called Gavvy but also referred to as *Cactus,* due to his sometimes abrasive personality, stood little over 5'10" tall and weighed 186 pounds. Though he entered the majors in 1908, he was up and down for a few seasons, not even appearing in a big league game in 1910 and 1911. He didn't become a regular until the Phillies obtained him in 1912 and then, a year later, he suddenly became baseball's most prolific home run hitter.

In 1913, Cravath led the majors with 19 home runs and 128 RBIs, while hitting .341. Ironically, it was Home Run Baker who led the American League that year, slamming 12 homers and driving home 126. Cravath's numbers, however, would even look pretty good in today's game. As a hitter, he knew how to go to the opposite field and often took advantage of the short right foul line at Philadelphia's old Baker Bowl, which was only 272 feet from home plate. His 19 homers were a new major league record, and he showed it wasn't a fluke by leading the league with another 19 the following season, a year in which Baker led the American League with just nine.

Then in 1915, the same year that Boston's young lefthanded pitcher, Babe Ruth, hit his first big league home run, Gavvy Cravath amazed the baseball world of the day by slamming 24 home runs. That was 11 more than his nearest rival in the N.L., the Cubs Cy Williams, who had 13. The American League leader was a player named Braggo Roth, who was traded from Chicago to Cleveland during the season, and who wound up with a grand total of seven home runs. What made Cravath's achievement even more amazing was that he hit more home runs than four National League teams hit combined, while two other clubs tied him with 24. In the American League, Cravath's 24 round trippers were more home runs than six of the eight teams could manage. It was quite a dominating performance and, in effect, really made this largely unknown figure baseball's first home run slugger.

Cravath's last three home run titles would come from 1917 to 1919, though he would only hit 12, 8, and then 12 in those three seasons. When he retired after the 1920 season, ending his career at the same time the dead ball era ended, he had 119 home runs, making him baseball's all-time leader in a category that still didn't mean much to the purists of the time. After all, the game's greatest players to that time—Cobb, Wagner, and Speaker—weren't paid to hit home runs. It just wasn't that kind of game. But the prevailing attitude would soon begin to change and, for a number of reasons, a confluence of events would all come together at the same time during two very pivotal seasons for the game, and for the home run. They were the seasons of 1919 and 1920.

THE BLACK SOX

The dead ball era might have had its end hastened by one of the best teams of that time, the 1919 Chicago White Sox. The Sox had won 100 games and an American League pennant in 1917, then defeated the New York Giants in six games to take the World Series. The club slumped the next year when their star, "Shoeless" Joe Jackson, was limited to sixty-five games because he decided to leave the team for draft-exempt employment at the Bethlehem Steel shipyards near Wilmington, Delaware. With World War I raging, Jackson had been classified 1-A but opted to work in the steelyards. In 1919, the war over, the White Sox were all the way back, winning another A.L. pennant and immediately installed as heavy favorites to defeat the Cincinnati Reds in the upcoming World Series.

Despite their success and a handful of real stars, such as Jackson, pitchers Eddie Cicotte and Claude "Lefty" Williams, second sacker Eddie Collins, outfielder "Happy" Felsch, and third baseman Buck Weaver, the Sox were an unhappy lot. The reason was simple. The team's owner, Charles Comiskey, was a known tightwad who paid his players far less than the going rate on other teams. Jackson, for instance, a player with the stature of a Ty Cobb or Tris Speaker, was making just $6,000 a year during the 1919 season. Other players also felt they were being stiffed, as Comiskey not only paid anemic salaries but also gave them less for meal money than the other ballclubs.

Back in 1919, gambling on sports was a heavy-duty proposition, with organized crime heavily involved. Yet very few people felt that Cincinnati, despite winning ninety-six games in the regular season, had much of a chance against the Sox. When the Reds shelled Cicotte and won the first game, 9-1, then took the second by beating Lefty Williams, 4-2, the whispers began. Something just didn't look right. The White Sox were playing sloppy baseball. Chicago won the third game, 3-0, behind young Dickie Kerr, but when they were shut out in both the fourth and fifth, 2-0 and 5-0, making five errors in the process, more suspicions were raised. People began wondering if this World Series was on the up-and-up.

It wasn't over yet because baseball was in the first of a three-year experiment to see if the series would work better in a best-of-nine format. Kerr and the Sox bounced back to win game six in 10-innings, 5-4, and then Cicotte went the distance to win the seventh game. But just when it looked as if the Sox were back on track, Lefty Williams was shelled for four runs in a third of an inning and the Reds went on to win, 10-5, clinching the championship in eight games, 5-3.

After the series ended, the whispers and suspicions continued. Had some members of the White Sox taken bribes from gamblers and intentionally "thrown" the series? Baseball's "best" team had made twelve errors in eight games and its two top pitchers, Cicotte and Williams, did not pitch well with the exception of game seven, which Cicotte won. When the 1920 season began, many fans began to openly question the integrity of the game. To restore respectability, the owners appointed baseball's first commissioner, Judge Kenesaw Mountain Landis, who was given a lifetime contract and complete autonomy to rule the sport. Landis immediately began to investigate the allegations that the fix was in during the previous World Series.

In 1920, the White Sox were engaged in a dogfight with the Cleveland Indians and New York Yankees for the American League pennant. At the height of the race, word came down that eight members of the White Sox were being indicted for their role in a conspiracy with known gamblers to fix the series.

The eight were Joe Jackson, Buck Weaver, Happy Felsch, Chick Gandil, Swede Risberg, Eddie Cicotte, Lefty Williams, and Fred McMullen. The Sox finished the season with a 96-58 record, two games behind Cleveland and one ahead of the Yankees. Jackson hit .382 with 12 homers and 121 RBIs, while Felsch batted .338 with 14 homers and 115 ribbys. The team also had four, twenty-game winners—Red Faber, Cicotte, Williams, and Kerr. They were still a great ballclub, but it was all about to come crashing down.

Though the players actually went to trial and were acquitted—some say by a jury of White Sox fans—Judge Landis felt he had to make an example, especially since it now had been revealed that there indeed was a conspiracy. Chicago gamblers were alleged to have hatched the plot with the major backing coming from the notorious New York gambler and underworld figure, Arnold Rothstein. Only a few of the players actually got any money and, when promises were not kept, they might have tried to turn it around. But it was too late. Landis then banned the eight players from baseball for life. Joe Jackson, who some say received $5,000, still hit .375 in the series, best on both teams. Buck Weaver never agreed to participate but was banned because he knew of the plot and didn't report it. As part of the punishment, none of the eight players has ever been eligible for the Hall of Fame, though many people feel that after all these years Joe Jackson should be elected.

This incident soon became known as the Black Sox Scandal and it certainly played a role in the dead ball era coming to an end. Both the White Sox and Reds teams of 1919 were typical of those of the times. The Sox led the American League with a .287 team batting average, but they hit just twenty-five home runs. The Reds had a .263 team batting mark, hitting only twenty home runs along the way. Nothing had changed very much on the field since the early days of the century, but because a number of White Sox players had conspired to throw the World Series, fans would begin to look at every error, every bad play, and every poor pitching performance and wonder if a player (or players) was trying to dump a game. Despite the fact that baseball was still inhabited by many great stars, the men who ran the sport wondered if some kind of tonic was needed after this terrible gambling scandal that rocked the foundation of the game.

A NEW HOME RUN KING

Though the Black Sox Scandal took over the baseball headlines following the 1919 World Series, there was yet another story in 1919 that foreshadowed what was to come in the very near future. George Herman Ruth, the young lefthanded pitcher of the Boston Red Sox, was suddenly making news of another kind. Ruth, already called *Babe* by some, had proved himself something more than a fine pitching prospect. In fact, he was well on his way to becoming one of the best pitchers in the game. Ruth was 18-8 his rookie year of 1915, the year he hit his first home run. He followed that with seasons of 23-12 and 24-13. In 1916, he also had the league's best earned run average, a microscopic 1.75, and led the American League with nine shutouts.

But the Red Sox saw something else in the Babe. He was also developing into an outstanding hitter, and the team was soon getting him more at bats than the average pitcher. They began using him as a pinch hitter and, in 1918, with the team fighting for another pennant, started playing the young Babe in the outfield when he wasn't on the mound, even skipping some of his scheduled starts to keep his bat in the lineup. He wound up the season with a 13-7 record, making only twenty starts as opposed to forty-one the year before. The reason was simple. He played fifty-nine games in the outfield and another thirteen at first base, winding up with a .300 average in 317 at bats. Even more surprisingly, perhaps, was the fact that Babe Ruth hit 11 home runs. He not only tied a player named Tilly Walker for the league lead, but the number represented a major league best. Gavvy Cravath led the National League with just eight.

That wasn't all. The 235 home runs hit in the majors in 1918 were the fewest ever, since records for the two leagues began in 1901. It was a drop of 100 homers from the season before, so the dead ball era was actually alive and well with no sign that anything would change in the immediate future. Pitchers continued to dominate and teams kept scratching for runs, using the stolen base and hit-and-run plays as batters still followed the old 'Wee Willie Keeler axiom to *hit 'em where they ain't*. After the season ended, the Boston Red Sox made a decision that would eventually lead up to the biggest strategic change since the game began.

It was Red Sox centerfielder Harry Hooper who had originally suggested that Ruth be allowed to play more in the outfield in 1918. The Sox liked his bat so much that they decided to sacrifice his pitching prowess for even more time in the outfield when the 1919 season began. So this multitalented player, who was being called the best lefthander in the American League between 1915 and 1917, was suddenly a part-time pitcher who would start just seventeen games in the 1919 season. He was still good enough to compile a 9-5 record, but that wasn't what everyone was talking about. That was because this twenty-four-year-old lefthanded batter was doing something that no one in the game had done before him—hitting a lot of home runs. The Babe played 111 games in the outfield that season and another four at first base. The result was a new home run mark as he topped Cravath's best of 24 by slamming 29 four-baggers!

Not only did the Babe lead the league in homers, he hit more as an individual than ten other teams and also led the majors with 114 runs batted in while compiling a .322 batting average. By contrast, the National League leader in RBIs had just 73 that year. Despite Ruth's sudden power burst, there were no light bulbs going off giving people the idea that the home run could be something special. In fact, some thought it was an aberration, that maybe this big, strong, pitcher-outfielder had a career year and wouldn't duplicate that kind of season again. The White Sox, after all, appeared to be baseball's best team and didn't hit a lot of home runs. But this was the same year the Sox would lose the World Series to the Reds, raising all kinds of eyebrows and leading up to the playing out of the Black Sox Scandal after the following season. In fact, the 1920 season would prove a pivotal one—for baseball, the Babe, the home run, and the future of the game.

2

The Babe and the Home Run Change Baseball, 1920–1927

Prior to the 1920 season, there was still little indication that the game would really change or that the home run would rise from rarity to revelation. Before the season started, there was still no evidence about players taking money to throw the 1919 World Series, only suspicions. Baseballs were left in play despite being discolored by tobacco and licorice, scuffed, cut, and slammed repeatedly by the hitters. Almost all the idiosyncrasies of the dead ball era were still in place. But there was one major rule change. Before the season, baseball decided to outlaw trick pitches such as a spitball. It was determined that seventeen pitchers, who basically made their living by using the spitball and were considered spitball pitchers, would still be allowed to throw it for the remainders of their careers. Burleigh Grimes was the last of the legal spitball pitchers, retiring after the 1934 season. Besides those seventeen designated spitball pitchers, however, others could no longer throw the wet ones. Of course, there are still pitchers today who try to get away with illegal pitches, but as of 1920, they would no longer be an accepted part of the game.

There were two additional rule changes, as well, both of which would eventually help home run hitters to a degree, but they wouldn't really alter the style of the game. As of 1920, if a player hit a home run in the bottom of the ninth or bottom of an extra inning with the winning run on base, all the runners, including the batter, would be allowed to score. The batter would now be credited with a home run. Before that, only the winning run was allowed to score and the batter credited with the hit that allowed the runner to cross the plate. If the winning run was on second and the batter hit one over the fence, he was only credited with a double and would lose the home run.

The other change involved the place a potential home run ball landed. The change allowed that a ball hit over the fence would now be judged fair or foul in respect to where it was when it passed over the fence instead of where it landed. In other words, if a player today curved one around the foul pole, the ball passing on the fair side and then landing in foul territory, it would have been judged foul by the old rules. The new rule made it a home run. So both of these rules give just a little more advantage to the home run hitter. But because there were no real home run hitters at the time, none of the rule changes led anyone to believe that the upcoming campaign would be too different from any other.

However, there was a deal made before the 1920 season began that would alter the entire landscape of the game forever. In December of 1919, Red Sox owner Harry Frazee needed money, supposedly to fund a Broadway production. He decided to part with his most valuable commodity and sold Babe Ruth to the New York Yankees for $125,000, as well as securing an additional $300,000 loan. The selling price alone was more than twice what had been paid for any ballplayer previously and was a transaction that would forever be ingrained in the minds of both Red Sox and Yankees fans for generations to come.

When the deal was completed, it gave the Yankees—up to that time a rather unsuccessful franchise—a player they felt would help them immensely. The team decided that the Babe would become a fulltime outfielder despite his obvious pitching prowess. In fact, after his trade to the Yankees, he had only five more pitching decisions for the remainder of his career. In typical fashion, he won them all. But as an outfielder, he could also take advantage of the short right field fence in the bathtubshaped Polo Grounds, which the Yanks then shared with the National League New York Giants.

Still, no one was quite prepared for the thunderbolt the Yankees would unleash on the rest of the American League in 1920.

The Babe always used heavy bats, but because he had unusually small hands for an otherwise large man, he always had the handles made thinner than the average bat of the day, and perhaps for that reason was able to generate more bat speed than other players. He also had a beautiful lefthanded swing, smooth and powerful with a slight uppercut, and often hit high, majestic drives, unlike the liners that many other top hitters used to spray around the field. It was obvious right from the start that Ruth's 29 home runs the previous year were not a fluke. For in 1920, the Babe began hitting home runs at a pace that fans, fellow players, managers, and those who followed and wrote about the game never dared dream about. While everyone else played the old game, Babe Ruth seemed to be inventing a new kind of baseball, riding the ball a country mile and out of every ballpark in the league.

Not only was Ruth hitting home runs, he was hitting more by himself than just about every other team in the league. Unlike today, when everyone in the league seems capable of reaching the fences, Ruth was literally a one-man show. The Yanks even got in the pennant race that year, and while they came up short, finishing third to the Cleveland Indians, the Babe was the big news. He finished the 1920 season with an unheard of 54 home runs. That wasn't all. In his first year as a fulltime outfielder, he batted .376, lead the league with 137 runs batted in, scored an amazing 158 runs, and recorded a slugging percentage of .847, a major league record that would stand for more than eighty years. With the Babe working his magic, Yankees attendance at the Polo Grounds more than doubled to 1,289,422 fans, a one-year record until the Yanks broke it in the first post-war year of 1946.

In the era when everyone else was still playing small ball, the Babe had ascended to a new and lofty perch as baseball's first true home run hitter. His 54 home runs were more than every other team hit collectively in both leagues with the exception of the Philadelphia Phillies, who finished with a total of 64. Runner-up to the Babe in the American League was George Sisler with 19, while the National League leader was Philadelphia's

Cy Williams, who hit just 15. What a disparity. Ruth's home run hitting dominance would be like having one National Football League back rush for 1,500 yards while no other runner reached 500, or an NBA player averaging 50 or 60 points a game while everyone else was struggling to reach 20. That was the reason fans in every city in the league began pouring out to watch him play. They all wanted to see this twenty-five-year-old who could hit a baseball higher and farther—and more often—than any player before him. And they all came hoping to witness the same thing—Babe Ruth hitting a home run.

Ruth's incredible slugging prowess, however, didn't change the game overnight. For one thing, as of 1920, no one could be sure that the Babe would continue to hit a ton of home runs. Maybe he was just on an amazing roll and would never hit that many again. He had belted 29 the year before and was obviously great box office, but baseball had already endured for two decades with players like Honus Wagner, Ty Cobb, Tris Speaker, Walter Johnson, Christy Mathewson, and Grover Cleveland Alexander—all incredible talents, record setters already looked upon as all-time greats.

The Babe's home runs, however, weren't the only baseball story during and after the 1920 season that would profoundly affect the future of the game. On August 16, the Cleveland Indians were playing the Yankees at the Polo Grounds in New York. The Yanks had submarine-throwing righthander, Carl Mays, on the mound facing Cleveland's fine shortstop, Ray Chapman. Chapman batted out of a crouch and crowded the plate and Mays was one of those pitchers who never hesitated to come inside. He fired a fastball that was slightly high and tight, typical chin music perhaps, but not that far off the plate. For some reason, Chapman seemed to freeze, making little or no effort to get out of the way, and the ball struck him flush on the side of the head, bounding back toward the mound. Mays actually fielded it and threw to first before anyone realized that Chapman had been hit. The shortstop collapsed, was revived several minutes later, and then started walking toward the cen-

The Natural

In the movie version of the Bernard Malamud novel, *The Natural*, Hollywood heartthrob Robert Redford played the fictitious lead character, the baseball player Roy Hobbs, who started out as a phenom of a pitcher, was shot and seriously wounded, then reemerged as a top slugger years later. That, of course, never happened. But if any ballplayer in the whole history of the game was a real natural, it had to be Babe Ruth. Seeing old, grainy, black-and-white films of the Babe today, fans will observe a slugger with thin legs and a pot belly, trotting around the bases taking quick baby-steps. But the Babe was much more than that. He was a complete talent, and a guy who had little formal baseball training.

At age seven, young George was sent to the St. Mary's Industrial School for Boys in Baltimore, a Catholic school, because he was already classified as incorrigible. Once there, he came under the guidance of Brother Matthias, who became, among other things, his unofficial baseball coach. In 1914, the nineteen-year-old Babe was signed by Jack Dunn, owner of the then minor league Baltimore Orioles. He was signed as a pitcher and by June of that year was in a Boston Red Sox uniform. With virtually no minor league experience, Ruth emerged as one of the top lefthanded pitchers in the league and, had it not been for his prowess with the bat, he undoubtedly would have gone to the Hall of Fame as a pitcher. His overall pitching record was 94-46, a winning percentage of .671, and his earned run average was a very impressive 2.28. Today, 714 home runs later, the Babe is still known as the Bambino or the Sultan of Swat, a truly great power hitter. But don't forget what he did on the mound. He was just as good when he toed the rubber, making him arguably the most natural and complete ballplayer of all time.

terfield clubhouse. At second base, he collapsed again. Rushed to a hospital, Ray Chapman died twelve hours later, the only player in major league baseball history to be killed by a pitched ball.

Many vilified Mays, accusing him of throwing at Chapman intentionally. But those on the scene, including Yankees catcher "Muddy" Ruel, disputed that, saying that Chapman simply froze and didn't try to evade the pitch. Mays, too, denied emphatically that he was trying to injure Chapman intentionally. Then, another possible reason for the tragedy arose. Umpires

World Series Slam

While Babe Ruth's incredible 54 home runs were the biggest baseball story during the 1920 season, the home run also made headlines in the World Series between Cleveland and Brooklyn that year. This was another best-of-nine series and, when the two teams met at Cleveland's old League Park on October 10, the series was tied at two games apiece. Jim Bagby started for the Indians while spitballer Burleigh Grimes was on the mound for the Dodgers.

In the very first inning, Cleveland outfielder Elmer Smith came up with the bases loaded. Smith had hit 12 homers in the regular season and this time he caught a Grimes pitch just right, driving the ball into the seats for the first grand slam homer in World Series history. Later in the game, pitcher Bagby hit a three-run shot, becoming the first pitcher ever to hit one out in the series. And to put a capper on a game of firsts, Indians' Bill Wambsganss made the first World Series unassisted triple play in the fifth inning. Cleveland went on to win the game, 8-1, and take the series in seven.

Billy Evans and Bill Dinneen pointed to the continual use of scuffed and dirty baseballs. They issued a statement that said the following.

"A short time ago the club owners complained to [league] President [Ban] Johnson that too many balls were being thrown out. President Johnson sent out a bulletin telling the umpires to keep the balls in the games as much as possible except those which were dangerous."

Before 1912, even balls hit into the stands were retrieved so they could remain in play and the same ball that started the game often was still in use at the end. Yet, even after fans were allowed to keep baseballs, it wasn't unusual for the ball in play to become discolored and scuffed, making it more difficult to see and often tougher to hit. Chapman's death led to a change the following season when umpires were directed to keep a clean, white ball in play at all times. This not only made the game a bit safer but also gave the hitters the advantage of being able to see the ball a lot better.

Then, at the end of the 1920 season, the Black Sox Scandal

broke wide open and while the eight players involved were acquitted by a jury, baseball commissioner Landis declared them out of baseball permanently before the start of the 1921 season. That brought about the question of credibility within the sport. How many other games might be "fixed," and what was to say it wouldn't happen again? That was the overriding reason Judge Landis felt he had to make such a harsh decision regarding the future of the players, and it also marked the point when gambling became baseball's biggest anathema. The owners were rightfully concerned that the fans would develop distrust for the game and begin to stay away.

By today's standards, baseball attendance was rather modest in the early days of the game. In 1901, the first year of the two leagues, a total of 1,683,584 fans attended American League games, an average of just 3,067 a contest. The National League drew slightly more with 3,423 fans per game. In 1917, before U.S. involvement in World War I, the American averaged 4,596 fans per game while the National was at 3,778, not a whole lot different from 1901. Then in 1919 with the war over, the American League attendance jumped to 3,654,236 fans, an average of 6,535 a game, while the National rose to 2,878,203, or 5,158 per game. A year later, when Ruth erupted for 54 homers, the A.L. was up to a record 8,240 a game, while the National rose to 6,542.

At that time, it appeared that baseball was poised for a post-war boom. The decade that would become known as the Roaring Twenties was beginning and, especially in the big cities, America was about to embark on a period of economic growth as well as an unprecedented growth in the popularity of sports. The twenties would be the first decade in which top athletes became full-blown celebrities. Thanks to improved communications, the beginnings of radio, and unprecedented newspaper coverage, fans all over the country would know the names of Ruth, boxer Jack Dempsey, tennis star Bill Tilden, Olympic swimming champ Johnny Weissmuller, golfer Bobby Jones, Notre Dame football coach Knute Rockne, running back Red Grange, and even a horse named Man O' War. Not surprisingly,

baseball wanted to take full advantage of the economic and so-
cial changes in the country, but with the abolition of the eight
members of the White Sox, there was reasonable concern.

That made the home run-hitting exploits of the Babe even
more important. His presence not only gave fans a reason to
follow the game, but a desire to come out and watch this big
guy hit. In 1920, the year Ruth walloped his 54 homers, there
were 630 home runs hit in the big leagues. Take away the
Babe's blasts and it still would have been a record. In the wake
of the Black Sox Scandal, more than one baseball official had
to wonder if the long ball might not be an answer, adding a new
dimension to a game that needed some excitement and new heroes. With all those pieces in place, yet another debate would
arise, one that would continue periodically for more than
eighty years. It involved the baseball and the home run and
began with a question that would be asked more than once over
the intervening years.

Was the baseball juiced?

To this day, the 1920s are considered the beginning of the
lively ball era in baseball, with the implication that the ball was
somehow constructed differently so that it would carry farther,
encouraging more hitters to emulate the Babe and begin to
swing for the fences. It certainly helped that new, clean baseballs were now on the field at all times. When the ball was left
in play for perhaps the whole game, it not only became more
difficult to hit as it became discolored and scuffed, but it also
softened by repeated contact with bats and carried even less as
the game wore on. But in addition to keeping a clean baseball
in play, the baseballs that were used in the 1921 season were
seen as being different.

All baseball officials would admit at the time is that the balls
were being made with a better quality of wool, were wound
tighter, and were stitched with new and improved machinery
that also tightened them. Baseball historian Bill James is one
who thinks any so-called juicing of the baseball in 1921 was
purely accidental. "There was no such switch in baseballs,"
James wrote. "A better quality of yarn was available after

World War I, and may have accidentally increased the resiliency of the ball, but that was incidental, and its effect was not dramatic."

James feels that the difference was simply that the lords of baseball saw the excitement created by Ruth's titanic blasts and decided to capitalize on it, not discourage it. In the past, they had always taken steps to reduce scoring and allow the pitchers to dominate, the circumstances of the game leading to *small ball* offense. But now the combination of the outlawed spitball and other trick pitches, clean balls being constantly put in play, worry over the fallout from the Black Sox Scandal, the more tightly wound baseball, and the arrival of Babe Ruth all came together to create conditions more conducive to increased home run production.

With all this in place, the Babe and the batters in general began to dominate the game in 1921. In a real sense, this was the season in which the dead ball era really ended, though many of the players who excelled during those earlier years were still performing at a high level. So it didn't happen all at once. Rather, it was a gradual change. But the fans certainly had a new hero, the guy who was hitting more home runs than anyone had ever thought possible. Not only was Ruth living up to the standard he had set the year before, he was exceeding it. He continued to hit long home runs at a pace that not only more than doubled that of any other player in both leagues, but he was also on track to top the mark of 54 he had set the previous season. Better yet, he had the Yankees driving toward an American League pennant and a possible World Series meeting with their co-tenants at the Polo Grounds, John McGraw's New York Giants.

The Babe notwithstanding, the 1921 season saw the beginnings of the gradual change in the overall game. Ruth may have been far and away the game's biggest slugger, but more players were hitting the ball into the seats as both leagues were on pace to hit more home runs than ever before. Many of the same players had been in the majors a scant two or three years earlier when precious few home runs were hit, so there can be a strong case made for the aforementioned changes—outlawed trick pitches, clean baseballs, and a more tightly wound ball—as working to the advantage of the hitters and making it more difficult for those who pitched the baseball.

When the season ended, Babe Ruth was sitting atop the baseball world and was quickly becoming the most recognizable and popular athlete in the country. Not only had he broken his own home run record by blasting an incredible 59, but he set a new record for runs batted in with 171. He also led the league in runs scored with 177, another modern record that still stands today. In addition, he batted .378, had 204 hits, a slugging average of .846, walked 144 times, and struck out only 81 times in 540 official at bats. It was an incredible year that simply earmarked the Babe as *the* athlete of the 1920s. He was truly becoming a living legend and, while he was obviously an outstanding, all-around ballplayer, it was the home run that was already putting a punctuation mark on his career.

There was also little doubt that hitting was up all over the league. The 1921 season saw major league batters belt 937 home runs, breaking the record of 630 the year before. Babe, of course, was head and shoulders above the rest. In the American League, Ken Williams of St. Louis and Bob Meusel of the Yanks were tied for second with 24, while in the National the leader was George Kelly of the Giants with 23. To set a major league record, there must have been more players beginning to hit between 10 and 20. The Babe still hit more by himself than seven other teams in both leagues, but the gap was closing if by just a bit.

The rising home run totals were not the only indication that the dead ball era was fast becoming a thing of the past. In the American League, Detroit's Harry Heilmann won the batting title with a .394 average. Teammate Ty Cobb was next at .389, the Babe third, George Sisler fourth at .371, and Tris Speaker fifth at .362. These were all future Hall of Famers, with Cobb and Speaker being two of the best from dead ball days. In addition, more players were driving in over 100 runs and getting more than 200 hits. The league as a whole batted .292, compared with just .254 only three years earlier. The National wasn't far behind. Hornsby won the batting title by hitting a sizzling .397 and also knocked in 126 runs. The senior circuit had a league batting average of .289, up from .254 in 1918. To further show the dominance of the hitters, only one American League pitcher had an earned run average under 3.00, and no National League hurler was under 2.59.

The ascension of Babe Ruth, the home run, and more hitting also coincided with the beginning of sports most enduring dynasty. The New York Yankees finished the season with a 98-55 record under Manager Miller Huggins and won the American League pennant by four games over Cleveland, their first since the franchise debuted as the Highlanders in 1903. Though John McGraw's Giants beat the Yanks, 5-3, in the last of the best-of-nine World Series, the Babe had one of the four homers hit in the fall classic that year. But Ruth and the Yanks would be back and with a vengeance.

THE DRIVE TO THE MAGIC 60

As home run totals began mounting in the 1920s, stolen base numbers began going the other way. In 1911, big league runners swiped a total of 3,403 bases, an average of 211 per team. By 1920, the number was down to 1,720, and by 1926 had dipped to a low of 1,275 thefts, an average of just under 80 for each ballclub. These numbers further reflect the changing style of play, and much of that can be attributed to the excitement caused by Babe Ruth and the home run. In addition, between 1920 and 1925, big league hitters reached the .400 mark seven times (three of them by Rogers Hornsby, including an all-time best of .424 in 1924), and on six occasions hitters finished at .390 or above. After 1925, the coveted .400 mark would be reached only twice more, by the Giants' Bill Terry in 1930 and Boston's Ted Williams in 1941. The gradual falling off of mile-high batting averages was still another mark of the home run's increasing importance. More young players would try to mold themselves after Babe Ruth rather than Ty Cobb.

A conflict with Commissioner Landis about barnstorming

after the 1921 season led to the Babe's being suspended for six weeks in 1922. He came back in a surly mood and was suspended three more times before the season ended. Because of the missed time, he wound up with just 35 homers in 315 at bats as Ken Williams won the home run crown with 39, while in the National, Rogers Hornsby proved you could hit .400 and still be a slugger. The Rajah batted .401 and finished with 42 home runs. These were numbers only the Babe was reaching just two years earlier. The Yanks had won the pennant again despite Babe's subpar year, but they were swept in the Series by the Giants. The team and its superstar now wanted to climb that final mountain.

Home run totals continued to escalate. Despite the Babe's off year in 1922, big leaguers went over the 1,000 mark with 1,055 home runs and then topped it again in 1925 with 1,169 despite an even bigger crash by the Babe. That was the year of the big bellyache. Many thought it was the result of the Babe's huge appetite for food and drink. In truth, he was operated on for an intestinal abscess and didn't start his season until June 1. He wound up hitting just .290, down from the .393 and .378 of the previous two seasons, and had just 25 homers. Because of his excessive lifestyle, many felt he was already on the downside, an old thirty, and they wondered if anyone could take his place. There was still no other hitter approaching 50 homers, with Hornsby's 42 in 1922 and Cy Williams's 41 the following year the best any National Leaguer could do.

But the Babe came to spring training in 1926 in great shape and seemingly determined to prove he still had a lot of baseball, and home runs, left in him. This time he had a potential partner. Lou Gehrig was signed out of Columbia University in 1923, where he was both a football and baseball star. A strong, rock-solid six-footer, Gehrig was a lefthanded batter, like Ruth, but was more of a line drive hitter than the Babe. His first full season was 1925, and he checked in with 20 homers, 68 RBIs, and a .295 batting average. With Ruth missing a huge part of the year, the Yanks finished seventh, but the young first baseman was already showing a world of promise.

The House That Ruth Built

Thanks to the slugging exploits of the Babe, the Yankees began to outdraw the National League Giants at the Polo Grounds in 1920. That's when the Giants gave them the boot and told them to find their own home. Yankees owner Jacob Ruppert decided this was his chance to build a state-of-the-art ballpark. The site was an old lumberyard in the Bronx, just across the Harlem River from the Polo Grounds. The new ballpark was baseball's first triple-deck stadium that held nearly 75,000 fans. Both original foul lines were relatively short, 281 feet to left and 295 to right. But left sloped out quickly to 460 feet in leftcenter—a large piece of turf later dubbed *death valley,* the place fly balls go to die—and a carnivorous 490 feet to dead center. For a lefthanded pull hitter like the Babe, however, the new ballpark was made to order.

There was even some talk about calling the new ballpark Ruth Field, but that idea was scrapped in favor of Yankee Stadium. Only it also had a nick name. Sportswriter Fred Lieb dubbed it *The House That Ruth Built.* The first game was played on April 18, 1923, with the Yankees hosting the Boston Red Sox before a record crowd of 74,200 fans. The Yankees won it, 4-1, the margin of difference a three-run homer by—who else?—the one and only Babe Ruth. The opening of Yankee Stadium marked the dawn of yet another new era in baseball and at season's end ushered in the first *Subway Series.* It was the Yanks and Giants once again and this time the Yankees won it in six, their first championship, with the Babe becoming the first player in history to hit three home runs in a World Series. Ironically, the Giants had won the opening game the old-fashioned way. Casey Stengel, who would manage the Yankees some thirty years later, hit an inside-the-park homer to break a 1-1 tie, a stark contrast to the Babe's big blasts, but just as effective.

If anyone thought the Babe's dominance and this first era of the home run was coming to an end, they were wrong. Though the 1926 season saw the number of homers drop by 306 from the year before, the Babe came back to lead the league with 47. It was almost like the early years, though. The next best slugger was Philadelphia's Al Simmons with 19, and the National League leader, Hack Wilson, had just 21. In addition, the Babe's 47 was a number that nine other big league teams could not reach that year. The Boston Braves were the most anemic, hitting just 16 home runs as a team the entire year. So while the game had changed considerably and several other players had gone over the 40 mark, with a number of others hitting 30 or more, it still wasn't a time when home runs would have made the ESPN highlight films day after day. There simply weren't that many of them.

The Yankees had come all the way back to win another pennant, but they were then beaten by the St. Louis Cardinals in seven memorable games. The Babe, of course, made the most news. In game four, he became the first player ever to hit three homers in a single World Series game. The big guy's flair for the dramatic seemed unending. He was even involved in the final play of the series when he was thrown out trying to steal second with what could have been the tying run. But by 1926, no player other than Ruth had established himself as a bonafide, consistent, big league slugger. It was still all Ruth's show and what was about to happen the following year would forever cement his legend in the minds of baseball fans then and in future generations.

The Yanks had built a powerful team. In addition to Ruth and Gehrig, they had an outstanding young second baseman in Tony Lazzeri and two hard hitting outfielders in Bob Meusel and Earle Combs. All five could bang the baseball and the supporting cast was solid. Waite Hoyt, Wilcey Moore, Herb Pennock, and Urban Shocker were a tough quartet of starting pitchers. This was the team that, after the 1927 season, would earn the nickname *Murderer's Row*.

It was obvious from the start that this was a special Yankees ballclub. They got out of the gate so fast that within weeks it was apparent that no American League team could catch them. And then, as April turned into May, then dissolved into June, the entire baseball world began to focus on not only the Babe but also young Lou Gehrig, who had emerged as a true star and the most dangerous home run threat since . . . the Babe himself. Ruth hit his first of the year in game four against Howard Ehmke of Philadelphia and, by the end of May, had 16 homers.

That was expected. What Gehrig was doing, however, was a surprise to many.

In his first two full seasons, the man who would come to be known as *The Iron Horse* for his refusal to come out of the lineup had hit 20 and then 16 homers. Because he hit such vicious line drives, as opposed to the Babe's soaring blasts, no one expected him to be a huge home run hitter. He was quiet for the first week of the season, but in the sixth game against Boston, Gehrig blasted a pair of homers that drove home five runs in a 14-2 New York rout. By the end of May, Gehrig was the number two home run hitter in the majors behind Ruth. He already had 12 and was just warming up.

The pace really began to pick up in June. The Babe continued to hit them and talk about him possibly breaking his 1921 record of 59 was in the air. He hit nine homers that month to end it with 25. But Gehrig did even better. Hot as a pistol, Gehrig blasted 13 four baggers that month and also finished the month with 25. The two sluggers were tied and no other player in the majors was even close. The Yankees continued to win at a record pace, the pennant already a foregone conclusion, and now the attention of the baseball world focused on the two sluggers. Since the Babe had emerged with 54 home runs in 1920, no one had come close to challenging his dominance as a slugger. Suddenly, there was another player making a statement, and it was a teammate. With the Babe hitting third and Gehrig batting cleanup behind him, the home run race between the two sluggers captivated the public in a way that wouldn't happen for another thirty-four years.

New York fans flocked to the games; others ran to grab the newspaper to see if one or both sluggers had hit another. At the end of July, Gehrig had 35 and the Babe 34. There was even talk about both of them breaking the old record, but that was beginning to seem unlikely. Now it seemed a matter of which one would wind up the home run champion. When Gehrig smashed his 38th homer on August 9, in the team's 109th game, he actually had a three-homer lead over baseball's greatest slugger. As hard as it was to believe, the kid was ahead of the old master. But the Babe was about to reestablish himself with one of the most incredible final months ever.

He began picking up the pace in mid-August. From the sixteenth to the end of the month he walloped seven to finish August with 43 homers. Gehrig only hit three in the final weeks, checking in with 41 as the final month of the season approached. In September, it became the Babe Ruth show. By the time he slammed three against Boston on September 6, and two more at Fenway the next day, he had 49 to Gehrig's 45. But Lou's season would suddenly slow to a crawl for a reason very few knew at the time. Fred Lieb, a reporter who covered the Yanks in 1927 and a personal friend of Gehrig's, said that Lou's mother fell ill and needed a very dangerous operation that September. Gehrig's mind was on his mother so often that if affected his play on the field. At one point he told Lieb, "I'm so worried about Mom that I can't see straight."

How his mother's illness affected Gehrig is hard to say. But he didn't hit a single home run from September 6 to September 27, and then he hit only one more after that to finish with 47. For the Babe, it was different. He hit his 50th on September 11 in the team's 134th game. So he had twenty games remaining to try to break his record. It wouldn't be an easy hill to climb. But he then hit a pair on September 13, another on the 16th, and one more on the 18th to give him 54 with seven games left. When he hit his 57th on September 27, off of the great Lefty Grove of Philadelphia, he had just two games left.

But the Babe always had a flare for the dramatic. In the 153rd game against Washington, he slammed two more, one a grand slam, tying his old mark of 59. And the next day, batting against southpaw Tom Zachery of Washington, Babe Ruth blasted his 60th and final home run of the season, quickly saying, "Let's see someone top that." He had set a new record, one that must have seemed almost impossible back in 1927. Gehrig's 47 represented more home runs than any other player had ever hit before . . . except for Ruth. The third-best slugger in the American League that year was the Yanks' Tony Lazzeri,

An Obscure and Little-Known Homer Mark

In 1927, rookie Lloyd Waner joined his older brother Paul as a member of the Pittsburgh Pirates. The two future Hall of Famers were a devastating combination that year. Paul batted .380 and Lloyd .355. They had 460 hits between them, Paul getting 237 and Lloyd a rookie record 223. But neither was a slugger and between them they had only 10 home runs, eight by big brother Paul.

But in a game on September 4 that year, the Waners decided to take a chapter out of the Ruth-Gehrig book. They both slammed home runs in the same inning, making them the only brothers in major league history to achieve that distinction.

who had only 18, so you can see just how incredible the two sluggers had been.

The Yanks set an American League record that year, finishing at 110-44 and a full nineteen games ahead of the second place Philadelphia Athletics, a team with seven future Hall of Famers on their roster. Ruth and Gehrig had put on one of the greatest two-man displays in the game. Besides his 60 homers, the Babe batted .356 and drove in 164 runs. Gehrig hit .373 and led the league with 175 RBIs. Sportswriter Fred Lieb felt that Gehrig not only had a chance to approach 60 homers, but also might have driven in 200 runs had it not been for the September illness of his mother. Harry Heilmann of Detroit was third in RBIs with 120, showing again the tremendous run production of the home-run hitting duo.

The 1927 Yanks as a team hit .307 for the year. Lazzeri batted .309 with 18 homers and 102 RBIs. Bob Meusel hit .337 with eight homers and 103 runs batted in, while Earle Combs batted .356 and led the league with 231 hits. In the World Series that year, the Yanks swept the Pittsburgh Pirates in four games. Legend has it that before the first game began, Pirates players watched Ruth, Gehrig, and the other Yanks take batting practice. They saw the two big sluggers bang ball after ball into the seats and were totally intimidated. Lloyd Waner, who along with brother Paul were the Pirates big stars, disputes that tale. Said brother Lloyd years later: "I don't think Paul ever saw anything on a ballfield that would scare him."

The Yanks were simply better. They won a pair by one run and then scored the winning tally in the final game on a wild pitch. There were just two homers hit in the fall classic that year. Not surprisingly, the Babe had them both. It was a magical year for the Yankees, maybe the real start of the dynasty by a Murderer's Row ballclub that is still often called the best ever.

Ironically, the 1927 season was not a huge year for home runs. There were 922 hit in both leagues, but Ruth and Gehrig, with 107 between them, hit roughly one-quarter of all the American League homers (439) and together out-homered every other team in both leagues except the New York Giants, which hit 109. But there were some surprisingly low totals as well. While the Yanks blasted 158 home runs, the Cleveland Indians had just 26, the Red Sox 28, and the Senators 29. In the National, Cincinnati had just 29, the Boston Braves 37, and Brooklyn Dodgers 39.

The common perception is that Babe Ruth waltzed up to the plate in 1920, began hitting home runs, and almost single-handedly saved baseball from the specter of the Black Sox Scandal, which broke the following year, and that shortly afterward there was a baseball boom as all the hitters began swinging for the fences. Not so. As the stats clearly show, the Babe was almost a solo act for the first half of the 1920s. A couple of other players had some strong home run hitting seasons, such as Rogers Hornsby's 42 in 1922. But there was no parade of sluggers and, while the number of homers had more than doubled from dead ball days, there were still teams hitting very few and relying on the old style of play.

But Babe Ruth was such a Herculean figure, a larger-than-life personality who dominated the game and became a huge part of the big-city sports boom of the 1920s, that it almost seems as if baseball had gone home run crazy. But until Lou Gehrig came along to give the Babe a running mate in 1927, the big guy was virtually doing it alone. What he accomplished was to show everyone how the game could change and would change in upcoming years. When the Babe hit his epic 60 in 1927, the stars of an earlier era like Ty Cobb and Tris Speaker were finishing up their great careers. Soon, new players would be coming to the fore and many of these players looked to Ruth, Gehrig, and the Yankees for inspiration. In the upcoming years leading up to World War II, baseball would change, the home run would become increasingly important, and the dead ball era would finally be gone forever.

3

Power Dominates the Game, 1928–1940

Though Babe Ruth had been whacking home runs since 1920, if any one season could be marked as the fulcrum of change it had to be 1927. That was really the first time a power team had dominated the league and won it all. This was not John Mc-Graw's Giants or the great White Sox teams that crumbled to scandal in 1919. No, this was the New York Yankees, Murderer's Row, a team that blasted an unheard of 158 home runs during the season and now had the two most productive home run hitters in baseball history. The team had four players driving in 100 or more runs and as a group had scored 130 more runs than any other team in the majors. They had done it with pure power, not speed and finesse. They didn't *hit 'em where they ain't*. Instead, they hit them where they couldn't be caught.

There's certainly little doubt that other owners, managers, and players took note of what the Yanks had done with Ruth and Gehrig sitting in the middle of their lineup. Of course, a Ruth and Gehrig don't come along every day, but soon more young players would be arriving with the ability to drive the baseball further and more often than those of the previous generation. In addition, the country was about to experience a radical change. When the stock market crashed in October of 1929, a decade of growth and prosperity would end, replaced by a difficult period of widespread poverty and struggle now known as the Great Depression. Baseball, of course, would have to find a way to survive and continue to bring fans through the turnstiles.

The 1928 season was almost a continuation of the year before, but without any records being set. The Murderer's Row Yankees won another pennant with a 101-53 record. The Babe had yet another colossal season, leading the league with 54 homers and 142 runs batted in. It was the fourth time in his career the Bambino had been over the 50 mark as he continued to build his reputation as an almost superhuman slugger. He doubled Lou Gehrig's total as his teammate fell back to 27 homers in the runner-up spot. But Gehrig was becoming an RBI machine. He tied the Babe with 142 ribbys and was third in the league in hitting at .374. There was no doubt that he had achieved star status.

In the World Series that year, Ruth and Gehrig again showed what power could do for a team. Playing against a very good St. Louis Cardinals ballclub that boasted the coleader in the National League home run race, Jim Bottomley, who tied Chicago's Hack Wilson with 31, and the guy who finished third, Chick Hafey, who clubbed 27, the Yanks dominated. As they had done a year earlier against the Pirates, the New Yorkers swept the fall classic in four games. Ruth put on a clinic. He batted .625 in the series with three homers and nine RBIs. Gehrig drove in just five runs, but he did it by hitting four homers. So the twin terrors of the Yanks clubbed seven homers between them, while Bottomley and Hafey managed just one.

There was little doubt why the Yankees had become baseball's biggest attraction. It started with Ruth and ended with Gehrig. Sure, there were other fine players on the team, making it one of the best ever. But it was the two guys who could hit it out—the Babe with his titanic moon shots and Gehrig with those liners that kept rising and rising. They were the heart and soul of baseball's greatest team. Who could ever hope to beat them with these two guys swinging those power bats? Maybe, however, the rest of baseball was getting a clue. In 1928, big league batters hit 1,093 home runs, up 169 from the year before. And in Philadelphia, Manager Connie Mack, a relic from the dead ball era, was putting together a ballclub to challenge the Yankees in 1929, a pivotal year for the sport in a number of ways.

Born in 1862, while the Civil War was still raging, Connie Mack was a player and then a manager, beginning his career behind the bench in 1894. By 1901, when the American League season yet with a .345 average, 39 home runs, and 159 RBIs. Those would be MVP type numbers even today, but despite his great year, no one was prepared for what Hack Wilson would do in 1930.

All Wilson did was produce one of the greatest slugging seasons in history, putting on a record-breaking performance that not only saw him threaten the Babe's record of 60, but also set another amazing record that stands to this day. Hack Wilson finished the 1930 season with 56 home runs, a .356 batting average, and a record 190 runs batted in. His RBI record still stands and it has even grown by one. In 1999, statisticians found an error in a box score and it was determined that Wilson actually drove home 191 runs that year. You can make a case that Wilson simply exploded for one nearly perfect season. But when you look at what happened around the rest of the major leagues, you've got to believe that the baseball had to be different, had to be *juiced*, in 1930.

Wilson, of course, was the majors homer and RBI champ, but he didn't win the National League triple crown because the Giants Bill Terry batted .401. Right behind Terry was Babe Herman of Brooklyn at .393, Chuck Klein of the Phils at .386, Lefty O'Doul of Philadelphia at .383, and Fred Linstrom of the Giants at .379. In fact, there were eleven National Leaguers with a batting average of .350 or better that year and seventeen players who drove home 100 or more runs. Six of the eight teams had batting averages over .300, and the league average was an incredible .303. National League hitters slammed 892 homers, including a record 171 by the Chicago Cubs, a team that finished second to the Cardinals in the final standings.

The American League wasn't far behind. Ruth and Gehrig were one-two in homers again with 49 and 41. Jimmie Foxx had 37, as did Goose Goslin of Washington, while Al Simmons had 36. Gehrig was the RBI champ with 174, and Simmons won the batting title at .381, two points better than Gehrig. The A.L. hit 673 homers and had a .288 league batting average with three teams hitting over .300. Eight American League hitters batted over .350 and fifteen hitters drove home 100 or

was founded, he became the manager and part owner of the Philadelphia A's and, by 1914, had already led the team to six pennants. By 1929, Mack was still managing, sitting on the bench in his customary civilian clothes, perhaps the only twentieth-century manager who never wore a uniform. He was sixty-seven years old then, but still young enough to change with the times. His A's ballclub had power. Al Simmons had been one of the best hitters in the American League since his second season in 1925, when he hit .384 with 29 home runs. Now he was joined by Jimmie Foxx, another powerful righthanded hitter who hit 13 homers in 1928 but was finally a regular and expected to blossom as a slugger.

The team had other fine position players such as outfielders Mule Haas and Bing Miller, catcher Mickey Cochrane, and veteran utility infielder Jimmy Dykes. Mack was smart enough not to forget about pitching. The staff was led by Lefty Grove, who would become one of the best ever, and righthander George Earnshaw. Years later, a national sports magazine would do an article about the 1929 A's, calling them *the team that time forgot*, the theme being that this was one of the great teams of all-time, a ballclub that has been somewhat obscured by Ruth, Gehrig, and the Yankees. In 1929, however, the team came into its own, winning the American League pennant with a 104-46 record and beating the Yankees by seventeen games.

They did it in a year when the hitters began dominating as never before. Ruth was still the home run champ with 46, Gehrig finishing second with 35. But the next two were Simmons and Foxx of the A's, with 34 and 33 respectively. Simmons also took the RBI title with 157, three more than the Babe. The A's as a team hit .296 and they had 122 homers, just 20 fewer than the Yankees. The American League hit a collective .284 and clubbed 595 homers. When the A's beat the Cubs in the World Series in just five games, there was little doubt that the best teams were continuing to come out of the junior circuit. But oddly enough, there was even more hitting going on in the National.

Suddenly, the N.L. was producing its own sluggers. Chuck

Klein of Philadelphia was the home run champ with 43. Another newcomer, Mel Ott of the Giants, was right behind with 42, while Hack Wilson and Rogers Hornsby had 39 each. Had Wilson and Hornsby both hit one more, it would have marked the first time any league had produced four hitters with 40 or more home runs. Almost incredibly, the National League slammed a record 754 homers, with the Phillies leading the majors with 153, just five short of the record set by the 1927 Yankees. The major league home run total for 1929 was a record 1,358, and it was now becoming very apparent that the game was changing big time.

That October, a month after the World Series ended, the stock market crashed and it began to appear that the country would soon fall into an economic slide. Yet, prior to the 1930 season, it was announced that Babe Ruth has signed a new contract for $80,000. He was by far the highest paid player in the game, making far more than the best pitchers, the top hitters for average, and the great defensive players as well. It was becoming very obvious that hitting home runs had rewards other than winning games. When someone commented to the Babe that he was making $5,000 more than the President of the United States, he gave his now classic reply. "I had a better year than he did," he quipped.

As the 1930 season approached, baseball was worried. Ironically, it was almost a decade since the lords of the game had a similar worry due to the impending Black Sox Scandal. Would the fans come back? That time the veracity of the game was in question. Now it was a matter of simple economics. With the country heading into a depression, how many fans would want to fork over the price of a ticket? It was felt that the home runs of Babe Ruth had kept the fans coming out after the Black Sox Scandal. If home runs were the magic ingredient then, maybe even more home runs would do the same thing now. That led to yet another controversy about the ball, especially when the hitters in both leagues began teeing off as never before as soon as the 1930 season began.

This time, however, it appears that the secret wasn't really a secret. The lords of baseball certainly knew about the Babe's effect on the sport and they were hoping that an even bigger explosion of hitting might induce fans, who were worried about spending during these troubled times, to forsake something else and still come out to the ballpark. By all accounts, the baseball that was put in play didn't have the usual raised stitches. Rather, the stitches were almost recessed and the cover of the ball was wound so tight that the ball was difficult to grip. Flat or recessed stitches would also make it difficult for pitchers to throw sharp breaking pitches and, in those days, the curve was the pitch used most often to offset the fastball. With this kind of ball in play, it isn't surprising that the hitters had a feast.

Suddenly, everyone was hitting. There were more home runs, more base hits, and more runs scored. Almost all the pitchers were getting tattooed with the exception of a select few. Once again the ball was suspect. When Ruth and Gehrig set the game on fire just three years earlier, there were few other real home run hitters. Now there were a slew of players hitting more home runs than they had ever hit before, as well as a number of players challenging the coveted .400 batting mark. Ruth and Gehrig were up to their usual tricks, running one-two in homers in the American League. But in the National League, a totally unlikely player was setting the league afire with his slugging.

Lewis Robert Wilson, better known as "Hack," didn't look like a typical baseball slugger. Standing just 5'6", but possessing a barrel chest, an 18-inch neck, and thick, muscular arms, Wilson was often described as "top heavy." Below his huge torso that held most of his 190-pounds were short legs and almost tiny, size 6 feet. Wilson joined the Giants in 1923 but didn't start to blossom until he was traded to the Cubs prior to the 1926 season. A hard-drinking, sometimes erratic player, he was a righthanded hitter who always took a mighty cut at the ball. With his huge upper body, he could hit it high and far when he connected. From 1926 through 1929, Hack Wilson hit 21, 30, 31, and 39 homers, also hitting over .300 and driving in more than 100 runs each year. So there was no doubt about his ability. In the hot hitting year of 1929, Wilson put together his best

more runs. Philadelphia, with its great team from a year earlier, won the pennant once more with 102 victories.

With all this hitting, what happened to the pitchers? If the ball used in 1930 didn't have raised stitches, well, the hurlers obviously struggled. The National League had just two twenty-game winners. Dazzy Vance of the Dodgers was the only pitcher with an earned run average under 3.00 at 2.61. Carl Hubbell of the Giants, a future Hall of Famer, was next at 3.76. The Phillies, a team that led the league in hitting with a .315 average, saw their pitchers give up an average of 6.71 earned runs a game. The league earned run average was 4.97.

Maybe the American League didn't hit quite as much because their pitchers were just a little better. The great Lefty Grove had the best season of them all, finishing at 28-5 with a league best 2.54 ERA. There were four other twenty-game winners, but the league earned run average was still 4.65. And, as further evidence that the old pitching and speed game was disappearing, major leaguers stole just 1,080 bases, the lowest number since both leagues began play in 1901. In the World Series, however, the old axiom that good pitching can stop good hitting again prevailed. Aces Grove and George Earnshaw won two games each as Philadelphia defeated St. Louis in six games.

In one other respect this season of enormous hitting seemed to pay off. Both leagues belted a record 1.565 home runs and the fans seemed to respond. Despite the deepening economic depression, National League attendance increased from 4,925,713 in 1929 to 5,446,532 in 1930. The American went up as well, but not as much, increasing to 4,685,730 from 4,662,470 the year before. The question, however, was what to do for an encore. It didn't take a genius to see that there was simply too much hitting in 1930. This season, more than any other, was at the complete opposite end of the spectrum from the game that had been played pretty much into the 1920s. After all, there had been quite a bit of hitting in 1929, but there was still a balance. If this kind of hitting kept up, who in his right mind would want to be a pitcher?

The consensus seems to be that by spring training of 1931,

the baseball had reverted back to 1929 style. That's really the only explanation for the hitting to fall off the way it did. All the numbers were down, but the player who took the most disastrous drop was Hack Wilson. After a record-setting 1930 season, Wilson proved he was no Babe, following it with a season in which he hit .261 with just 13 homers and 61 RBIs. The year before he was handled extremely well by manager Joe McCarthy, but the following year he had to play under the prickly Rogers Hornsby and it didn't work. In fact, Wilson would be out of baseball after the 1934 campaign and would hit only 51 homers after blasting his record 56 in 1930. That number, however, stood as the National League standard for sixty-eight years until Mark McGwire and Sammy Sosa both blew past it in 1998.

The National League that year had an even bigger dropoff than the American. In 1931, the senior circuit hit 399 fewer home runs than the preceding year. The batting champ, Chick Hafey, edged out Bill Terry by a hair, both finishing at .349, 51 points lower than Terry's .401 in 1930. The league average of .277 was 26 points lower than the .303 mark of a season earlier. The pitchers had an aggregate earned run average of more than a full run less; the 4.97 from 1930 was down to .386 in 1931. The dramatic drop in the numbers was further evidence of the ball being not only juiced but difficult for the pitchers to grip properly in 1930.

Oddly enough, there wasn't quite the same disparity in the American League, showing that, while perhaps not being that much better overall, it certainly had the bigger superstars. Ruth and Gehrig tied for the home run crown with 46, while the next best was Cleveland's Earl Averill with 32. Lou and the Babe also ran one-two in RBIs, finishing with 184 and 163 respectively. Gehrig, in fact, mounted a challenge to Hack Wilson's 191 of a year earlier, setting an A.L. record that still stands today. The league average of .278 was down just 10 points from the year before and the A.L. hit just 97 fewer home runs. More hitting in the American resulted in a higher league ERA than the National—the American League pitchers checking in at 4.38, but still down from the 4.65 of 1930.

In the World Series, the A's dynasty came to an end with a 4-3 loss to the St. Louis Cardinals. But by this time, the game of the 1930s was firmly established, the altered baseball of 1930 notwithstanding. Players were stealing fewer bases and that trend would continue right into the 1960s. Ruth and Gehrig were now being joined by a bevy of potential sluggers who were capable of belting the ball over the fences, and more teams were looking for the big inning or the three-run homer more often than scratching and clawing for runs. As the country sunk deeper into the Great Depression over the next several years, baseball attendance would drop, hitting a low in 1933, but not because of the product on the field. Rather, it was the economic conditions of the times. Through the remainder of the decade, however, the home run would continue to make the news as talented players entered the game. Many from this next generation would continue what the Babe had started as more and more fine, all-around players also had the ability to hit the ball out.

While the 1932 season saw the Yankees once against rise to the top, the Ruth-Gehrig-led Bronx Bombers winning 107 games, Yankee fans had something to worry about all season long. There was yet another player threatening to break the Babe's epic record of 60 home runs. He was the A's young slugger, Jimmie Foxx. In his three seasons since becoming a regular, Foxx had hit 33, 37, and 30 homers. Though Foxx was establishing himself as a power hitter, no one was ready for what the twenty-four-year-old from Sudlersville, Maryland, would do in 1932.

Jimmie Foxx was a powerful six-footer who weighed about 200 pounds. It was his massive arms and shoulders that led to the nicknames *The Maryland Strongboy* and *The Beast*, though many simply called him *Double-X*. Unlike Ruth and Gehrig, he was a righthanded batter, but like the Babe, Foxx's long home runs became legendary. Maybe that's why some looked at him as a righthanded version of the Bambino. He was surely baseball's first major righthanded slugger and he had already hit massive home runs in Chicago, New York, St. Louis, and Detroit that had fans marveling at his strength. The one he hit in Yankee Stadium came within 20 feet of going out of the ballpark. When Lefty Gomez, the Yankee hurler who served up the pitch, went out to the deep left field stands to see where the ball landed, he found the seat it hit had shattered. "I thought it was impossible," Gomez said, "but old Double-X did it. He even has muscles in his hair."

But in was in 1932 that Foxx really made the baseball world stand up and take notice. He began hitting homers early and jumped into the league lead over the Babe and Gehrig. It was soon obvious that they weren't going to catch him. The question then became how high would he go? Though he didn't come out of the lineup, a wrist injury in August slowed him a bit. He picked it up at the end and finally fell just short of the Babe, finishing the season with 58 home runs, more than any player had ever hit except for the one and only. Unlike the Babe, however, Foxx never capitalized on his hitting prowess, which would continue for much of the decade. Though his 58 home runs came just five years after the Babe's 60, timing and luck were never with him.

For years, those who saw him said that Foxx really should have set a new record in 1932. Had he not injured his wrist in August, he might have hit a few more right then and there. But looking at some of the changes that occurred in the ballparks between 1927 and 1932, you can see how luck was not on Jimmie Foxx's side. For openers, he lost two homers to rainouts, hitting them early in the game before the rains came, then not hitting a homer when the games were made up. On five occasions, he hit balls off a screen in right field at Sportsman's Park in St. Louis. That screen was not in place in 1927. There was also a screen erected in left field at Cleveland that was not in place back in 1927. Foxx hit that one three times during the season. So, had 1927 conditions prevailed, Foxx would have had at least 66 home runs in 1932. That's how good he was.

Because the county was moving toward a depression, Foxx also didn't make the big dollars that the Babe did. Ironically, he was even forced to take a pay cut after his great season. Attendance was dropping by then, and because so many people were worried about jobs, food, and surviving during this difficult period, Foxx never received the adulation that had always been given to the Babe. He was always a big spender, which made money in short supply, and his heavy drinking would lead to a premature ending of his career. Yet for more than thirty years, Jimmie Foxx would be considered the greatest righthanded slugger of them all until the modern day player began to surpass him. He would finish his career with 534 home runs, which at the time would also be second best to the Babe.

The next few years were difficult ones for baseball. The sport was mired in the Great Depression and the game was changing at the same time. Attendance would bottom out in 1933 to pre-1920 levels. At the same time, the hot-hitting seasons of 1929 and especially 1930 seem to complete the conversion to a power game. In 1932, stolen bases in the majors dropped below the 1,000 mark for the first time in history. They would continue to stay at that low level into the 1940s and 1950s, barely nudging back to 1,027 in 1937 and then to 1,010 in the war year of 1943 before falling off even farther and reaching a low of 650 in 1950. So the station-to-station game was taking hold with everyone waiting for the next guy to get a hit. If that hit happened to be a home run, so much the better.

The early 1930s was also the end of another era. Babe Ruth's career was winding down. The Babe had his last truly big year in 1931, tying Gehrig for the home lead with 46, batting .373, and driving in 163 runs. A year later he was still a force with a .341, 41, 137 season, but in 1933 age and hard-living were beginning to take its toll. He hit only 34 home runs, batted .301, and drove in just 103 runs. A year later the handwriting was on the wall. A struggling Ruth had just 22 homers and 84 RBIs, coupled with a .288 average. He was thirty-nine years old and, considering the way he lived, the fact that he lasted so long was a tribute to his great natural ability.

Babe's post-playing goal was to manage the Yankees, but the offer never came, especially after he refused to manage the minor league Newark Bears of the International League to get

The Babe Calls His Shot . . . or Does He?

Despite Jimmie Foxx's heroics in 1932, the Yanks regained the American League crown over the A's and went on to meet the Chicago Cubs in the 1932 World Series. Right away, there was bad blood between the two teams. Ex-Yankee Mark Koenig had been traded to the Cubs, and the Babe, especially, didn't like the way Koenig was being treated and let the Cubs players know it. At one point in the third game, the Babe hollered over to the Cubs' bench with a reference to bandbox Wrigley Field: "I'd play for half my salary to hit in this dump all year," he said.

That set the stage. By the fifth inning of the game, the Yanks were down 4-3 when the Babe came up to face the Cubs' Charlie Root. As the legend goes, the Babe took the first two pitches for strikes, and each time held up a finger to show everyone that he knew the count. Then, before Root was ready to pitch again, the Babe held out his bat, almost as if he was pointing to the centerfield stands. Some say he was simply indicating that he had one strike left, but he turned to catcher Gabby Hartnett and said, "It only takes one to hit it."

Sure enough, Ruth went after the next pitch and hit it high and deep into the centerfield stands. As he rounded the bases, he taunted the Cubs bench and crossed home plate with a big smile on his face. Many felt that his gesture meant he was going to hit a home run to centerfield, in effect, calling his shot. Pitcher Root said that if he thought Ruth was trying to show him up like that, he would have put the ball in his ear. But the legend persists that the Babe, indeed, called his shot. After all, he was the only one good enough to do it, to almost hit a home run at will. P.S.—The Yanks won the Series in four straight games.

some experience. So the Yanks refused to sign him for the 1935 season, in effect cutting him loose. When the Boston Braves offered him a contract to play—as well as being an assistant manager and vice president with the implication that he'd eventually be made the team's manager—he went to the National League. But the Braves just wanted him as a gate attraction despite the fact that the forty-year-old slugger was just a shell of his former self. By the end of May, the Babe was struggling and looking awful at the plate. He had just three homers and his batting average was below .200. On May 25, Boston was playing the Pirates at the enormous Forbes Field in Pittsburgh. Those in attendance would never forget what they saw that day.

Legend has it that the Babe stayed out on the town almost all night with a local reporter, who then told Pirates manager Pie Traynor about it. When Traynor was going over the Braves lineup, he supposedly told his team, "Don't worry about Ruth." Sitting at that meeting was Waite Hoyt, Ruth's old teammate with the Yanks who was finishing his pitching career with the Pirates. When he heard Traynor make his pronouncement, Hoyt allegedly spoke up and gave the Pirates a word of caution. "I wouldn't say that," he warned his manager.

His first two times up that afternoon, the Babe turned back the clock and hit two long home runs, much to the chagrin of Traynor and the Pirates. The third time up he singled, then came up again in the seventh. This time he really put the wood to the ball, driving it over the right field roof at Forbes and hitting what was always considered the longest home run at that old, mammoth ballpark. It was a final touch of glory, showing everyone one last time what Babe Ruth and the home run was all about, and how much he had meant to the game. After playing just another handful of games, the Babe retired for good.

He left with a slew of hitting records, including his single season mark of 60 home runs and a lifetime 714 four-bag blasts. He also had a .342 lifetime batting average, one of the best ever, and collected 2,860 hits and a record 2,211 RBIs. And don't forget those 94 pitching victories. To this day, he is still often called the greatest of all players, and he's certainly the measuring stick for every slugger that followed. Perhaps more importantly, Babe Ruth was the single greatest influence and brought the game full cycle, from the small-ball style of the dead-ball era to a slugger's game in the 1930s. The reason was simple. Fans loved it when he hit one high and far and into the distant stands for yet another home run. And he did that more than anyone at the time could really believe possible.

As the Babe bowed out, Lou Gehrig continued his tremendous hitting with the Yanks. In 1934, the Babe's last season with the New Yorkers, Gehrig was baseball's premier slugger with 49 home runs and 165 runs batted in. Jimmy Foxx was still on the scene, chasing Gehrig all year and winding up with 44. The National League leaders were Mel Ott of the Giants and Rip Collins of the Cards, with 35 each. Both leagues hit about the same number of homers that year, 688 in the American and 656 in the National. A colorful Cardinals team, known as the Gas House Gang, won the World Series. Collins and Joe "Ducky" Medwick were St. Louis's primary power hitters, and Dizzy Dean, who won thirty games, was the star pitcher. While they were a hustling bunch of guys, they stole just 69 bases as a team, once again showing how power hitting had come to dominate the sport.

By 1935, another big slugger was starting to assert himself into the mix. Hank Greenberg of the Tigers shared the A.L. home run lead with Jimmie Foxx at 36 and led the league by a mile with 170 RBIs. He would continue to excel in the upcoming years, joining other new sluggers, like Cleveland's Hal Trosky, who slammed 42 home runs and had a league best 162 RBIs in 1936. That same year the Yankees brought up a slender, graceful centerfielder named Joe DiMaggio, who could also hit a ton. As a rookie, DiMaggio joined Gehrig to lead the Yankees to yet another pennant. Gehrig hit 49 homers once again, driving in 152 runs, while the rookie hit .323, with 29 homers and 125 RBIs. He was already being acclaimed as baseball's next great huge star.

DiMaggio really began to dominate the next year, leading the league with 46 homers and finishing second to Greenberg with 167 RBIs, though he would never quite become the super slugger many people thought he would be. Home runs numbers were continuing to rise slowly, with the American hitting 182 more than the National. The American was still the place where most of the big sluggers lived and in 1938 two of the best brought the home run and the Babe to the top of the sports pages once again. This time it was Greenberg and Foxx, both of whom began tattooing the ball as soon as the season began.

Hank Greenberg, the son of Rumanian Jewish immigrants,

grew up in New York City and went to the public schools there. He matured into a strong 6'3½", 215-pounder, but he was far from the natural Babe Ruth had been. The big kid was clumsy and awkward, so he worked extra hard to refine his skills because he didn't want to look foolish. The hard work and hours of practice paid off, and Greenberg soon began developing into quite a player. Yankee scout Paul Krichell took Hank to his first major league game in 1929, telling him that in a few years he could be the Yankee first baseman. But Greenberg was smart enough to see that Lou Gehrig would be ensconced at first for years. The Giants also wanted him. John McGraw figured a big Jewish kid would be a huge star in New York with its large Jewish population. But Hank fooled everyone and ended up signing with Detroit.

By 1938, Greenberg was already a slugging star. He played in the World Series in both 1934 and 1935, helping to bring a championship to Detroit in 1935. He also had to endure a brace of ethnic taunts, similar to the racial animosities that would greet Jackie Robinson in 1947. But he persevered to become one of the most feared sluggers in baseball. Oddly enough, Greenberg began the early part of 1938 in a batting slump. His batting average the previous four seasons was close to .340. Now he was hitting under .300, but it was the singles, doubles, and triples he wasn't getting. The home runs were still coming.

"There was a nine-game stretch when I got just five hits," Greenberg said in later years, when he looked back at the season. "But all five were home runs."

Then, right after the All-Star break, Greenberg began to pick it up, putting some distance between him and Jimmie Foxx. He had three multi-homer games in the first half of the season, then eight more in the second half, his eleven multi-homer games establishing a new record. Finally, with five games left, Greenberg hit his 58th home run, tying Jimmie Fox for the most homers ever this side of Babe Ruth. Could he tie or pass the Babe in those five games?

The first two games were against the St. Louis Browns. An erratic lefty, Howard Mills, walked Greenberg four times in the first game, leading to the claim that pitchers wouldn't give him anything to hit in order to protect the Babe's mark. Mills, however, had walked 116 batters in 210.1 innings that year, so he did have control problems. In the second game, veteran Bobo Newsome held Greenberg to a single in four at bats. Now the Tigers traveled to Cleveland for the final series of the year. On Friday, Indians' righthander Denny Galehouse held the slugger hitless at old League Park. Then the Indians decided to rearrange things a bit.

They called off the Saturday game and announced that a doubleheader would be played on Sunday, not at League Park, but at the new, huge Municipal Stadium. The stadium, that held nearly 78,000 fans, opened in 1932 and was only used then for Indians' Sunday and holiday games. By scheduling a Sunday doubleheader, the Indians hoped for a huge gate as Greenberg took his final aim at the record. It was a dark, dismal day in Cleveland with nineteen-year-old fastballer Bob Feller on the mound in the opener. All Feller did that day was become the first pitcher in baseball history to strike out eighteen hitters in the game. Greenberg fanned twice and again failed to hit a homer.

In the second game, Hank had a pair of doubles off Johnny Humphries, one of them ringing off the left centerfield fence, some 420 feet away. That one would have been a homer at League Park. Finally, with darkness approaching in the sixth inning, umpire George Moriarty had to call the game, actually apologizing to Greenberg. "I'm sorry, Hank," he said. "This is as far as I can go."

Greenberg, worn down by the homer chase and discouraged by his failure to do it one in the final five games, answered, "This is as far as I can go, too."

But it had been another epic season. Greenberg finished with 58 homers and 146 RBIs. Jimmie Foxx wound up with 50 round trippers, making it the first season ever that two players hit 50 or more, and old Double-X also led the league with 175 RBIs. American League hitters banged out 864 homers. The National again lagged behind, with only 611. Mel Ott was the leader with 36. The senior circuit still hadn't produced a slug-

The Homer in the Gloaming

The National League had a hot pennant race in 1938 with the Chicago Cubs chasing the front-running Pittsburgh Pirates. Late in the season, the Cubs thirty-eight-year-old catcher, Gabby Hartnett, took over as player-manager. Hartnett was coming to the end of a Hall of Fame career that began in 1922. He was an outstanding backstop who would wind up with a .297 batting average. Not a slugger in the classic sense, the most homers he had were 37 in the souped up 1930 season. But when he took over the managerial reins, he had the Cubs hot on the Pirates' tails.

On September 28, the Cubs had closed the gap to just half a game and were playing the Pirates at Wrigley Field. Pittsburgh had a 5-3 lead in the eighth when the Cubs tied it. As the teams went to the ninth, darkness was beginning to envelop the ballfield. If the game ended in a tie, they would have to play a doubleheader the next day. In the bottom of the ninth, which would be the final inning, Phil Cavarretta flied to Lloyd Waner and then Carl Reynolds grounded out. Hartnett was next. Reliever Mace Brown was on the hill. Brown had a fine curve and, being a catcher, Hartnett felt he would stick with it despite the fact that it was getting dark fast.

Hartnett swung at the first pitch and missed. Brown quickly threw a second curve and Gabby fouled it back. Strike two. Instead of wasting a pitch, Brown went back to the curve a third time, and this time it broke over the plate. Hartnett swung and hit a deep drive to left. Many of the fans would say later that it was so dark they couldn't even follow the flight of the ball. But a veteran hitter like Hartnett could sense it. "I got the kind of feeling you get when the blood rushes to your head and you get dizzy," Hartnett said. "I knew it was gone."

Gone it was. Hartnett had hit a ball he could hardly see, and it forever became known as the Homer in the Gloaming. It gave the Cubs the lead and they went on to win the pennant. Three years later, Gabby Hartnett retired.

ger the likes of Ruth, Gehrig, Foxx, or Greenberg. Hack Wilson's 56 in 1930 was an obvious aberration, coming the year the ball was changed and juiced. But the National was still playing the new, station-to-station game. In 1938, National Leaguers stole just 354 bases, their lowest total ever, with Stan Hack the leader with only 16.

While the 1938 season was a great one for the home run,

there was development that surprised a lot of people. Lou Gehrig, the Yanks great first sacker, had an off year. After batting .351 with 37 homers and 159 RBIs in 1937, a typical Gehrig season, he finished the 1938 season at .295, with 29 homers and 114 ribbys, good for most other players, but far below Gehrig's standards. Most felt it was an off year and the Iron Horse would be back. Sure he was thirty-five years old, but he still appeared to be in great shape, and he had never missed a single game since becoming the Yanks regular first baseman back in 1925. Maybe he just needed a day off now and then. But the following spring, Gehrig seemed a shell of his former self. He wasn't moving well and seemed to have little of his old coordination, both in the field and at the plate. He played just eight games, hitting .143, before taking himself out of the lineup after a record 2,130 consecutive games, 493 homers, a .340 lifetime batting average, and 1,990 runs batted in, second only to the Babe at the time of his retirement and still third all-time.

Soon the entire baseball world got the devastating news. Gehrig was suffering from amyotrophic lateral sclerosis, a debilitating and fatal disease. He was given a grand day at Yankee Stadium; made his now-famous speech, in which he referred to himself as "the luckiest man on the face of the earth"; and subsequently died in June of 1941 just weeks before his thirty-eighth birthday. One of the great early sluggers and great all-around players the game had ever seen was gone.

Gehrig's retirement and passing also heralded the end of yet another era. Foxx and Greenberg were one-two in homers in 1939, but they had just 35 and 33 respectively. In third place was a slender rookie with the Boston Red Sox, Ted Williams, who hit 31, one more than DiMaggio. The National League also had new blood. Big John Mize of St. Louis was the senior circuit's home run king with just 28, but he looked as if he'd hit a lot more before he was done. He proved it by taking the 1940 title with 43 while driving in 137 runs. Greenberg and Foxx continued to be the top sluggers in the A.L., starting the new decade with 41 and 36 homers, with Greenberg the RBI king with 150.

The 1940 season also saw a record 1,571 home runs hit in the major leagues, finally topping the record of 1,565 set in the juiced-ball year of 1930, and that number included a record 883 banged out by American League hitters. The game had fully turned from the 1920s, when the big blasts of the Babe gave it a new direction. Baseball also seemed to be getting healthier again. The American League had set a new attendance record in 1940, drawing 5,433,791 fans, an average of 8,778 a game, breaking the old mark set back in 1924. The National drew 4,389,693, fewer than the two previous seasons, but up from the middle of the decade when the Great Depression gripped the nation.

What was the difference in the two leagues? Bigger ballparks? Not really. Very few of the parks were filled. Could it have been that the American League was hitting more home runs and had the big name sluggers, a lineage from Ruth to Gehrig to Foxx to Greenberg to DiMaggio that the National couldn't match? No National Leaguer besides Hack Wilson had ever reached the 50 home run mark, and Wilson's achievement was tainted by the doctored ball in 1930. If that was true, it was the home run that was filling seats and the big sluggers who were drawing the crowds. There was no reason to think that anything would change.

Only it would. By 1940, war was breaking out in Europe and it wouldn't be long before America was embroiled in World War II. Many of the great stars would enter the service and the game would change for several years. The question was how the game would react when the war ended. Would it remain a game where the home run would continue to play an increasingly major role in the sport's popularity as well as the way the game was played on the field? Only time would tell.

4

A New Breed of Sluggers, 1941–1960

At the beginning of the 1941 season, thirty-year-old Hank Greenberg had become the highest paid player in the major leagues. But soon, all of that would mean very little to Hank and a score of other players. In the autumn of the previous year, Selective Service was launched to draft young men into military service. With the nefarious happenings in Europe, there was a feeling that the U.S. involvement in the war was inevitable. Greenberg was still a bachelor then and, like so many others, was eligible for the draft. In early May of 1941, after hitting a pair of home runs in a game against the Yankees, Hank was called. He was only the second big league player to be called to military duty.

While he lost the balance of the 1941 season, Greenberg learned in early December that a new provision allowed the discharge of men over the age of twenty-eight. He left the army on December 5. Two days later, the Japanese attacked Pearl Harbor and everything changed. The United States was now fully involved in a world war and Hank Greenberg quietly re-enlisted, this time as an officer candidate in the Air Corps. He eventually became a captain and served with distinction in India and China. Among other things, he was the administrative commanding officer of the first B-29 Superfortress base established on foreign soil (in China) and was part of the first land-based bombing of Japan in June of 1944.

He also lost nearly five full seasons of his baseball career!

Of course, baseball paled in importance to World War II. But Hank Greenberg's story was repeated many times over as both huge stars and journeyman players went off to war over the next four years. Big names like Greenberg, Bob Feller, Joe Di-Maggio, and Ted Williams lost three, four, or five seasons of what would have been the primes of their careers. All left great records behind, but they would have been even greater had the country not become embroiled in a war. With so many players serving their country, baseball had to make do with aging veterans, journeyman players who might not have otherwise reached the majors, and others who were disqualified from service for one reason or another. There was even some talk about shutting the game down while the war raged, but President Franklin D. Roosevelt asked that baseball be continued to create a feeling of normalcy at home as well as a diversion from the difficult conditions in Europe and Asia.

During the first five years of the new decade, baseball sunk increasingly into survival mode as more and more players left to enter the service. There really wasn't any emphasis on changing the game since everyone worried about simply keeping it in operation and putting the best possible product on the field. With each succeeding year, new players had to be found to replace those leaving for the war. Some were drafted later than others because of the number of children they had. Others simply realized the magnitude of the conflict and how much was at stake, and volunteered. But it was apparent that the game slowly deteriorated in quality between 1942 and 1945.

The effect of the war wasn't felt in 1941. With the exception of a couple of players, such as Hank Greenberg, the game was still intact. And what a season it was. That was the year that young Joe DiMaggio set the baseball world on its ear by hitting in an incredible fifty-six straight games. When the streak ended, it took two great plays by Cleveland third baseman Ken Keltner to do it, whereupon DiMag went out the next day and started another seventeen-game streak. Had Keltner not made one of those two plays, Joe D. would have hit in an even more amazing 74 straight. As is, his record 56 straight is considered one of baseball's records least likely to be broken.

That wasn't all. The 1941 season was also a real coming-out party for Boston's Ted Williams. The Splendid Splinter didn't turn twenty-three until August 30 that year. By then he was threatening to become baseballs first .400 hitter since Bill Terry in 1930. Williams, however, was not a punch-and-judy hitter, looking to place basehits all over the field. He was also a slugger who was vying for the home run title while making a run at .400. A 6'4" lefthanded hitter, Williams was not only a natural, he also worked his tail off, often taking batting practice until his hands bled. There were no batting gloves in those days. He kept up his pace all year and, going into the final doubleheader of the season, his batting average was at .399955. It had dropped from .413 earlier in September and his manager, Joe Cronin, offered to sit him, pointing out that his average would officially be recorded as .400.

"No," Williams barked at the suggestion he sit out the final two games. "I don't want to be a .400 hitter by my coattails."

Showing the great player he was, Williams then went out and got six eights in eight at bats in the final twin bill and finished the season at .406. He also led the American League with 37 homers and his 120 RBIs were five short of DiMaggio's leading 125. Otherwise, he would have taken the triple crown. Though the league had just a pair of twenty-game winners, hitting was down a bit from the year before. The league hit 149 fewer homers, but the war had not yet had an impact. The Yanks, under Joe McCarthy, won 101 games and another pennant, and they would go on to beat the Dodgers in the World Series.

In the National there still was no major slugger emerging who could dominate the league. Dolph Camilli of the Dodgers was the home run king with just 34, the only player to go over the 30 mark, and just four senior circuit hitters drove in 100 or more runs, Camilli again leading the way with 120. The league had a couple of twenty-game winners, but it did not have a young, dominating starter who could match Bob Feller. It was still the American League that had the big stars, with the excitement in 1941 being provided by DiMaggio, Williams, and Feller, who won 25, struck out 260 batters, and threw six shutouts. In the annual All-Star Game, which was started in 1933, the American League also dominated, winning six of the first nine played through 1941.

The next year the ranks began to thin. Bob Feller was gone

to the service, taking away the game's most exciting pitcher. But Ted Williams was back and this time he did win the triple crown, hitting .356, belting 36 homers, and driving in 137 runs. Yet he was the only A.L. player with more than 30 as the number of homers continued to drop. Veteran Mel Ott led the National with 30 homers and only two players, Johnny Mize and Camilli, had more than 100 RBIs. The two leagues combined for 1,071 homers, the lowest number since 1931. The game seemed to be in a leveling off period. Attendance was dropping and so were the batting averages. The National League hit just .249 and the American .257. There didn't seem to be enough big stars and now the war was beginning to take more of them. Perhaps the biggest excitement was caused by the pennant race in the National League, where the St. Louis Cardinals won 106 games and needed every one of them to top the Dodgers by just two games. The Cardinals also unveiled a rookie outfielder named Stan Musial, who hit .315 with 10 homers and 72 RBIs. He would get much, much better. When the Cardinals beat the Yanks in five games to win the title, they proved they were baseball's best that season.

By 1943, Ted Williams was gone. He would become a fighter pilot, losing three full seasons and most of two more when he was called back into action during the Korean War in the early 1950s. The Cards and Yanks met again that fall with the New Yorkers reversing fortunes in the Series, 4-1. Musial emerged as a star by winning the N.L. batting crown at .357. The American League had just four .300 hitters and three players with 20 or more homers, while the National had just one, Bill Nicholson with 29. A year later the war had really sapped both leagues of many stars. DiMaggio was gone by then and teams were scraping the barrel to fill rosters. The Dodgers used seventeen-year-old Tommy Brown at shortstop for forty-six games with regular Pee Wee Reese in the service, and the Reds allowed fifteen-year-old Joe Nuxhall to pitch two-thirds of an inning, also in 1944. A year later the St. Louis Brown played Pete Gray for seventy-seven games in the outfield. He hit .218 with 6 doubles and a pair of triples. They put him out there despite the fact that Pete

Gray had only one arm! That's what wartime baseball was all about.

It was difficult to see the direction of the game during the war. The 1945 season saw the two leagues pretty much decimated of stars. Stan Musial was probably the last of the big names to go. Stan the Man had several children and because of that was way down on the draft list, but he was finally called. When the war ended that summer, the players began returning. One of the first back had been one of the first to go. Hank Greenberg donned a Detroit Tigers uniform instead of khakis for the first time in nearly four years on July 1, 1945. In front of some 50,000 screaming fans, Greenberg didn't disappoint. He hit a home run to help the Tigers to a victory, and on the final day of the season, he whacked a dramatic grand slam with darkness approaching to give the Tigers a 6-3, ninth-inning win that clinched the American League pennant. Maybe, at last, things would be getting back to normal.

Greenberg hit 13 home runs in 270 at bats in 1945, but the American League leader was St. Louis's Vern Stephens with just 24, the only player to go over the 20 mark. Nick Etten of the Yankees had 111 RBIs, the only American Leaguer over the century mark in that category. The League hit .255 and for once was outhit by the National. Tommy Holmes of the Braves had 28 homers and Dixie Walker of the Dodgers led in RBIs with 124 as the senior circuit batted .265. Home runs stayed at wartime levels, with just 1,007 being hit. But with all the top players returning for the 1946 season, the winds of change were not far behind, in more ways than one.

A NEW BREED OF PLAYER

The American League set a new attendance record in 1945 and the National was up as well. As soon as the war ended, fans seemed to be flocking back to the ballparks in droves. There would be even a bigger jump in 1946, a season that saw some of the old and a little of the new. Players like Musial and Williams came back seemingly without missing a beat. Stan the

Man won the National League batting title at .365 and a Pittsburgh rookie named Ralph Kiner was the homer champ with 23, beating out Johnny Mize by a single round tripper. The St. Louis Cardinals, perhaps the best team of the 1940s, won yet another pennant.

In the American, Ted Williams returned from the war every bit the player he had been before. He was second in batting at .342, second in homers with 38, and second in RBIs with 123. As for turning back the clock, thirty-five-year-old Hank Greenberg put up some prewar numbers. Carrying the mantle of Ruth, Gehrig, and Foxx, the slugger topped the American League with 44 homers and 127 RBIs. In a glimpse of what would become the future, Greenberg was the first player in big league history to hit more than 40 homers without hitting .300. He finished at .277, and after the season the Tigers unceremoniously released their longtime star because they didn't want to raise his salary to $75,000. Greenberg wasn't even notified personally. He heard about it secondhand on the radio.

League averages stayed about where they were a year earlier, and home runs were up, but still below the levels reached in 1941 before the players began leaving. Stolen bases remained down and were no longer really a factor in the game. In the World Series, St. Louis beat Boston in a hard-fought seven games. Ironically, it was speed that decided the series as Enos Slaughter raced from first to home with the winning run in the eighth inning of game seven. When it was all over, it was apparent the game was back. In the following year, baseball would see one of the biggest changes since 1901, an event that would ultimately change the entire makeup of the game. At the same time, baseball would begin to evolve once again and, in the ensuing five years, the sport would slowly enter the modern era with the home run playing a greater role than ever before.

In 1947, the Brooklyn Dodgers unveiled Jackie Robinson to the baseball world amid protests and threats of team boycotts. Robinson, of course, became the first African American to play in the major leagues. By now, his story is well known. Jackie was a terrific ballplayer, not a slugger but an igniter who could do it all on the ballfield. He had to withstand tremendous verbal and physical abuse, but he prevailed. Before the 1947 season ended, Larry Doby had joined the Cleveland Indians as the first African American to play in the junior circuit. That didn't mean there were a flood of players jumping from the old Negro Leagues or flocking out of minors immediately, and a few teams didn't sign black players for years. But those that came over the next decade were destined to make their mark on the shape of the game. Because the National League was quicker to sign top African Americans players and then Latin Americans, it changed the balance of power between the two leagues in the 1950s.

The 1947 season also saw the National League begin to dominate the American in the number of home runs hit. In fact, the senior circuit would have more four baggers for the next thirteen seasons. While there were certainly some great players in the game during these years, baseball continued to be played station-to-station as more teams waited for the big slugger to hit one out. Stolen bases hit an all-time low in 1947 with just 760 thefts in both leagues. The number would dip to 730 in 1949 and then bottom out at 650 in 1950. In fact, between 1932, when steals dropped below 1,000 for the first time, and 1961, when they topped that mark again for good, big leaguers swiped more than 1,000 bases in just two seasons, 1937 and the war year of 1943. And they didn't get over the 1,000 mark by much, just a combined 31 bases. So over this three-decade period, teams were not really clawing and scratching for runs, they were just sitting back and hoping their hitters would do the job.

In 1947, the New York Giants personified that style of play close up, setting a new team record by slugging 221 home runs. John Mize was the leader with 51. In fact, he shared the league lead with Pittsburgh's Ralph Kiner, the first time that two National Leagues went over the 50 mark in the same season. Joining Mize in the Giants homer parade were Willard Marshall with 36, Walker Cooper with 35, and Bobby Thomson with 29. Yet despite their long ball prowess (they also led the league with

830 runs scored), the team finished fourth, thirteen games behind the pennant-winning Dodgers, proving once again that
slugging wasn't the answer to everything.

Kiner also emerged as a full-fledged, prime-time slugger with
51 round trippers. The Pirates had spent $100,000 to bring
Hank Greenberg to Pittsburgh in order to tutor the young slugger. Greenberg, playing part-time because of injuries, hit the
final 25 homers of his career. He would retire with 331 four-
baggers, far short of Ruth's 714 and the 534 slugged by Jimmie
Foxx. Many feel, however, that had Greenberg not lost nearly
five full prime seasons to military service, and stayed a bit
healthier, he would have approached or gone over the 600
homer mark. Also retiring after 1947 was Mel Ott, who was
managing the Giants that year and played in just four games.
Ott retired with 511 homers, yet he went over the 40 mark just
once in a twenty-two-year career. Though he was elected to the
Hall of Fame in 1951, he is often overlooked, especially today,
when people talk of the game's great sluggers. Greenberg, however, isn't.

Slugging in the American League was down in 1947. Ted
Williams won another triple crown but had just 32 homers and
114 RBIs, the only American League to surpass the 100 mark.
While the game on the field might not have been the best, the
crowds came as postwar enthusiasm continued. The National
League set a record, going over the 10 million mark for the first
time and averaging 16,756 fans per game. They wouldn't reach
that mark again until 1960. The A.L. drew almost 9,500,000,
giving the two leagues a new mark combined. The game seemed
to be getting healthier and it was about to have an infusion of
talent on a scale never seen before.

Joe DiMaggio had his last huge year in 1948, leading the
American League with 39 homers and 155 RBIs while batting
a solid .320. Then, a year later, Ralph Kiner created some real
excitement by slamming 54 home runs for the Pirates. Many
began to ask whether this strong righthanded hitter had the
ability to threaten Ruth's record. With Kiner leading the way,
the National League set a new mark with 935 homers and base-

Maybe the Greatest Slugger Ever

A very great baseball player died in January of 1947, though there was little fanfare and the average fan had no idea just how great he was. But there are still those today who say that Josh Gibson might have been the greatest slugger who ever lived. Unfortunately, Gibson played his entire career in the Negro Leagues and died at the age of thirty-six from a brain tumor, several months before Jackie Robinson became the first African American to play in the majors. Even if Gibson had lived, he would have had just a couple of years in the majors at best, and like so many other outstanding African American players, major league baseball would never see his true talent.

Just how good was Josh Gibson? He was a righthanded hitting catcher who they say slammed line drives that just kept rising and rising. Records and statistics from the Negro Leagues were sketchy at best, but it has been estimated that Gibson hit upward of 800 home runs in his career and as many as 75 in a season. Roy Campanella, the African American catcher who joined the Dodgers in 1948 at the age of twenty-six, describes Gibson's ability this way:

"When I broke in with the Baltimore Elite Giants in 1937, there were already a hundred legends about him," Campy said. "Once you saw him play, you knew they were all true. I couldn't carry his bat or glove. The stories of his 500-foot home runs are all true, because I saw them. And he was one of those sluggers that seldom struck out. You couldn't fool him; he was too quick with the bat."

Like Lou Gehrig, Gibson died much too young. But had he been given the opportunity to play his career in the majors, there's little doubt he would be among the slugging elite. In 1972, Josh Gibson was elected to the Hall of Fame—finally.

ball finally topped the record it had set back in 1940 with 1,704 round trippers. At the same time, Jackie Robinson led the league both in hitting with a .342 average and in stolen bases with 37. Robinson probably could have swiped a lot more if baseball was playing a running game then. He drove pitchers to distraction every time he got on base, giving the game a glimpse of the past and the future at the same time.

But the hitters still prevailed. By 1950 there were more batters ever going past the 20-homer mark. Many of them were not bona fide sluggers but hard hitters going with the flow and doing what many more batters now did at the plate—swing for the fences. A quick look around the majors revealed a number of these heavy hitters, many just coming into the league. The Dodgers had Duke Snider, Gil Hodges, and Roy Campanella and would lead the league with 194 homers. The Phillies had Willie Jones, Del Ennis, and Andy Seminick, while the Giants had Bobby Thomson, Hank Thompson, and Wes Westrum. Earl Torgeson, Bob Elliott, and Sid Gordon were connecting for the Braves, while the Cards had the already great Stan Musial. Big Ted Kluszewski was hammering homers for the Reds, while the Cubs had Roy Smalley, Andy Pafko, and big Hank Sauer. The cellar-dwelling Pirates had the home run champ in Ralph Kiner, with 47, and Wally Westlake. All of the above players had 20 or more homers in 1950. A few are in the Hall of Fame, although most are now largely forgotten.

It was much of the same in the American. The Yanks had DiMaggio and Yogi Berra, as well a veteran from the National League, John Mize. Detroit had Vic Wertz and Hoot Evers, while the Red Sox had Walt Dropo, Bobby Doerr, Vern Stephens, and Ted Williams. Cleveland had Luke Easter, Al Rosen (the league leader with 37), and Doby, while the White Sox boasted Eddie Robinson and Gus Zernial. The St. Louis Browns had Don Lenhardt, while the A's had Sam Chapman. Again, all these guys were over 20 homers, making a total of 36 players reaching the 20-homer mark. Compare those numbers to 1927 when the Babe hit 60 and Gehrig had 47. That year, only four other players, all in the National League, had 20 or more four baggers. Yet they called the 1920s the lively ball era. It was pretty apparent that the game had changed. To make the change complete, 1950 was also the year in which stolen bases reached an all-time low.

In 1950, National League batters combined to hit 1,100 homers, the first time a league had gone over 1,000. The American wasn't far behind with 973, and the two leagues broke the 2,000 barrier for the first time with 2,073 circuit shots. Why had the game changed at mid-century? The biggest trio of vet-

More Big Homers

With more homers hit in 1950 than ever before, two achievements still stand out. On August 31, Gil Hodges, the big first baseman of the Dodgers, became just the second player since 1901 to hit four home runs in a game. Lou Gehrig had done it back in 1932. Facing the Phils that day, Hodges had five hits in six at bats, his homers producing nine RBIs. But as great as his achievement was, it was topped when the same two teams met on October 1. This time, the National League pennant was at stake. With the game tied at 1-1 in the top of the tenth inning, Phils' first baseman Dick Sisler came up. Sisler was the son of the great George Sisler, a two-time .400 hitter, but the son was simply not the hitter the father was. Except in this at bat. Sisler picked out a Don Newcombe fastball and hit it into the left field seats for the three run homer that won the National League pennant for the Phillies, their first in thirty-five years. It was a hit to remember and showed once again the kind of instant excitement and euphoria a game-winning home run could produce.

eran stars—Williams, DiMaggio, and Musial—were all very great players. All three were genuine .300 hitters. Williams had hit .406 back in 1941, while DiMaggio topped out at .381 in 1939, and Musial won a batting title with a .376 mark in 1948. Unlike the great players in the early days of the game who hit for a high average, these three guys hit home runs as well. Williams was considered the biggest slugger, but each was a fine, all-around hitter in the mold of a number of players from the late 1920s and through the 1930s. But not all the players beginning to hit home runs in the late 1940s also hit .300. Unlike those players of the past, the new breed of slugger was not necessarily also a great hitter.

There was no radical change in the equipment. The bats may have been a bit smaller than those used by Home Run Baker and the Babe, but they were nothing like the lightweight, thin-handled bats used today. Most of the old ballparks were still in use. Some had moved the outfield fences in over the years, but not in the 1940s. No, it was simply of matter of more players approaching the game differently. Obviously, emphasis on the stolen base was greatly diminished by 1950, and with it small ball became a lost commodity. Ruth, Foxx, and Greenberg had shown what the home run could do. Sluggers were already getting more "ink" and making the big bucks. So by 1950, more players were simply swinging harder and looking to hit the ball as far as they could. And, in truth, the late 1930s and 1940s were not an era of great pitchers. Sure, there were a few, such as Bob Feller and Warren Spahn, and a number of very good ones. But there simply weren't that many who could consistently dominate a game. In other words, it was a very good time for hitters, and the trend would continue through the 1950s.

MORE GREAT HITTERS ARRIVE

In 1951 two players arrived on the scene, both of whom would leave a huge mark on the game, and three years later they would be joined by a third. They were, of course, Willie Mays, Mickey Mantle, and Henry Aaron. But before we begin to talk about them, here's a quick look at some other top sluggers who arrived on the scene between 1951 and 1960. These players, and the year they began making their mark, include Eddie Mathews and Ernie Banks (1953), Al Kaline (1954), Roberto Clemente (1955), Frank Robinson and Rocky Colavito (1956), Roger Maris (1957), Orlando Cepeda (1958), Willie McCovey and Harmon Killebrew (1959), Frank Howard, Ron Santo, and Billy Williams (1960).

Including Mays, Mantle, and Aaron, eight of the above players would wind up with 500 or more home runs in their careers. To say a new era of slugging was about to begin is an understatement. There were also others, of course, fine players who didn't hit as many home runs but certainly began making their mark on the game, and there were also plenty of veterans continuing to hit the long ball as well as younger players who would have been considered sluggers twenty years earlier. But the group mentioned above were really the tip of the iceberg, for they were the first of the modern sluggers. Not all of them were complete, five-tool players, but they could all hit the ball a ton and would dominate the game (along with more newcomers) into the 1970s.

Mays and Mantle both made a huge splash when brought up to the New York Giants and New York Yankees in 1951. Each played just part of the season but was already being lauded as can't-miss, future superstar. Both were centerfielders with tremendous speed and power. Mays was charismatic from the start, making his nonchalant basket catch in center, yet running down everything in the gaps as his cap inevitably flew from his head. Mantle was a switch hitter with tremendous power from both sides of the plate, but so fast he could drag a bunt and easily beat it out. Neither set the world on fire as rookies, Mays hit .264 with 20 homers and 68 RBIs, while Mantle batted .267, slammed 13 homers, and drove home 65 runs. But there was much more to come.

Mays would miss almost two years to military service (most of 1952 and 1953), while Mantle would take a couple of years to really come into his own. By the time they were ready to erupt in 1954, they were joined by Henry Aaron, a twenty-year-old rookie rightfielder with the Braves. Aaron may not have had the flair and charisma of the two New York stars, but he was a multitalented player who would join the others to make the trio, in a sense, the Musial-Williams-DiMaggio of their generation. And they would soon be joined by a brace of players who were almost as good.

The 1951 season was routine except for the National League pennant race. That seemed all but over in mid-August when the Dodgers opened up a 13½ game lead over their bitter rivals, the New York Giants. But the Giants, under Leo Durocher, went on a late-season tear as the Dodgers faltered, and they caught them at the wire, necessitating a best-of-three playoff for the pennant. The Giants won the first game, 3-1, behind the pitching of Jim Hearn. Then young Clem Labine shut out the New Yorkers in the second contest, 10-0. The third and deciding game was set for the Polo Grounds on October 3. Amazingly, there were some 20,000 empty seats at the old ballpark that day, but millions were watching on television. The Dodgers took a 4-1 lead into the bottom of the ninth behind big Don Newcombe, setting the stage for one of the most dramatic home runs in baseball history.

Al Dark and Don Mueller started the rally with singles. Then, after a Monte Irvin pop out, Whitey Lockman doubled, driving home Dark and putting the tying runs on second and third. That's when Dodgers manager Chuck Dressen replaced Newcombe with hard throwing righty Ralph Branca. Up stepped third sacker Bobby Thomson. Thomson already had 31 homers on the year, so he could hit the long ball, but he certainly wasn't considered a top slugger. Before he came to the plate, Manager Leo Durocher said to him, "Bobby, if you ever hit one, hit one now." It seemed like a last ditch, desperate request, and all Thomson wanted to do was put some wood on the ball. He didn't know it then, but he was about to become part of baseball history.

Branca's first pitch was right down and middle and Thomson took it for a strike. "Watch and wait," Thomson kept reminding himself, "Watch and wait." With his second pitch, Branca intended to put one up and in, hoping to set Thomson up for a curve down and away. Only the pitch wasn't quite as high and tight as he hoped, and Thomson went after it. He hit a sinking drive to deep left that cleared the wall for a pennant-winning home run. As Thomson circled the bases, Giants announcer Russ Hodges screamed over and over again to his radio audience:

THE GIANTS WIN THE PENNANT! THE GIANTS WIN THE PENNANT! THE GIANTS WIN THE PENNANT!

Bobby Thomson's Shot-Heard-Round-the-World home run is now considered one of the most dramatic in baseball history, and it is always ranked in the top five in almost every opinion poll, often topping off in the number one spot. Thomson would retire with 264 career homers, a nice number, but the other 263 would not come close to the one hit on that gray, October day. And because the times were so different then, Thomson went from the ballpark to appear on the Perry Como Show, for which he was paid $1,000, then took the Staten Island Ferry home, and walked from the Ferry to the firehouse where his brother worked, then continued home . . . alone. Imagine a player hitting that kind of dramatic homer today. He wouldn't have a moment's peace for weeks and the endorsement opportunities would be endless.

Ralph Kiner led the National League with 42 homers in 1951, Brooklyn's Gil Hodges was next with 40. The American League leader was Gus Zernial with 33. Ironically, Zernial was traded from Chicago to Philadelphia shortly after the start of the season. But big Gus, who stood 6' 2½" and weighed 210 pounds, was typical of the kind of solid slugger who played in the 1940s and 1950s. He reached the majors when he was almost twenty-six, spending a number of years in the minors as most players did then. He didn't hit for much average, being a .265 lifetime hitter, but he hit as many as 42 homers in a season and during his eleven-year career had 237 rounds trippers. There were a number of players like him at the time, not stars and largely forgotten. But they could hit the long ball. Another was American Leaguer Roy Sievers, who played from 1949 to 1965, averaged just .267, but hit 318 homers with a best of 42. Hank Sauer played in the National League from 1941 to 1959, had a .266 lifetime batting mark, but hit 288 home runs with a high of 41. These were the kind of sluggers entering the game at the time. They didn't set records and didn't hit for a high average, but they flourished in the station-to-station game of the day. The new breed sluggers would be even better.

One great player retired at the end of the 1951 season. Joe DiMaggio called it quits after thirteen seasons, a victim of injuries and declining skills at the age of thirty-six. Yet the Yankee Clipper is considered one of the all-time greats, a graceful player, fine hitter, and smooth outfielder. He retired with a lifetime .325 batting average and 361 home runs. DiMag was really not a pure slugger. Had he played in, say, Fenway Park with that short left-field wall, he certainly would have hit more. In Yankee Stadium, with deep Death Valley in left center, Joe D. simply became a fine, all-around hitter. During his career, he struck out just 369 times, only eight more strikeouts than homers, a truly amazing statistic. Can any modern-day slugger come close to that?

In 1952 and 1953, the Yankees again won the World Series, making it five straight for the latest version of the Bronx Bombers. In 1953, the National League and the Majors set another new home run record. Senior circuit hitters slammed out 1,197 round trippers and the big league total was 2,076, three more than in 1950. A new slugger was also born as Eddie Mathews of the Braves walloped 47 homers to lead the league in just his second season. Duke Snider and Roy Campanella of the Dodgers had 42 and 41 respectively, and big Ted Kluszewski of Cincinnati had 40 as the hitters took advantage of the smaller ballparks in the N.L. By this time it was apparent that the home run was on the rise. The 1954 season saw six National Leagues hit 40 or more, led by Kluszewski with 49, yet in the American League only Larry Doby with 32 hit as many as 30.

The Giants captured the National League pennant that year with Willie Mays back from the service and immediately becoming a star. Mays batted .345 with 41 homers and 110 RBIs and won the National League Most Valuable Player prize for his efforts. In game one of the World Series, against highly favored Cleveland, Mays made an unbelievable catch off the bat of Vic Wertz, running the ball down 440 feet from home plate and grabbing it while running full speed with his back to home plate. There were two on at the time, and Willie wheeled and got the ball back to the plate so quickly that neither runner could advance. His catch saved the game, but a home run won it, and it came from an unlikely source.

With the game tied at 2-2 in the bottom of the tenth, the Giants put a pair of runners on against Bob Lemon. Manager Leo Durocher called on pinch hitter Dusty Rhodes, who had hit .341 with 15 homers and 50 RBIs in a part-time and pinch hitting role. It was one of those magical years when Rhodes always seemed to find the hole. Against Lemon, he found the stands, but just barely. He hit the ball close to the right-field line, the shallowest part of the old ballpark, and it went into the first row, some 258 feet from home plate. Short homer or not, it was of the walk-off variety, and the Giants took the opener, then went on to sweep the Indians to become world champs. For James Lamar "Dusty" Rhodes, it was his ultimate moment in the sun.

Then in 1955, the young sluggers began taking over. Willie Mays belted 51 homers to lead the National. Big Kluszewski had 47, a slim shortstop named Ernie Banks, in just his second full season, slammed 44 for the Cubs, the veteran Snider had 42, and Eddie Mathews slugged 41. Batting averages were down. The league hit just .259 with the Phils Richie Ashburn, a singles hitter, leading the league at .338, the only player over .320. Not surprisingly, the senior circuit set another home run record with 1,263. In the American, Mantle was beginning to emerge, winning his first homer title with 37. But only one other American Leaguer, Gus Zernial, had 30 or more, and he hit the mark right on the nose. The league hit 961—not a record, but combined with the National, it set a new big league home runs standard of 2,224. It wouldn't last long. The hitters were beginning to dominate and the name of the game was long ball.

If 1955 marked Willie Mays's coming-out party, then the 1956 season belonged to Mickey Mantle. Though the American League had lagged behind the National in slugging, they slowly began closing the gap and Mantle was a big reason. Showing tremendous power from both sides of the plate, Mantle began hitting some of the longest home runs seen in many years. Some even say the phrase *tape measure home run* was created to gauge some of Mantle's long homers. He had a long, powerful swing and hit high, majestic drives similar to those of the Babe. The successor to Joe DiMaggio as the Yankees centerfielder, Mickey was playing arguably the most glamorous position in the game, and his powerful hitting turned the fans on, especially in 1956 when he began fulfilling his tremendous potential.

Besides leading the Yankees to yet another pennant, Mantle won the triple crown with a .353 batting average, 52 home runs, and 130 runs batted in. He also led the league in slugging

The Say Hey Kid

Willie Howard Mays got his unique nickname because he had trouble remembering names. Whenever he would come upon someone, he would simply greet them with, "Say, hey." But this native of Westfield, Alabama, never forgot anything on a baseball field. He had an innate sense of the game and rarely made a mistake on the diamond. When he went after a fly ball, he always knew the game situation and where his throw had to go. In fact, he's often called the greatest centerfielder ever. He ran the bases with controlled abandon and, if a fielder hesitated for a moment, Willie would take the extra sack. Born in 1931, he was so good that he signed with the Birmingham Black Barons of the Negro Leagues in 1948, at the age of seventeen. Fortunately, for all of baseball, Jackie Robinson had broken the color line the year before, and by 1951 Mays was with the New York Giants and beginning one of baseball's great careers.

Mays was not a huge man, standing just 5'11" and weighing 180 pounds, so he wasn't the prototype slugger. But he had tremendous strength in his hands and arms and exploded at the ball from the right side of the plate. No pitcher intimidated him and during his long career he faced the best. Knock him down and he didn't charge the mound or even give a threatening glare at the pitcher. He knew this was part of the game and his answer was to get a base hit. He played the game with an enthusiasm and a boyish exuberance that was perhaps unmatched in the annals of the sport, and in his early years with the Giants, before the team moved to San Francisco, Mays often showed up in Harlem and played stickball with the local kids right out on the streets. He retired after the 1973 season, leaving a great legacy and 660 home runs among his many baseball achievements.

percentage, home run percentage, and runs scored. The Mick had 20 more homers than the next American Leaguer, Vic Wertz with 32. Still, the league cracked the 1,000 mark for the first time and both leagues hit 2,294, a new record, with the National League leader Brooklyn's Duke Snider with 43.

To further indicate just how much the home run was coming to dominate the game, the Cincinnati Reds tied the all-time record of 221, set by the New York Giants of 1947. The Reds were led by a rookie outfielder named Frank Robinson, who tied Wally Berger's long-standing rookie record of 38 homers.

He was followed by Wally Post with 36, Ted Kluszewski with 35, Gus Bell with 29, and Ed Bailey with 28. The slugging Reds almost won the pennant, finishing just two games behind Brooklyn. The Yankees, by contrast, let the A.L. with 190. Though they didn't have a great pitching staff, the Reds led the National League in runs scored and showed that a team of sluggers could challenge for the pennant.

Though home run totals would level off for the remainder of the decade, the young sluggers continued to assert themselves. In 1957, Henry Aaron of the Braves won his first home run crown with 44, followed by Ernie Banks of the Cubs with 43. Aaron also took the RBI title with 132 and became the league's MVP as the Milwaukee Braves won the pennant and went on to beat the Yanks in the World Series. Dependable Roy Sievers won the A.L. crown with 42, but the big news in the junior circuit was made by Ted Williams. Some sixteen years after becoming baseball's last .400 hitter, the thirty-nine-year-old Splendid Splinter flirted with the magic mark again, winning the batting title with a .388 average. Williams also clubbed 38 homers and led the league with a .731 slugger average. It was an amazing performance by a great hitter at an advanced baseball age. And in the National, thirty-six-year-old Stan Musial won another batting title with a .351 average, adding 29 homers and 102 RBIs. So baseball's two senior stars showed they could still compete with the young turks and further cemented their place in baseball history.

A year later, Ernie Banks put to rest forever the perception that shortstops were punch-and-judy hitters. Banks belted 47 homers, paving the way for the hard-hitting shortstops that would emerge years later. But he was the first, adding 129 RBIs and winning the first of two straight Most Valuable Player awards. He would hit another 45 the following season, losing the home run crown to Eddie Mathews by one, while Aaron had 39, Frank Robinson 36, and Mays 34. The players who had come in during the 1950s were now not only starting to dominate the game, but also showing the baseball world that they were destined to become all-time, Hall of Fame greats.

Another pair of newcomers tied for the A.L. homer crown in 1959. Harmon Killebrew of the Senators and Rocky Colavito of the Cleveland Indians smacked 42 apiece. Unlike Mays, Mantle, and Aaron, both of these guys would become outstanding sluggers but not quite the all-around players the others were. Killebrew would wind up with 573 homers, making him an elite slugger and Hall of Famer, but doing it with just a .256 lifetime batting average. Colavito's career lasted just fourteen years. He was a good outfielder with a great throwing arm, and wound up with just 374 homers and a .266 lifetime average. Rocky never made the Hall of Fame as the home run criteria for almost automatic induction became the 500 mark for the modern slugger.

The 1960 season would begin a new decade in a very dramatic way and set the stage for what was to follow a year later. Prior to the season, the Yankees had made a trade with Kansas City, bringing outfielder Roger Maris to the team. Maris was a fine all-around player, a lefthanded hitter with good power and an excellent rightfielder, but he was also considered a cut below the so-called superstar level. Teamed with the superstar Mantle, he would give the Yankees a new, one-two punch. Mantle, Maris, and the Yanks would again be the class of the league and were the big story right until the final at-bat of the entire baseball season. That at-bat would result in one of the most dramatic home runs in baseball history, and it would be hit by a very unlikely player.

Not surprisingly, the Yanks cruised to the American League pennant. Mantle won the home run crown with 40, followed by Maris with 39. Roger also led the league in RBIs with 112 and won the MVP. As a team, the Yanks hit 193 homers and again lived up to their reputation as the Bronx Bombers. The National League had a surprise winner. The Pittsburgh Pirates, led by MVP shortstop Dick Groat and emerging superstar Roberto Clemente, beat the Braves by seven games. But they were considered downright underdogs to the hard-hitting Yanks in the World Series.

It was a strange fall classic right from the start. Pittsburgh won games 1, 4, and 5 by scores of 6-4, 3-2, and 5-2. The

Going Out in Style

Following the 1960 season, one of the greatest ballplayers ever finally hung up his cleats at the age of forty-two. Ted Williams retired with a .344 lifetime batting average and 521 home runs. He won six American League batting titles, was the home run champ four times, and led the league in RBIs on four occasions. And, of course, he had that incredible .406 season in 1941. Had Williams not lost nearly five full seasons to military service, he undoubtedly would have hit well over 600 home runs and might have even challenged Ruth's 714.

Not surprisingly, Williams went out in style. At the age of forty-two he was still good enough to hit .316 with 29 home runs. And, in his final at bat ever at Fenway Park in Boston, Williams said goodbye to baseball by hitting the last of his 521 homers. There are some, even today, who consider Ted Williams the greatest hitter who ever lived. He was that good.

Yanks won games 2, 3, and 6 by scores of 16-3, 10-0, and 12-0, all blowouts with two being complete game shutouts by ace lefty Whitey Ford. Through six games the Yanks were in the process of setting all kinds of hitting records. Mantle had three homers, Maris a pair, but the Bombers still had to win game seven at Forbes Field in Pittsburgh to become champs. This one was back and forth from the start. The Pirates jumped off to a 4-0 lead after two, but by the sixth inning the Yanks had taken a 5-4 advantage, thanks to a three-run homer by Yogi Berra. The Yanks upped the lead to 7-4 in the top of the eighth and it began to look as if it was over.

In the bottom half of the inning the Pirates got a break. What looked like a routine grounder to short took a bad hop and hit Tony Kubek in the throat. Kubek had to leave the game and the Pirates jumped on their good fortune to score five runs and take a 9-7 lead. But they still couldn't hold it. The Yanks came back with two runs in the top of the ninth to knot the game once again. In the bottom of the ninth, Manager Casey Stengel stayed with righthander Ralph Terry, who had come on to get the final out in the eighth. Terry was essentially a starter who was 10-8 during the season. Leading off for the Pirates was second sacker Bill Mazeroski, a solid hitter and great fielder, who hit .273 with 11 homers and 64 RBIs during the regular season. In other words, Maz wasn't considered a big home run threat even though he had hit a two-run homer in the opening game.

Mazeroski took the first pitch for a ball and then jumped on the second one. He hit a Terry fastball deep to left . . . and over the ivy-covered wall for a World Series winning, walk-off home run. It was the only time in baseball history that game seven of a World Series ended with a home run in the bottom of the ninth inning. Mazeroski triumphantly circled the bases as his teammates waited to rejoice at home plate. And the Yanks, who had slammed a record 91 hits in the series, left the field dejected losers.

Even today, some polls rank Mazeroski's home run as the greatest of all-time. It certainly was a moment to remember and, in a sense, it served as a prelude. It showed baseball fans everywhere how exciting a game-winning homer could be. There probably wasn't a single player in the big leagues or, for that matter, a baseball player anywhere who wouldn't have traded places with Maz at that moment. Yet while his lightning-strike of a homer had produced instant excitement, what was about to happen the following year would put the home run on center stage with a drama that would grip the entire nation.

5

The M & M Boys Excite a Nation, 1961

By 1961, the style of play was poised to change once again, but the landscape of the game was already changing. It began back in 1953, when the Boston Braves, their attendance flagging badly, moved the franchise to Milwaukee. It was the first change of any kind in the basic structure of the game since 1903, when the American League New York Highlanders (later the Yankees) joined the league, displacing the original Baltimore Orioles. Then in 1954, the Orioles returned, but only because the St. Louis Browns also threw in the towel and moved east. But the biggest shakeup came four years later.

After the 1957 season, Brooklyn Dodgers owner Walter O'Malley heeded the advice dispensed by journalist Horace Greeley back in the nineteenth century. Greeley was quoted as saying, "Go west, young man," referring to the potential of the then undeveloped West Coast of the nation. O'Malley also saw gold on the West Coast, only it was dollars, not nuggets, and he decided to move the beloved Brooklyn franchise—which had won six pennants and a World Series since 1947 to Los Angeles. Almost as soon as O'Malley made his decision, New York Giants owner Horace Stoneham reacted similarly. Attendance was also down at the antiquated Polo Grounds and Stoneham, following O'Malley's lead, decided his team would prosper in San Francisco, rekindling immediately the old and deep rivalry between the two ballclubs on the west coast. Before that, baseball never ventured west of St. Louis, but beginning in 1958, the Major League Baseball stretched from ocean to ocean.

If that wasn't enough, New York was suddenly without a National League team after having two competing franchises for decades. Now the Yankees were left alone to rule supreme.

From 1947 to 1960, there had been seven so-called *subway series*, World Series between the Yanks and either the Dodgers or
Giants. Now, the two clubs were gone. Three years later, when
the 1961 season began, there was an even more radical change
in place. The lords of the game felt it was time for baseball to
grow. Now that the game had roots on the West Coast, baseball
decided to add more teams, in effect to expand. So when the
American League season began, there was a new team in Los
Angeles (the Angels) and a new team in Washington as well.
The old Senators, an American League original, moved to Minnesota that same season to become the Twins and were replaced
immediately by an expansion franchise. So baseball had also
moved to the upper Midwest. Plans also included the addition
of two new National League teams the following season, one in
Houston and the other in New York.

To accommodate the new ten-team league, the schedule makers added eight games, making the 1961 American League season 162 games instead of the traditional 154. At the time this
change was announced, no one thought much of it. Sure, there
were eight more games, a little more than a week's worth—
some extra baseball for everyone. Yet before the season ended,
those eight games would figure in one of the greatest debates
the game has seen in years. At the core of the debate would be
Babe Ruth's home run record of 60, set thirty-four years earlier,
in 1927.

When the season began the Yankees were once again considered baseball's best team. The seven-game loss to the Pirates in
1960 was looked upon as an aberration, something that
couldn't happen again, especially because of the way the Yanks
hit in the games they won, setting records with 91 hits and 55
runs. This was a powerhouse team from top to bottom. The
Yanks had a great infield with Bill "Moose" Skowron at first,
Bobby Richardson at second, Tony Kubek at short, and Clete
Boyer at third. Kubek and Richardson were a great double play
combination, and Boyer was an acrobatic performer, a guy who
could make spectacular plays and had a great arm. Skowron

was a good hitter capable of between 25 and 30 homers. The team also had the luxury of three catchers. The veteran Yogi Berra was still a threat at the plate, and Elston Howard, the Yanks first African American player, was in his prime. The third catcher, John Blanchard, was a powerful lefthanded hitter who could put the ball in the seats. To get all three playing time, new manager Ralph Houk let Howard do the bulk of the catching and also spell Skowron at first on occasion. Berra played a lot of left field and still caught a number of games. Blanchard also caught some and played some outfield as well. He was also the team's top lefthanded pinch hitter. In 1961, it worked like a charm.

Then there were the two other outfielders, Mickey Mantle in center and Roger Maris in right. Both were coming off fine seasons in 1960 and expected to be the focal point of the offense once more, although no one realized at the time just how focal they would be. To complement the outstanding hitting, the Yanks also had a fine pitching staff led by ace lefty Whitey Ford, righthander Ralph Terry, and a fine little southpaw relief pitcher named Luis Arroyo. Houk had replaced the venerable Casey Stengel after the 1960 season, so he was in his first year at the helm. But, as a former Yankee backup catcher, he knew the team and the system. Everything was in place for a potentially big season.

The American League was loaded with hard-hitting sluggers that season. With two new teams and more young and untried pitchers, it figured to be a good year for batters from the beginning. The Detroit Tigers were the team expected to challenge the Yanks. Not only did the Tigers have a fine pitching staff, led by Yankee killer Frank Lary and Jim Bunning, but they could hit. Al Kaline was considered the club's best all-around player, but they also had a hard-hitting first baseman in Norm Cash and had acquired slugger Rocky Colavito in a trade with Cleveland several years earlier. The Orioles and White Sox also had good teams, but the consensus was that the Yanks were easily the class of the league.

Much of the first month of the season proved there would

indeed be a pennant race in the A.L. The Yanks and Tigers quickly showed they were the league's best teams, both winning five of their first six games. By the end of the month, the two continued running neck in neck, the Tigers at 10-4, leading the Yanks by a game. Mickey Mantle was off to a solid start. The Mick smacked seven homers during April, was healthy, and pointing toward another big year. Roger Maris, however, the reigning MVP, wasn't hitting. Maris didn't get his first homer until the team's eleventh game on April 26, helping the Yanks to a 13-11 win over Detroit. Mickey hit a pair that day, his sixth and seventh, and that's the kind of hitting from the two sluggers the team was hoping to see.

Because of Maris's slow start, Manager Houk also decided to make a change in the batting order. Mantle had been hitting third and Maris cleanup. Now Houk flipflopped them hoping Maris would get better pitches to hit, the theory being that who, in their right mind, would pitch around Roger Maris to get to Mickey Mantle. The switch worked to perfection and before long both sluggers began bashing the baseball. Maris woke up to hit 11 homers in May, while Mantle hit seven more. By the end of the month, the Mick had 14 and Rog had 12. But the team had not yet gone on a sustained winning streak and had a 23-17 record, still three and a half games behind the 29-16 Tigers.

Then in June, Maris really got hot. He would wallop another 15 home runs in June, with 10 of them coming on the road, to take over the league lead with 27. The Mick smacked 11 and trailed his teammate by two. Despite the heavy hitting, New York still lagged behind the Tigers by two games as Detroit was getting a career year from first sacker Norm Cash, the usual fine performance from Kaline, and Rocky Colavito was on a pace to hit more than 40 home runs. The pitching was also very good, so there was a pennant race after all. But more than that, the number counters were soon beginning to look at Maris and Mantle. When the All-Star break arrived, the hot Maris had 35 homers while Mantle wasn't far behind with 31. Maris had hit his 35th home run in the Yanks 86th game. Through eighty-six

games in 1927, Babe Ruth had just 30 homers, and both sluggers were now ahead of the fabled Ruth pace.

That's when the pressure began. Suddenly, the nation was
aware that not one but two sluggers had a chance to break
what was arguably baseball's most sacred record. Add to that
the fact that they were not only teammates but also New York
Yankees, Babe's team, and the story became huge. Shortly after
that, someone christened the two sluggers the M & M Boys, a
sobriquet for the duo that looked great in print. Then, by the
end of July, Maris reached the 40-homer mark with Mantle
keeping pace at 39. Roger had hit his 40th in the Yanks 96th
game. After ninety-six games, the Babe had just 33 homers, so
both Rog and the Mick were continuing well ahead of the
Babe's pace. With all that, the drama continued to build. Ruth,
of course, had set the record by having an incredible September,
hitting his final 17 homers in the last month of the season. That
was always where the few pretenders to the throne had faded.
But the M & M Boys were showing no signs of slowing down.

As the dog days of August approached, something unexpected began happening in New York. Up to this point, the fans
had been cheering for both sluggers. Now, with the record
seemingly within reach, there was a definite swing in popularity
to Mantle. In a sense, it was kind of unexpected. In his early
years with the Yanks, Mantle often heard catcalls, especially in
1952 and 1953 when the Korean War was raging. Fans saw this
strong, fast, young player who could seemingly do everything
on a ballfield and wondered why he wasn't in the service. Calls
of *draft dodger* came cascading down from the far reaches of
the stadium. What people didn't know then was that while
playing football in high school, Mantle had been kicked in the
lower leg and developed *osteomyelitis*, a bacterial infection of
the bone and bone marrow. It was this condition that led to his
being classified 4-F by the draft board, unfit for military service.
Seeing how he performed on the ballfield and not knowing
about this bone disease, many fans felt otherwise.

But that was in the past. By 1961 the Mick had been with the
Yanks for a decade, and with Ruth's record in sight, these same

fans felt that Mickey should be the one to break it. After all, he was the *true Yankee*, the successor to DiMaggio, who was the successor to Gehrig and Ruth. It was a natural lineage, one in which Roger Maris simply didn't belong. Maris was being looked upon as the newcomer, a guy who came in a trade the year before and wasn't a home-grown, full-blooded New York Yankee. Many felt he didn't deserve to break the record, and the fans began to turn on him. It may sound unbelievable now that with the Yanks still in a pennant race that fans would blatantly root against one of their own, but it happened. And it began weighing heavily on the psyche of Roger Maris.

A small-town guy who grew up in Fargo, North Dakota, where he was a three-sport star in high school, Maris was an outstanding halfback on the football team, and he was so good that Bud Wilkinson, coach of the Oklahoma Sooners, actually recruited him. He eventually chose baseball and signed with Cleveland, was promoted to the majors in 1957, and then was traded to Kansas City a year later. Before coming to the Yankees in 1960, Maris had never hit above .273, hadn't topped 28 homers, and never drove home more than 80 runs. He didn't hit long, tape-measure shots like the Mick and lacked the kind of charisma that the press and media liked. Mantle was used to dealing with the New York media, and his *aw-shucks* Southern drawl and self-effacing humor finally won over the writers. Maris often didn't know how to respond to their many questions, especially when the home runs began piling up. In fact, he was a guy who didn't aspire to greatness and seemed to be having a difficult time handling his newfound notoriety.

"I never wanted all this hoopla," Maris would say. "All I want is to be a good ballplayer and hit 25 or 30 homers, drive in a hundred runs, hit .280, and help my club win pennants. I just wanted to be one of the guys, an average player having a good season."

In the eyes of most, he was an average player or a slightly above average player suddenly having a great season, at least as far as home runs and RBIs were concerned. Maris had batted .283 in his MVP season of 1960, and in 1961, despite all the homers, was struggling to get his average above .270. Heck, when the Babe blasted 60, he also batted .356. Mantle, right behind Maris in homers, was flirting with the .320 mark and had already hit .365 and .353 in his career. Yep, he was the true Yankee, the guy who should break the Babe's record, if anyone was going to break it.

Mantle was also a small-town guy, having been born in Spavinaw, Oklahoma, on October 20, 1931. His family moved to Commerce, Oklahoma, when he was four and he wound up starring for Commerce High. His father, Elvin "Mutt" Mantle, was a miner and wanted his son to be a ballplayer from the start. He's the one who insisted Mickey switch hit. By the time he was a teenager, there were already stories of his mammoth home runs. He was a three-sport star in high school and then was discovered by scout Tom Greenwade, who eventually signed him for the Yankees. Coming to New York wasn't easy at first, but Mantle went through the tough times in the early 1950s and eventually learned how to handle and sometimes deflect the media. By 1961, he simply refused to let them bother him.

In that sense, there was more pressure on Maris than the Mick. Mantle had been dealing with the New York media for a decade and could be charming or evasive, depending on his mood, but rarely offensive. Maris, because of his innate lack or color or charisma, was perceived as dull and, as the questions mounted, finally as evasive and even confrontational. Certain members of the press also turned against him, joining the many fans who were rooting outwardly for Mantle. The media even tried to claim a feud between the two, something that couldn't be further from the truth. The two men, opposites in so many ways, genuinely liked each other and pulled for each other to succeed.

By July 30, the Yanks had finally eased ahead of the Tigers, leading by one and a half games. They would slowly increase the lead, though not really shake the Tigers, until early September. Despite a close pennant race, more and more attention turned to the home run chase because both sluggers continued

Mickey Mantle and the Tape Measure

Many still say that it was the immense power of Mickey Mantle that led to the phrase *tape measure home run*. It may have started way back in 1953, Mantle's third year in the league. On April 7, the Yanks were playing at old Griffith Stadium in Washington when Mantle came up batting righthanded against Senators' lefty Chuck Stobbs. The Mick got the pitch he liked and sent a rocket that went clean out of the old ballpark and just seemed to keep going. Someone saw where it landed and the blast was ultimately measured as landing 565 feet from home plate. Some still call it the longest documented homer ever hit.

"I never saw a ball hit so far," said Yank lefty Bob Kuzava. "You could have cut it up into 15 singles."

Soon, the Mick's power became legendary. In May of 1955, he hit three homers in a game at the Stadium, all three going into the centerfield bleachers, and each clearing the 461-foot sign that adorned that distant fence. In 1963, Mantle came within of foot of hitting the first fair ball out of Yankee Stadium, something that still hasn't been done. He hit a high drive to right which arched above the third tier of stands and bounced off the right field facade about a foot below the top. Experts looking at the trajectory of the baseball have estimated that, had it traveled unimpeded, it would have gone some 602 feet.

That was the power of Mickey Mantle. Even the top sluggers of the modern era, behemoths like Jose Canseco and Mark McGwire, would have trouble matching the consistent, long home runs that were hit by the Mick back in the 1950s and 1960s.

to stay ahead of the Babe's pace. When Mantle hit three homers on August 6, he took the lead, 43-41. Many felt that the Mick would now command center stage and Maris would fade, as Lou Gehrig had in 1927. But the resilient Maris picked up the pace, blasting two homers on August 13 and two more on the 16th. He now had 48 homers in 119 games, once again taking over the lead from Mantle, who had 45. The Babe, after 119 games, had 39 home runs. So both sluggers continued to run ahead of Ruth's pace.

By September 1, the Yanks still only had a game and a half

lead on Detroit, but the New Yorkers were about to embark on a thirteen-game winning streak that would break the pennant race wide open, increasing their lead to twelve games. And with the final month of the season looming, Roger Maris had 51 home runs with Mickey Mantle still on his heels with 48. It was becoming the greatest two-man race for the home run record in baseball history to that time. Fans would not see anything else like it for another thirty-seven years. Even in cities where there was no major league baseball, people grabbed the newspapers and tuned into radio and TV newscasts to see if either of the M & M Boys had hit another home run. The name and image of the Babe, who died in 1948, was being brought up more often than it had in any time since his death. It was almost as if the Bambino and his record had been brought back to life.

That's when the possibility of the record being broken began spawning yet another debate and controversy. It started in the press and it spread quickly to the office of Baseball Commissioner, Ford Frick. Suddenly, the new 162-game schedule became an important issue. What if either Mantle or Maris broke the record, but didn't do it until those extra eight games? Not fair, said some defenders of the Babe. Among them was Commissioner Frick, who had been a personal friend of Ruth's. Finally, Frick made a controversial ruling. He said that for a new home run record to count, it would have to be set within the first 154 games of the season. If the record-breaking home run was hit in the final eight games, it would appear in the record book with an asterisk alongside it, saying it was set in a 162-game schedule. In other words, there would be two separate records.

Not everyone agreed, sparking yet another debate. Would this asterisk ruling apply to any baseball record set in the final eight games of a 162-game schedule? American League President Joe Cronin, who played in Ruth's era, said he saw no logic in Frick's ruling, adding that, "A season is a season, regardless of the number of games."

None of this debate helped Roger Maris with his growing angst. He was not only perceived more than ever as the villain, the interloper, but he was also having an increasingly difficult time with the media, having to answer questions such as why he thought so many more fans were rooting for Mantle to break the record or how he could possibly compare himself to the great Babe Ruth, something he really never did.

"I don't want to be Babe Ruth," he said. "He was a great ballplayer. I'm not trying to replace him. The record is there and damn right I want to break it, but that isn't replacing Babe Ruth."

The pressure and stress became so intense over the final month of the season that Maris's hair actually began to fall out in clumps. Doctors assured him it was stress and nothing else, but it was a very disconcerting situation. In what should have been his greatest season, one that he could revel in and enjoy, going after the Babe's record was turning into a personal hell. On September 9, Maris belted his 56th home run off Jim "Mudcat" Grant of Cleveland, giving him the same number Hack Wilson had hit in 1930. A day later, on September 10, Mantle hit number 53. At that same point in the season, the Babe also had 53. So it was getting close. There were eighteen games left, but only ten if they were going to do it within 154 games. Then, fate took over and the record chase would be left in the hands of a single player.

First Mantle came down with a cold he couldn't seem to shake. It lingered and it weakened him. Finally he went to see a doctor who was recommended to him and received an injection in the area of his lower hip. The point of the injection soon became infected and had to be cut open and lanced, the developing sore making it difficult for him to play. He wouldn't hit another home run for almost two weeks, and when he smacked his 54th on September 24, it was the last one he would hit all season. He wound up missing eight games due to the hip infection and was obviously not at full strength in a number of others. Maris, then, was left to carry on alone.

Considering the tremendous pressure he was under, Rog made a gallant effort. He hit number 57 in game 151, off a tough pitcher, Frank Lary of Detroit. Then, the next day, he slammed number 58 off Terry Fox of the Tigers. Finally, he went into game number 154 at Baltimore still needing three homers to break the record within the boundary set by Commissioner Frick. That night he slammed number 59 off Milt Pappas and barely missed number 60 when another long drive went foul. When he came up for the final time, he had to face Hoyt Wilhelm, one of the best knuckleball pitchers of all time. He hit a check-swing grounder to first and that part of his chase was over.

But there were still eight games left and no reason to quit. Rog didn't hit one over the next three and then, facing Jack Fisher of the Orioles, he became the second man in the history of baseball to hit 60 home runs in a season, slamming one into the right field seats at Yankee Stadium. The fans cheered as he circled the bases. With Mantle out of the chase, some of the animosity against Maris had disappeared. Now, he had four games left to try to get past the Babe, Frick's asterisk notwithstanding. Once again he was stifled for three straight contests, the pressure building. Finally, the Yanks were hosting the Boston Red Sox in the final game of the season. The Sox had righthander Tracy Stallard on the mound and interest was high to see if Roger Maris could do it.

In the fourth inning, Maris stepped in for his second at bat. Stallard threw a fastball and Roger swung the bat the same way he had all year. He hit a drive to right that cleared the wall and went about 340 feet into the right field stands. Home run number 61! He had done it. Maris rounded the bases the same way he had all year, no faster, no slower. There wasn't a large crowd at the stadium, but those there cheered and, once in the dugout, his teammates had to force him out for a curtain call. Fittingly, the Yankees won the game, 1-0, completing their season with a 109-53 record, giving them an eight-game advantage over a very good Detroit team.

Like him or not, count it as a new record or not, Roger Maris has done something remarkable. He put together a season in which he hit 61 home runs and drove home 142 runs, the best in the majors. His detractors pointed to the fact that he only hit .269, but that was emblematic of the changing game. Sluggers no longer had to hit .350, just pound out the home runs. Mantle finished with 54, hit .317, and drove home 128 runs, another great season for Mickey. Had he not developed the hip infection, who knows? He might have also gone over 60 or pushed Maris to go even higher. That, we'll never know.

As great as the season was for Maris, the pressures and personal attacks from both the press and fans made it one he couldn't enjoy. He put it in perspective when he said, "As a ballplayer, I would be delighted to do it again. As an individual, I doubt if I could possibly go through it again."

It was also an interesting season in other ways. The powerful Yankees, riding the wave created by the M & M Boys, set a new major league record with 240 home runs. Bill Skowron had 28, Yogi Berra 22, Elston Howard and John Blanchard 21 each in the sports of the M & M Boys. American League hitters on the whole set a new mark with 1,534 four baggers. Jim Gentile of Baltimore had a career year with 46, the same number as Harmon Killebrew of the Twins. Rocky Colavito of Detroit slammed 45 and teammate Norm Cash, the batting champ at .361, hit 41. So six A.L. players had gone over the 40 mark, and 22 players had hit 20 or more.

National League hitters had 1,196, not quite up to the record 1,263 they hit in 1955, but combined with the American, big league hitters set a new mark with 2,730 home runs. In the senior circuit, Orlando Cepeda of the Giants led with 46, while Willie Mays followed with 40. Some nineteen N.L. hitters were over the 20 mark. Interestingly, many pointed to expansion as the reason so many homers were hit in the American League, saying that the pitching had become diluted as the staffs on the new clubs had the highest earned run averages in the league. But the National hadn't expanded yet and actually had a higher league batting average than the American, .262 compared to .256.

If the pitching was so bad, why weren't the batting averages up? The reason was that the game was still changing. With Maris and Mantle getting a ton of ink for their home run chase, everyone began swinging for the fences. The fact that there were more home runs but a league batting average that was only one point higher than 1960, before expansion, points out once again that the home run was continuing to occupy a more prominent place in the game than ever before. Asterisk or not, Roger Maris had shown everyone that 60 wasn't sacred. It could be topped. Seeing what he had done, every great slugger in the game probably was thinking, why not me?

The Yanks, by the way, won the World Series easily, topping the Cincinnati Reds in five games, including two more shutouts by Whitey Ford, who was 25-4 during the regular season. Maris had just two hits, one of them a homer, while Mantle only played in two games and had a single hit. But the rest of the Yanks picked it up with the supporting cast hitting six home runs, showing that they were a great team top to bottom, even without major contributions from the M & M Boys.

As for Roger Maris, hitting 61 home runs was not only something he couldn't totally enjoy when he hit them, he couldn't enjoy them for years afterward either. The following season Maris didn't live up to expectations. He hit just .256 with 33 homers and 100 RBIs. After that, a series of injuries reduced him to little more than a good journeyman ballplayer. He never hit more than 26 homers or drove in more than 71 runs again. After the 1966 season, in which he hit just .233 with 13 homers and 43 RBIs, and was booed mercilessly by the New York fans, he was traded to the St. Louis Cardinals, where he helped win two pennants and a World Series, but with very modest numbers. He retired after the 1968 season with a .260 lifetime batting average and 275 home runs, and his immediate memories of his days in New York weren't good ones.

"Every day I went to the ballpark in Yankee Stadium as well as on the road people were on my back," he said. "The last six years in the American League were mental hell for me. I was drained of all my desire to play baseball."

After retirement, he ran a successful beer distributorship in Florida. For a number of years he appeared bitter, once saying, "Now they talk on the radio about the records set by Ruth, Di-Maggio, and [Henry] Aaron. But they rarely mention mine. Do

you know what I have to show for the sixty-one home runs?
Nothing, exactly nothing."

Years later, after George Steinbrenner bought the Yankees in
the 1970s, Roger Maris finally agreed to return to Yankee Stadium. At long last he was greeted with warm cheers and af-
fection from the fans when he appeared at Old Timers Days,
something sorely missing in 1961. He seemed to genuinely appreciate it. Unfortunately, in the early 1980s Maris was diag-
nosed with lymphatic cancer and he died in December of 1985
at the age of fifty-one. He has never been elected to Baseball's
Hall of Fame.

Mickey Mantle also didn't travel a happy road after 1961.
Injuries and years of hard living began catching up to him. His
last big year was 1964, when he hit .303 with 35 homers and
111 RBIs. But he never led the league in any category again
after topping the league in walks in 1962. In his last two years,
1967 and 1968, he was little more than a shell of his former
self. His legs were gone, he couldn't run, and he often stumbled
at the plate. But the fans loved him. He was cheered vigorously,
even when he struck out. The Mick came to spring training in
1969, tried to play again, but simply couldn't. At age thirty-
seven, he decided to call it quits. In his retirement statement he
said:

"I can't play anymore. I can't hit the ball when I need to. I
can't steal second when I need to. I can't go from first to third
when I need to. I can't score from second when I need to. I have
to quit."

Mickey Mantle retired with a .298 lifetime batting average
and 536 home runs. He is still considered the greatest switch
hitter ever to play the game and it's generally acknowledged
that had he taken better care of himself his record would have
been a lot greater. Mickey admitted to heavy drinking and
many late nights on the town during his Yankee years. Because
his father, and a number of close male relatives, had died before
their fortieth birthdays, Mantle developed a fatalistic attitude
and decided to cram as much living as he could into a short

amount of time. Playing in New York, that was often very easy to do.

Always a beloved figure at Yankee Stadium, Mantle became a spokesman for alcohol abuse in his later years. He finally underwent a liver transplant in 1994 at which time doctors discovered an inoperable cancerous lesion. The Mick died on August 13, 1995, at the age of sixty-three. Elected to the Hall of Fame in 1974, his first year of eligibility, Mickey Mantle is still remembered as a great player and great slugger, a powerful hitter from both sides of the plate whose tape measure home runs helped to foster and encourage the generations of sluggers who followed.

And no one has ever forgotten the 1961 season, when Roger Maris and Mickey Mantle made the home run front-page news and showed, once and for all, that there was nothing more exciting in baseball than watching two players in an epic home run race, chasing each other and trying to establish a new record at the same time.

6

Don't Let the Pitchers Get Too Good, 1962–1972

After the great home run race in 1961, it's not surprising that more hitters viewed the fences as a road to fame and maybe even riches, at least the riches of the day. There were plenty of sluggers scattered throughout the big leagues who had not only watched the excitement generated by the M & M Boys but had also contributed to what turned into a record year for four baggers. No one had any doubt that this fence-busting behavior would continue. The National League had followed by a year in adding two new teams. One of them, the New York Mets, had been created to fill the void left five years earlier when the Dodgers and Giants went west. The other, the Houston Colt-45's, later renamed the Astros, brought Major League Baseball to Texas. So baseball was ready for another banner season in 1962, undoubtedly featuring a lot of home runs. Then, an unexpected thing happened.

Maury Wills of the Los Angeles Dodgers stole 104 bases!

The stolen base numbers had gone down steadily beginning in the 1920s, not coincidentally when Babe Ruth started hitting home runs all over the lot. They bottomed out in 1950 when big league runners stole just 650 bases collectively. Then the numbers began rising slowly. In the late 1950s, shortstop Luis Aparicio of the White Sox began stealing more bases. In 1959, he swiped 56, something not seen in many years. By 1960, shortstop Wills of the Dodgers also pilfered 50 sacks, and a year later big league runners went over the 1,000-steal mark for the first time since 1943 and only the third time since 1931. When Wills ran wild in 1962, he broke the forty-seven-year-old record of 96 steals, set by the great Ty Cobb back in 1915. It didn't herald a return to small ball or a widespread running game, but led by Wills, National League baserunners stole 788 sacks, the most since way back in 1923.

Wills also began setting the tone for an outstanding Dodgers team that would dominate the National League through 1966. This was essentially a pitching, speed, and defense team that didn't rely on the long ball to win. When you have a Sandy Koufax and Don Drysdale at the top of your rotation, you can build a team without a ton of home runs. The trend would slowly escalate, especially in the National League during the early and middle sixties, as more great pitchers would begin to dominate the game. It would reach a point in 1968 where the men who run the sport decided they had to find a way to slow down the pitchers and help the hitters. But let's backtrack a bit first.

The 1962 season did see players swinging for the fences more than ever. Another new home run record was set as big leaguers whacked 3,001, a mark that would stay on the books for seven years. The American League reached a new high with 1,552 while the National hit 1,449, some 253 more than the season before. Yet there was no Maris-Mantle home run race, no one threatening to break any records, just more guys than ever hitting home runs. In the National, the two greatest players hit the most home runs, Mays with 49 and Aaron with 45. Frank Robinson had 39, Banks 37, and Cepeda 35. It was becoming "round up the usual suspects." The sluggers were doing it every year. The American saw Killebrew lead with 48, followed by Cash and Colavito with 39 and 37. Leon Wagner of the Angels had 37, while Gentile and Roger Maris had 33 each. As for Mickey Mantle, injuries limited him to just 377 at bats and he finished the season with 30 homers.

Despite the falloff by the M & M Boys, the Yanks won another pennant, beating out Minnesota by five games. In the National, the Giants and Dodgers waged an old-fashioned war, just like the old days in New York and Brooklyn. The two teams wound up in a tie and met in a best-of-three series for the pennant. As happened in 1951, they split the first two games, then the Dodgers took a 4-2 lead into the ninth inning of the third game only to see the Giants rally and win it, 6-4. But these were two distinctly different teams. The Giants were built for power, hitting 204 homers, second in the majors to Detroit's 209. Besides Mays and Cepeda, Filipe Alou had 25, Willie Mc-Covey 20, and Tom Haller 18. By contrast, the Dodgers relied more on pitching. Don Drysdale won twenty-five games and, had Sandy Koufax not been sidelined by a circulatory problem the second half of the season after getting off at 14-7 with a league best 2.54 ERA, the Dodgers probably would have won it. Los Angeles did get 31 homers and 119 RBIs from big Frank Howard, while outfielder Tommy Davis had a career year with a .346 batting average, 27 homers, and a league best 153 runs batted in.

The Dodgers, however, were giving the baseball world a glimpse of the future. The Yankees won the World Series once again, topping the Giants in seven games. The deciding game was a 1-0 contest, Ralph Terry going the distance in a tense game in which the sluggers were silenced. Average attendance was down slightly, though the National had more paying customers because of the two new teams. One of them, the New York Mets, set a record for futility by losing 120 games.

The following season a trend began that would increase over the next six seasons, culminating in the 1968 campaign, which will forever be known as the Year of the Pitcher. This gradual swing from hitting to pitching would signal the first real change in the way the game was played since the 1930s, when the hitters began dominating and slugging increased. Home runs didn't stop or diminish greatly until 1967, but the dominant team from 1963 to 1966 would be the L.A. Dodgers, a ballclub that won conspicuously without a lot of home runs.

It began in 1963 when lefthander Sandy Koufax emerged as the most dominant pitcher in baseball. Koufax had been with the Dodgers since 1955, when he was a nineteen-year-old called up to Brooklyn. He began starting regularly in 1958, but it took him another four years to get his great fastball and sharp-breaking curve under control. Once he did, he became almost unhittable. In 1963, he compiled a 25-5 record with a 1.88

earned run average, striking out 306 hitters while walking just 58. Behind Koufax, Don Drysdale, and the rest of the staff, the Dodgers won the pennant by six games over St. Louis, a team developing an ace of their own in righthander Bob Gibson, who was 18-9 that season.

Frank Howard, with 28 homers, was the only Dodger who remotely resembled a slugger. Tommy Davis was next with 16 homers. No Dodger drove in as many as 100 runs and the team hit only 110 home runs. Yet they won while the Giants, with 197 team homers, finished a distant third despite the presence of their own ace pitcher, righthander Juan Marichal, who was 25-8 on the year. The Dodger did, however, lead the league in stolen bases and their pitchers had the league's lowest earned run average. The Yanks, a team in transition, won again in the American League, but this year their top home run hitters were catcher Elston Howard with 28 and young first sacker Joe Pepitone with 27. Both Mantle and Maris were injured for much of the year, so the Bronx Bombers weren't quite the same.

Just two years removed from the greatest home run chase the sport had ever seen, the World Series was totally dominated by the Dodger pitchers. The once mighty Bronx Bombers managed just four runs as L.A. swept. Koufax won games one and four, striking out fifteen in the opener and allowing just a Mantle homer in the fourth game. Johnny Podres, the hero of the Dodgers only World Series win in Brooklyn, back in 1955, pitched a seven-hitter in the second game, which the Dodgers won, 4-1. Then big Don Drysdale shut out the Yanks and Jim Bouton, 1-0, in the third before Koufax wrapped it up with his second win over Whitey Ford, 2-1. The Dodgers managed 12 runs, but nine of them came in the first two games. So it was a pitcher's World Series, certainly not the direction the game had been going in for so long.

Maybe it was then that many teams began realizing all over again that the old axiom was still true, the one that says, "Good pitching always stops good hitting." Of course, there were too many good hitters, too many sluggers around, to completely turn the game over to the pitchers. But the Dodgers formula had worked and would work again, although not the following year. In 1964, only Mays with 47 and Killebrew with 49, topped the 40-homer mark, and the aging Yanks had a last hurrah with another pennant as Mantle had his last big year with 35 homers and 111 RBIs. In the series, they met the St. Louis Cardinals, a solid club but not a slugging one. The Cards long-time star, Stan Musial, retired the year before at the age of forty-two, leaving behind a .331 lifetime average, 3,630 hits, and 475 home runs. Stan the Man never hit 40 homers in a single season, but he was such a great, consistent, and feared hitter that he was always a long ball threat and obviously one of the greatest ever.

The World Series of 1964 was diametrically opposite that of the year before, more in keeping with the slugging trend. It went seven games. The Yanks and Cards combined to hit 15 home runs, including grand slams by the Cards' Ken Boyer and Yanks' Joe Pepitone. Mantle turned back the clock and blasted three, leading both clubs with eight RBIs. But the Cards had an equalizer. After losing the second game, Bob Gibson came back to beat the Yanks in game four, 4-2, and going ten innings to do it, then Gibby won the seventh and final game, 7-5, in another route-going performance. It was just a glimpse of what was to come from Gibson in big games.

Slugging totals stayed pretty much the same during the next two seasons. Mays hit 52 in 1965, but it would be the last time a player went over the 50 mark for a dozen years, and then it wouldn't happen for another thirteen years after that. It became more a matter of a lot of players hitting a good number of homers. For example, the Braves of 1965 had seven players with 20 or more homers, led by Aaron and Mathews with 32 each. In the A.L., young Tony Conigliaro of the Red Sox led with just 32 as the junior circuit hit 181 fewer than the year before. The year also marked the end of a dynasty, as the New York Yankees, their stars aging, crashed to 77-85, and a year later would finish an uncharacteristic dead last. Though they were still there, the M & M Boys were no longer a factor, both falling victim to repeated injuries.

A year later, Frank Robinson of the Reds was traded to the Baltimore Orioles, the Cincy brass saying he was "an old thirty." All Robinson did was win the American League triple crown with a .316 average, 49 homers, and 122 runs batted in. Aaron hit 44 to lead the National, followed by Dick Allen of the Phils with 40. While homers stayed at a steady clip, the American League batting average was dropping, going down to .242 in 1965 and .240 in 1966. The National was at .249 in 1965 and .256 a year later. So the pitchers were slowly beginning to dominate. And both the 1965 and 1966 World Series featured top pitching. The Dodgers beat the Twins in seven games in the 1965 classic, with Koufax winning twice, throwing shutouts in games five and seven, and in the finale doing it on two days rest. There were still 11 homers hit, but the next year those who like to see hitting in the World Series did nothing but yawn.

The Dodgers faced the Baltimore Orioles, which had a young pitching staff and didn't expect to match Koufax, Drysdale, and company. The Dodgers scored single runs in the second and third innings of game one . . . then never scored again. Reliever Moe Drabowsky pitched $6\frac{2}{3}$ scoreless innings to finish game one for the O's, then Jim Palmer, Wally Bunker, and Dave McNally all threw complete-game shutouts to wrap the series up in four straight. The final two games were decided by identical 1-0 scores. The Orioles scored 13 runs, the Dodgers only two as the losers ended the series with an anemic team batting average of just .142. But only baseball purists could have enjoyed the strings of goose eggs that were put on the scoreboard. The problem was that the situation would only get worse.

In 1967, batting numbers began to go down even more. Home runs dipped from 2,743 in 1966 to 2,299 in 1967. The National League batting average was down to .249 and the American dipped to .236. Hank Aaron led the National in homers with 39, while Harmon Killebrew and Carl Yastrzemski, who had replaced Ted Williams in left for the Red Sox in 1961, had 44 each. They were the only players over 40 in both leagues. The same two sluggers were also the only American League players to drive in more than 100 runs. The league earned run

Sandy

Though this is a book about the home run and the men who hit them, it's also worth mentioning a pitcher who stopped sluggers as well as anyone—Sandy Koufax. After the 1966 World Series, baseball's best pitcher abruptly announced his retirement just two months before his thirty-first birthday. He cited an arthritic left elbow that prevented him from throwing between starts, but some feel that this intensely private individual was also tired of the limelight.

Despite being injured for parts of two of his final five seasons, Koufax had a record of 111-34 between 1962 and 1966. He led the National League in earned run average each year, being under 2.00 on three occasions. He struck out more than 300 hitters three times, including a record 382 in 1965. And in his final season he was 27-9 with a 1.73 ERA, striking out 317 batters in 323 innings and completing 27 of his 41 starts. No wonder he was elected to the Hall of Fame in 1972 despite a relatively short career that saw him win just 165 games. But during those final five seasons, no one was better. And some say no one *ever* was better. The hitters were glad to see him go.

average for all the pitchers was down to 3.23, a far cry from the 4.02 of 1961. Though there were just five twenty-game winners in both leagues, pitchers were starting to dominate.

What was happening? Were too many players beginning to swing for the fences at the expense of good hitting? Remember, Joe DiMaggio hit 361 homers and struck out only 369 times in his entire career. That meant with two strikes, DiMag became a different hitter. He wasn't trying to slam the ball over the fence, he just wanted to get his bat on it. Lou Gehrig, who hit 493 homers, never struck out more than 84 times in a season and had several peak years where he fanned just 31, 38, and 46 times. He fanned just 789 times in 8,001 official at bats. By contrast, Mickey Mantle struck out more than 100 times in eight different seasons and retired with 1,710 strikeouts in 8,102 official at bats, more than twice as many K's as Gehrig in a comparable number of at bats.

There are countless other examples. Ted Williams, considered by many the greatest hitter ever, fanned just 709 times while walking on 2,019 occasions. The Splendid Splinter never struck out more than 49 times in a single season, while Stan Musial whiffed only 696 times in 10,972 official at bats, and never more than 46 times in a year. Yet Harmon Killebrew, one of the greatest sluggers of the 1960s, fanned more than 100 times in seven of nine seasons through 1967. Eddie Mathews, who would retire after the 1968 season with 512 homers, also fanned 1,487 times. Those sluggers who also hit close to .300 or above didn't seem to fan as much, except maybe for Mantle. But the new breed who could hit 40 homers while batting just .260 were often still flailing away with two strikes.

Ironically, while the sluggers continued to swing for the fences, more teams were again beginning to steal bases. The success of Luis Aparicio and then Maury Wills, who swiped another 94 in 1965 after setting his great record of 104 three years earlier, had shown once again that the running game could be effective. After cracking the 1,000-steal mark in 1961 for only the third time in thirty years, baserunners did not fall below that number again. By 1965, there were 1,449 thefts in both leagues and the numbers were getting higher. Beginning in 1966, Lou Brock of the Cards would be the National League's top thief eight of the next nine years, culminating his run with a record 118 steals in 1974. Teams were beginning to realize that the stolen base was one way to disrupt a hot pitcher. Against some of these dominant pitchers it often became necessary to manufacture a run, just as they had done so often in the dead ball era. So the steal was beginning to come back. Then, by 1968, the pitching dominance came to a head.

THE YEAR OF THE PITCHER

This turned into a legendary season. Did it come without warning? Not exactly. Hitting was down in 1967, but no one thought that there could be a year like this one, where pitchers would simply put the batters in a choke hold and refuse to let go. There were still plenty of good hitters around, as well as a brace of guys who could hit the ball in the seats. Most of the great sluggers who had come in during the 1950s were still playing and had been joined by more hard-hitting youngsters— guys like Bobby Bonds, Jim Ray Hart, Lee May, Tony Perez, Johnny Bench, Joe Torre, Willie Stargell, Johnny Callison, Dick Allen, and Jimmy Wynn in the National League. The American had Willie Horton, Bill Freehan, Boog Powell, Ken Harrelson, Reggie Jackson, Sal Bando, Reggie Smith, Tony Oliva, and Bob Allison among the younger players who could and would have big slugging seasons.

There were also a number of guys capable of hitting for big averages, such as Clemente, Pete Rose, Matty Alou, Oliva, Rod Carew, and Carl Yastrzemski. Yet with all these players swinging the bat, it was the pitchers who made the big news. Because there was so much pitching and so little hitting some of the best pitchers had almost mediocre won-lost records, but great earned run averages. In fact, seven big-league pitchers would have earned run averages under 2.00 at the end of the season, and several notable pitching records would be set. At the same time, the hitting totals at year's end would be abysmal, the worst ever.

Just for the record, the list of outstanding pitchers in the majors in 1968 included the following. In the National League there was Bob Gibson, Steve Carlton, Juan Marichal, Gaylord Perry, Ferguson Jenkins, Bill Hands, Jim Maloney, Phil Niekro, Bob Veale, Steve Blass, Don Drysdale, and Chris Short. Even the lowly Mets had a one-two punch in second-year right-hander Tom Seaver and rookie lefty Jerry Koosman. In the American there was Denny McLain, Mickey Lolich, Dave Mc-Nally, Sudden Sam McDowell, Luis Tiant, Mel Stottlemyre, Catfish Hunter, Dean Chance, Jim Kaat, Tommy John, and Camilo Pascual. They aren't all Hall of Famers, but they sure dominated during the 1968 season.

The only way to accurately gauge what happened is to look at both the numbers and then at some outstanding pitching performances. Here are the basics. The National League hit .243. No slugger hit as many as 40 homers. The leader was Willie McCovey with 36 and only three other players—Allen, Banks, and Billy Williams—went over the 30 mark. McCovey was the lone player to drive in more than 100 runs and he only had 105. Pete Rose won the batting title at .335 with Matty Alou at .332 and brother Felipe at .317. Alex Johnson (.312) and Curt Flood (.301) were the league's only other .300 hitters.

In the American league it was even worse. Big Frank Howard had 44 homers, while Willie Horton hit 36 and Ken Harrelson 35. Young Reggie Jackson was next with 29. Only Harrelson and Howard managed more than 100 RBIs and, amazingly, the batting title was won by Carl Yastrzemski, whose .3005 average was officially recorded as .301 and was the lowest league-leading average in baseball history. And, obviously, Yaz was the one-and-only .300 hitter in the entire league. The composite batting average in both leagues was .236, the lowest in the history of the sport. To make things even worse, home runs in the majors dropped to 1,995, the lowest number since 1954. And, remember, there were now four more teams than there were then, and all were playing a 162-game schedule. Homers had also dropped by a total of 748 in just two years, despite the presence of some great and consistent sluggers.

Want more proof that it was the year of the pitcher? Feast on this. In the American League, Detroit righthander Denny McLain won thirty-one games, becoming the majors first thirty-game winner since Dizzy Dean in 1934. He would also be the last. McLain had been a good but not great pitcher since 1965, compiling records of 16-6, 20-14, and 17-16. His ERA those last two years was 3.92 and 3.79, not the mark of a dominating hurler. But in 1968, McLain was almost unbeatable, going 31-6 with a 1.96 ERA. He completed 28 of 41 starts and fanned 280 hitters in 336 innings, throwing six shutouts along the way. McLain won both the Cy Young and MVP awards that year, followed it with a 24-9 record the next year, then frittered away his career through hard living and scrapes with the law. He would win just seventeen more games after 1969 and was out of baseball after the 1972 season.

As good as McLain was in 1968, Bob Gibson was even better. His record for the St. Louis Cardinals was 22-9, but that didn't fully tell the story of his dominance. The raw numbers tell a more incredible tale. Gibby completed 28 of 34 starts that year, pitched 304⅔ innings, struck out 268, and walked just 62. He pitched an amazing 13 shutouts and had a microscopic earned run average of 1.12, one of the best in baseball history, and the kind of ERA that was only compiled in the dead ball era many years before. That still wasn't all. At one point in the season he won fifteen straight games, which could have easily been sixteen but he had an 11-inning no-decision against the Pirates. During that streak he threw 47⅔ consecutive scoreless innings and in one 95-inning stretch he gave up just two earned runs!

In three of Gibson's nine defeats the Cards were shut out, including a four-hit effort against the Giants on September 17. He lost that one, 1-0, because the Giants' Gaylord Perry pitched a no-hitter. Knowing the kind of stuff he had all that year, Gibson even said, "I'm amazed that I lost nine ballgames." Not surprisingly, he was also both the Cy Young and MVP winner that year. But unlike McLain, Gibson continued having a great career. He won 20 or more five times, 19 on two other occasions, and ended his Hall of Fame career with a 251-174 record. Gibby was a fierce competitor, a great athlete, and a huge big-game pitcher who had a mean streak on the mound. There were few better, and in 1968 there was none better. His season was simply amazing.

Veteran Don Drysdale of the Dodgers also made news during 1968. At one point in the season Drysdale broke a sixty-four-year-old major league record by throwing six straight shutouts. He also threw 58⅔ consecutive scoreless innings, breaking the record of fifty-six set by the great Walter Johnson back in 1913. Yet because his own hitters couldn't support him, Drysdale finished at just 14-12 despite eight shutouts and a 2.15 ERA. When he didn't throw a shutout, his record was just 6-12. Again, no hitting support. And there were others. Juan Marichal of the Giants finished the year at 26-9. Rookie Jerry Koosman of the ninth place Mets had a 19-12 record with a 2.08 ERA. His teammate Tom Seaver was 16-12 with an ERA of 2.20. There were numbers like that all around the league.

The American League also had some great pitching stats. Luis Tiant of the Indians had a 21-9 record and a league best 1.60 ERA. Sam McDowell, also of Cleveland, had a 1.81 ERA to go with a league best 283 strikeouts. McLain, Dave McNally of the Orioles, and Tommy John of the White Sox also had earned run averages under 2.00. Ironically, the World Series that year between the Tigers and Cardinals featured more hitting with 15 home runs. Yet Detroit prevailed because Mickey Lolich won three games and beat Gibson in the seventh and deciding contest when Curt Flood misjudged a ball in the eighth inning. Gibson had won two previous games, setting a record with 17 strikeouts in the opener, and both he and Lolich had 1.67 ERAs in the series. The year before, Gibson had won three games against the Boston Red Sox, including the seventh and deciding game, compiling an ERA of 1.00. Gibby was simply one tough customer in big games.

But now baseball had a problem. The year of the pitcher saw attendance decline in the National League for a second straight year. From a high of 15,015,471 in 1966, it was down to 11,785,358 in 1968. Attendance in the A.L. had gone up in 1967 and down only slightly in 1968. Still, the lords of the game were worried. For one thing, they planned to add four more teams in 1969, two in each league, then break both leagues into two divisions of six teams each. That would add a round to the playoffs. The division winners would meet in a best-of-five series for the pennant, the winner going on to the World Series. That also meant four more expansion teams that wouldn't be very strong. If the pitchers continued to dominant, how would the fans react? Many felt that a 1-0 or 2-1 ballgame was considered dull by the average fan who wanted to be entertained by a lot of action. Only the real purists could appreciate the artistry of a pitching gem.

Not only was attendance down, but polls showed that fewer people were watching on television as well. There would be new National League teams in Montreal (the Expos) and in San Diego (the Padres). In the A.L., the Kansas City A's had moved to Oakland in 1968 and would be replaced by a new team in

Climbing the Home Run Ladder

Though the 1968 season will forever be known as the Year of the Pitcher, the modern-day sluggers were already beginning to make their mark as all-time great home run producers. Mickey Mantle, of course, retired before the 1969 season began. His career shortened by injuries and high-living, Mantle nevertheless retired with 536 home runs, topping by two the number hit by early slugger Jimmy Foxx. Foxx, when he retired, was second only to the 714 accrued by the Babe. But despite overtaking Foxx, Mantle was not in second place.

Willie Mays, at age thirty-seven, had hit 23 home runs in 1968, running his career total to 587 and putting him second behind Ruth. Some thought Willie had a chance to catch the Bambino, but he was on the downside and would eventually retire at the end of the 1973 season with 660 home runs among his many great accomplishments. But there was another player lurking just behind the dynamic duo of Mantle and Mays. The low-key Henry Aaron hit just 29 home runs in the Year of the Pitcher. Nonetheless, it brought Aaron's lifetime total up to 510 home runs. Hammerin' Hank was just thirty-four years old and still in fine shape. It was a foregone conclusion that he would pass Mantle. Where he would finish, however, was still a toss-up. But during the next eight years, Aaron and his quick wrists would surprise a lot of people as he would continue his assault on the home run record book.

Kansas City, the Royals. The other new team was the Seattle Pilots. They would last one year before moving to Milwaukee and becoming the Brewers. Later, the expansion Mariners would finally establish the game in Seattle. At any rate, with these new teams it was felt that more fans would come in to see the big sluggers hit the ball rather than top pitchers spin a shutout. Many felt that low scoring games were boring, the lack of action uninspiring. There simply wasn't any reason for fans to jump out of their seats and cheer.

That's when the rules committee got to work. If the hitters couldn't do it on their own, baseball would legislate hitting back into the game. In a sense, this was the first time baseball took an overt step to get more hitting since 1930, when they changed the baseball with catastrophic results for the pitchers. Before 1969 began, there were two changes put into effect, both of which worked to the advantage of the player with the bat in his hands. The first could be considered a radical one. The pitcher's mound, which had crested at 15 inches above the level of the playing field for years, was lowered by five inches, so that it would now be just 10 inches high.

By lowering the mound, it gave hitters a better angle from which to hit the baseball. A tall, overhand pitcher operating from a 15-inch-high mound is throwing the ball on a downward trajectory. Using the hands of a clock as an analogy, the ball is almost being thrown from twelve o'clock and crossing the plate at six o'clock. That is a more difficult angle from which to hit the ball hard. If it was delivered on a flat plane, from nine o'clock to nine o'clock, it's easier to see and to hit. With the lowered mound there was still an angle, but it had been reduced by a third. Advantage hitters.

In addition to the mound, the other change involved the shrinking of the strike zone. The traditional strike zone was the width of home plate horizontally, and vertically from the letters on the uniform, which were about at the shoulder, to the bottom of the knee. The vertical range was shortened. The new strike zone was from the armpit to the top of the knee. This change forced pitchers to throw more pitches that were easier to hit. Batters would no longer have to flail away at the high hard one for fear it would be called a strike. These were the two changes put in place at the start of the 1969 season. They worked. The so-called Year of the Pitcher would not become the Era of the Pitcher. It would remain a one-year phenomenon.

The result was a more all-around game. Over the next four years, the hitters would hit, the good pitchers would win, the runners would steal more bases, and new, swing-from-the-heels sluggers would come into the game. During these years, more of the old ballparks would disappear, being replaced by symmetrical, all-purpose concrete bowls that would become known as the cookie-cutter stadiums. All would feature something that

Robby and the Killer

Two of the most prolific home run hitters of the twenty-year era that stretched from the mid-1950s to the mid-1970s were Frank Robinson and Harmon Killebrew. They would both play for more than twenty years and finish their careers within 13 home runs of each other. At the time of their retirements, they ranked fourth and fifth on the all-time home run list. Yet they were two very different kinds of ballplayers and, in a sense, showed the way in which home run hitters were evolving.

Robinson was the throwback, the great all-around player who could do it all. He hit a high of 49 homers in 1966, yet he was also capable of hitting .330, stealing bases, and was an outstanding rightfielder with a great throwing arm. Robby played the game hard, and it was said he would take his own grandmother out at second base if it meant breaking up a double play. Born in Beaumont, Texas, in 1935, Robinson had a twenty-one-year playing career, became baseball's first African American manager in 1975, and is the only player to win the Most Valuable Player award in both leagues, retiring with a .294 lifetime average. As of 2004, he was the manager of the Montreal Expos and would be moving with the team to Washington for the 2005 season.

Harmon Killebrew was born in Payette, Idaho, in 1936 and would play for twenty-two years. At 6 feet and 195 pounds, he wasn't huge, but he was exceptionally strong through the arms and shoulders. In many ways, the "Killer" was a one-dimensional player. He wasn't a particularly fast runner and was simply adequate in the field. He also never hit .300 for a full season and retired with just a .256 lifetime batting average. But he was every bit the slugger Robinson was and always a threat to end a game with one big swing. Like most modern-day sluggers, he struck out a lot, but because of his enormous power, he was one of the most feared hitters in the game. Though far from the all-around player Frank Robinson was, Killebrew's achievements were recognized the same way Robinson's were—eventual election to the baseball Hall of Fame.

players grew to hate—artificial turf—and these changes also affected the way the game was played.

In 1969, a home run hitter began making big news for the first time since 1961. It was the perfect antidote to the Year of the Pitcher. Reggie Jackson, a twenty-three-year-old outfielder with the Oakland A's began hitting them early and often. Reggie had made his presence felt the year before, slamming 29 homers as the pitchers prevailed. He also, however, struck out 171 times, close to a record. In that sense, Reggie was emblematic of the new-age slugger. He went all out all the time, even with two strikes on him. Even when he swung and missed, he was exciting. But early in 1969, he was hitting a lot more than missing. During a weekend series against the Red Sox in Fenway that June, Jackson knocked in 15 runs in only 14 at bats. Ten of them came in one game when he also walloped two homers.

When he hit his 40th home run of the season on July 29, Jackson was twenty-three games ahead of the pace set by the Babe. Maris, however, also had 40 by the end of the same month. Still, there were those who felt Jackson had a chance. He was a powerful lefthanded hitter and, when he connected, the ball went a long way. But August turned into the cruelest month for him and Reggie connected just five times. With 45 homers on September 1, most felt the chase was over but that he would still become the first hitter since Mays in 1965 to go over the 50 mark. It didn't happen. His slump continued and he slammed just two more the rest of the way to finish with 47. But thanks to Reggie, home run excitement was back.

So was baseball. The first year of divisional play proved a success. With two division winners, it doubled the races and doubled the number of teams with a chance to win the World Series, so fan interest stayed high in more cities. Then, an amazing story began to unfold. The New York Mets, a team that had never finished higher than ninth since its inception in 1962, was the surprise of the baseball world. Led by Seaver and Koosman, their fine young pitchers, the Mets caught fire, passed the Cubs in September, and won the first ever N.L. East title. Then they swept the favored Braves in three straight games before upsetting the Baltimore Orioles in five to become World Champs. It was a great story and great for baseball when the game needed a boost.

The home run was also back. Jackson, who had made the big

news by hitting 40 by the end of July, didn't even end up with the A.L. home run title. In fact, he finished third as Harmon Killebrew hit 49 and Frank Howard checked in with 48. A pair of Red Sox, Rico Petrocelli and Yaz, had 40 each. At the same time, stolen bases were up, Tommy Harper of Seattle stealing 73 and Bert Campaneris of Oakland swiping 62. There were also six twenty-game winners in the American, led by McLain's twenty-four wins. So a case can be made for a more balanced game. The league hit .246, up 16 points from the previous year. In the National, McCovey and Aaron were over 40 homers, Rose won the batting title at .348 and five hitters were over the .320 mark. But the senior circuit also saw great pitching. Seaver won 25, with Phil Niekro, Marichal, and Fergie Jenkins winning more than 20. Marichal had a 2.10 earned run average, the Cards' Steve Carlton was at 2.17, Gibson at 2.18, Seaver at 2.21, and Koosman at 2.28. So there were still dominating pitchers. Obviously, though, lowering the mound and compressing the strike zone had helped even things out.

Just listen to the slugging numbers. In the year of the pitcher, big league hitters had just 1,995 home runs. A year later they set a new record with 3,119 balls going into the seats. With a new decade coming, the game expanding, and new ballparks being opened, it began to look as if baseball was getting healthy. The only surprise was the attendance. Despite two new teams, the average crowd in the National League increased by just a bit over 1,000 a game to 15,514, while the American, also with two new teams, dropped almost 1,500 per game to an average of 12,471.

Over the next three years most of the baseball news would not involve the home run. There were other changes in the game that took over the headlines and with the balanced game on the field, there was more emphasis on new ballparks, the division winners, and a lawsuit that would make baseball history and ultimately change the face of the entire sport.

One of the big changes was the introduction of a number of new ballparks, outdoor stadiums that were used for both baseball and football, and because there was so much on-field activity, they decided to install artificial turf. The first stadium to use this new surface was the indoor Houston Astrodome, which was opened in 1965. When the groundskeepers realized that grass simply wouldn't grow well indoors that first year, they switched to turf. That same year, 1966, Busch Stadium in St. Louis was opened to replace old Sportsman's Park. Grass was used for four years and in 1970 they, too, switched to artificial turf.

In the next two years three new National League parks opened, all symmetrical concrete stadiums used for both baseball and football. They had almost identical dimensions and artificial turf. Riverfront Stadium in Cincinnati replaced Crosley Field, Three Rivers Stadium in Pittsburgh made carnivorous Forbes Field obsolete, and Veterans Stadium in Philadelphia led to the wrecking-ball destruction of old Connie Mack Stadium. Busch and Riverfront had identical dimensions, 330 feet down both lines and 404 feet to center. Three Rivers was almost the same, 335 feet down the right and left field lines and 400 to center. Veterans Stadium was 330 down the lines and 408 to center. Jack Murphy Stadium, which opened in San Diego in 1969, had real grass, but those same dimensions, 329 down the lines and 405 to center. Even the Astrodome was 330, 400, 330.

By and large, the ballplayers didn't like artificial turf. It was hard on both the feet and knees. In a place like St. Louis, the turf became almost unbearably hot in July and August. There were seams in the carpet that often led to bad hops and on the tight, hard surface the ball traveled faster through the holes in the infield and between the outfielders when it was hit in the gaps. Turf teams needed speed on defense and it didn't hurt to have fast men on the bases, either. But it also didn't take a huge poke to get the ball into the seats. No more centerfield fences pushing 450 to 500 feet away as in the old days. And the symmetrical, almost antiseptic look of the outfields sometimes made one park indistinguishable from the others. Eventually the turf even covered the entire infield, except for dirt cutouts around the bases so the players could still slide. It would take twenty years or so, but eventually these cookie-cutter parks would be deemed bad for the game. They really didn't hurt the home run hitters, but the teams that played on turf felt they should be built around speed, not around sluggers. Having sluggers in the lineup was simply a bonus.

About the same time the new parks were opening, baseball had another diversion, something that would upset an apple cart of long standing. Curt Flood was the star centerfielder for the St. Louis Cardinals, an outstanding all-around player maybe just a cut below the superstar level. He was instrumental in bringing the Cards pennants in 1964, 1967, and 1968, as well as world championships in 1964 and 1967. When the Cards didn't repeat in 1969, management decided to make some changes and one of the moves was to trade Flood to Philadelphia. When Flood heard about the trade from a reporter, he bristled.

Flood didn't want to play in Philadelphia and felt he should have a choice. Players had been subject to baseball's reserve clause for years, mandating that they play where they are sent or retire. After consulting with attorneys and the Players' Association, Flood wrote a letter to Commissioner Bowie Kuhn which said, in part, "After twelve years in the major leagues, I do not feel I am a piece of property to be bought and sold irrespective of my wishes. I believe that any system which produces that result violates my basic rights as a citizen and is inconsistent with the laws of the United States. . . ."

Bottom line. Flood sued and it wound up going all the way to the Supreme Court, where the court ruled against him, 5-3, with one abstention. Flood had opened the doors at the cost of his own career. He sat out 1970, tried a brief comeback with Washington the following year, but retired after just a handful of games. However, it was his lawsuit that would ultimately lead to the creation of free agency in 1976, changing both the physical and financial landscape of the game forever. Today's multimillionaire players all owe a debt of gratitude to Curt Flood.

Back on the field it was business as usual. Between 1970 and 1972, Baltimore, Cincinnati, Pittsburgh, and Oakland were the dominant teams. The Orioles, Pirates, and A's would be the world champs over the next three years as the game leveled out. Attendance edged upward in the National League and stayed on an even keel in the American. Though there were more teams, stolen bases began reaching pre-1920 levels as the artificial turf stadiums encouraged more running. Home runs reached a new high of 3,429 in 1970, then dropped back for some seven years until 1977. Johnny Bench (45), Willie Stargell (48), and Bench (40) again were the National League homer champs during this three-year period, while Frank Howard (44), Bill Melton (33), and Dick Allen (37) were the American League's best.

If there was any trend during these three years it was back to pitching. By 1972 the National League hit just .248 and the American .239. The American had six twenty-game winners that year and the California Angels Nolan Ryan, who won nineteen, struck out 329 hitters. Luis Tiant of Boston and Gaylord Perry of Cleveland had ERAs under 2.00, while Catfish Hunter, Jim Palmer, and Roger Nelson were just over that low mark. Relief pitchers were being used more often and in more specialized roles. Sparky Lyle of the Yankees had 35 saves that year. In the National, Steve Carlton went 27-10 for a Philadelphia Phils team that finished last at 59-97. Lefty had a 1.97 ERA and fanned 310 hitters while pitching thirty games. His great performance with a very bad team might have overshadowed everything else that year.

Baseball also suffered a tragic loss. Pittsburgh's great Roberto Clemente, who was the star of the 1971 World Series, and who got the 3,000th hit of his great career in the final game of the 1972 season, was killed in a plane crash on December 31 while flying on a plane loaded with relief supplies for victims of a huge earthquake in Managua, Nicaragua. Clemente had organized the relief mission and lost his life trying to help the victims. It was a tragic loss for baseball. A pure hitter rather than a slugger, Clemente was one of the best ever. His slashing style produced four batting titles and 240 home runs.

In a sense, an era was ending. Many of the great sluggers who had come into the game in the 1950s were either gone or winding down their careers. Mantle and Eddie Mathews had retired after 1968 with 536 and 512 homers respectively. Ernie Banks called it quits after 1971, also with 512 homers. Mays returned to New York with the Mets in the 1972 season. A shell of his former self, he would play again in 1973, then retire with 660 home runs. Harmon Killebrew had 541 homers through the 1972 season, would play until 1975, and leave with 573 home runs. Frank Robinson hit 19 homers at age thirty-seven in 1972. He already had 522 homers and would play until 1976, his final two seasons as playing/manager of the Cleveland Indians, the first African American manager in baseball history. He would retire with 586 homers.

These sluggers all helped shape the modern game. Many of them became larger-than-life personalities, great players who commanded attention and showed just what the home run could mean to the game. But the way the game was changing in the early 1970s, with the cookie-cutter stadiums and artificial turf, there was some question as to whether their kind would be seen again, especially the way pitchers were throwing as the new decade got underway.

Obviously, we've also left one man out of the above equation. Henry Aaron was thirty-eight years old in 1972. The season before he had hit a career-best 47 home runs, and in 1972 he walloped 34 more, bringing his career total to 673 and propelling him into second place behind Babe Ruth. Hammerin' Hank was still in good shape and continuing his career. The Braves had moved from Milwaukee to Atlanta in 1966 and in Atlanta Stadium, Aaron had a very home run friendly stadium. Suddenly, baseball people saw the possibility of something that once seemed impossible. Could Hank Aaron possibly hit more home runs than Babe Ruth? At the end of the 1972 season, he was just 42 home runs away from achieving that milestone, and his chase in the upcoming seasons would once again put the home run squarely in the middle of the baseball map.

7

Hammerin' Hank Chases and Catches the Babe, 1973–1976

Despite the fact that Henry Aaron had pulled within 41 home runs of Babe Ruth's 714 by the end of the 1972 season, there still wasn't a lot of excitement about the possibility of him breaking this cherished record. Aaron, however, began to feel that he did have a shot at the once thought unreachable standard after hitting 81 home runs in 1971 and 1972. But he felt in order to do it, "I had to stay healthy and be surrounded by great ballplayers."

Why then wasn't there more excitement at the beginning of 1973? For openers, Atlanta wasn't considered a major market back in 1972. Attendance at Atlanta Stadium was spotty and the city wasn't really considered a "baseball town." Then there was Aaron's persona. Hammerin' Hank had been widely acknowledged as a great ballplayer since the middle of the 1950s, one of baseball's best. Though he was widely considered to be on a par with Mays and Mantle as one of a trio of great superstars from the mid-fifties to late-sixties, he had entered the league several years after the first two and in the minds of the public always lagged a step or two behind.

For one thing, Aaron didn't have the same kind of charisma as Willie and the Mick. They both played centerfield, the glamour position, while Aaron patrolled right. Fans knew Willie by his trademark basket catch and the way his cap flew off his head every time he chased one down in the gaps. He was the Say Hey Kid, having one of baseball's great nicknames. Mantle was the switcher, the guy who hit titanic home runs from both sides of the plate. When he first joined the Yanks, he was also the faster runner in baseball. He had an infectious grin and spoke with a pleasing southern drawl that could not be mistaken for anyone else. Both Mays and Mantle played in the media spotlight of New York, while Aaron was tucked away in Milwaukee, then later in Atlanta, where major league baseball was still a new kid on the block.

Both Mantle and Mays were confirmed sluggers, players who had gone over the 50-home run mark twice in their careers. Mantle, of course, had been engaged in that epic chase of the Babe with Roger Maris in 1961. Aaron was simply consistent and dependable, yet he never reached 50 homers in a season. He was also a low-key player. Like Joe DiMaggio before him, he made everything look easy, almost as if he wasn't even breaking a sweat. In addition, he was a quiet man, dignified and often humble in the eyes of the public. While he didn't seek the limelight, he nevertheless had a quality shared by the other two. He burned to succeed and to be the best he could possibly be. Henry Aaron never gave up an at bat. Each and every trip to the plate was important to him, an individual battle between him and the pitcher. The problem was that, as of 1973, very few baseball fans really knew a whole lot about this quiet and dignified superstar. But they would soon find out.

There was more news made at the outset of the 1973 season by a very controversial rule change making its debut in the American League. Because their attendance lagged behind the National League and had dropped slightly over the past three seasons, junior circuit officials felt their game needed some juice. Some juice usually meant more offense. To get it, they broke with what had been the basic structure of the game since the very beginning. They decided that the pitcher would no longer hit. Batting in his place would be a bench player who never went out into the field. They would call him the *designated hitter*, or *DH*, and he could bat anywhere in order, not necessary in the ninth spot where the pitchers almost always hit.

In other words, if there was an aging slugger or fine all-around hitter on the bench, a guy who perhaps couldn't cut it as a position player or was injured so that he couldn't play in the field, he would become the DH. If he had a big bat, he could be placed in the three, four, or five slot, normally run-producing positions, and give the offense a huge boost. With the DH, the ninth-place hitter could be a singles hitter, maybe a fast man who could also steal or take the extra base. With the leadoff hitter normally a similar kind of player, the nine and one slots would almost be interchangeable. Instead of having the pitcher lead off some innings, a team could almost have two leadoff men in the nine and one slots, a pair of table setters who could start rallies, get on base, and set things up for the power guys, one of whom could now be the DH.

Obviously, the designated hitter would alter the strategy of the game, not only with the lineup but also with the way managers handled their pitchers. Now a manager would not have to pinch-hit for his pitcher in a game he was, say, losing by a 2-1 or 3-2 score in the sixth or seventh inning. If the pitcher was still throwing well, he could stay in for another inning or two and, depending on the strength of the bullpen, perhaps give his team a better chance to win. For baseball, this was an extremely radical change, one not everyone would welcome with open arms.

In fact, National League officials saw the new rule and said no way. This isn't the way baseball is supposed to be played, they felt. But the American League didn't waver. They decided to try the new rule for three years. Now, some thirty-two years later, the junior circuit still uses the designated hitter, whereas the National has never adopted it, and it continues to be the one major difference between the two leagues. The Yankees Ron Blomberg became the first designated hitter in baseball history. Blomberg came to bat against Boston's Luis Tiant with the bases loaded in the first inning of the very first game of the 1973 season. He drew a walk to drive in a run and wound up with one hit in three at bats on the day. A new era in baseball was born.

To show the effect of the DH that first year you only have to look at the numbers. Attendance in the American League went up by nearly two million, to 13,433,604. National League attendance also rose, but only by about a million fans. In addition, the presence of the DH definitely resulted in more offense. American League hitters slammed 377 more home runs than the season before while the National increased by 191. The league batting average rose 20 points to .259 and, amazingly, the combined teams scored 1,873 more runs than they had the season before. So the DH served its purpose and after that there was never any real talk about abolishing it. Yet even today baseball purists will rail against the designated hitter, still claiming it takes some of the strategy out of the game.

So at the outset of the 1973 season, there really wasn't a great deal of excitement generated by Henry Aaron. The Braves didn't have a very good team that year, which also diverted attention from him, but they would hit a lot of home runs. The ball always carried very well at Atlanta Stadium and, despite being thirty-nine years old, Hammerin' Hank still had the quick and powerful wrists that always characterized his swing. He began hitting well right from the beginning of the season. Before long it started to become apparent that Aaron was not going to suddenly fade away and fall short of the Babe. The way he was hitting, there even seemed to be a chance he could pass the Babe's 714 before the season ended. And that's when the hate mail started.

The more homers Aaron hit, the more mail he received. Some, of course, was encouraging, but playing in the south in 1973, there was also mail of a very different nature. Plain and simply, there was an element that didn't want to see an African American break a record set by a white man. To illustrate just how voluminous his mail was, it reached a point in the summer where he was receiving some 3,000 letters a day. Surprisingly, much of the mail that contained racial slurs also came from northern cities. He was inundated with the same kind of racial epithets that Jackie Robinson had to endure twenty-six years earlier. He also received death threats, with some of the letters claiming he would be shot right out on the field. Aaron would admit later that the letters not only changed him but also kept him from enjoying the chase to the record.

"The threats and the controversy definitely made it difficult," he said. "My daughter was in college at Fisk University, and she wasn't able to enjoy it. And I had to put my two boys in private schools, so they weren't there to be bat boys. They weren't able to enjoy it. So I was deprived of a lot of things that really should have belonged to me and my family."

As a tribute to his talent and ability to concentrate, the hate mail and threats didn't affect his play on the field. Just being at the ballpark, in fact, served as a kind of respite from the real world.

"When I was at the ballpark, I felt there was nothing that could bother me," he said. "I felt safe. I felt like I was surrounded by angels and I had God's hand on my shoulder."

Aaron also admitted that because he played in Milwaukee and Atlanta, and was a low-key guy who never hit more than 50 homers, people probably never expected that he would be the one to chase the record. He was well aware that he had played most of his career in the shadows cast by Mays and Mantle.

"I was going to eventually do what I had to do, regardless of what those guys did," he said. "If the public had a choice of who they wanted to break Babe Ruth's record, it would have been Mickey Mantle. And if Mickey couldn't do it, they probably would have wanted Willie Mays. If you walked on the field in New York in the 1950s, there might be fifty guys with pencils in their hands taking notes. I played in a little town like Milwaukee and then we moved to a little bigger town, Atlanta. Both had just two newspapers and they were owned by the same company."

It may surprise fans today to learn that baseball simply wasn't as popular from the fifties into the seventies as it is today. There was no cable television, not as much media hype, and not as many fans flocking to the ballpark. Remember, there were some 20,000 empty seats at the Polo Grounds in 1951 when Bobby Thomson hit his Shot-Heard-Round-the-World home run in the third and final game of a pennant playoff. How much bigger can a game get than between two New York teams in the largest city in the world and still not fill the house. So despite the mountains of mail Aaron was receiving, the media hype wasn't what it would be in 1998, when Mark McGwire and Sammy Sosa would both threaten Roger Maris's single season record.

For a thirty-nine-year-old approaching a sacred record and receiving reams of threats and hate mail, Aaron produced a simply incredible season. After the all-star break it became increasingly apparent that not only was Henry Aaron going to break the Babe's record, but he might even do it before the 1973 season ended. He came *this/close*, finishing the season with 40 home runs and 713 for his career. He was within one home run of Ruth, setting up a highly anticipated drama for the start of the following season.

Though the Braves had finished fifth in the six-team National League West with a 76-85 record, they led the majors with 206 home runs and became the first team in baseball history to have three players top the 40-homer mark. Second sacker Davey Johnson set a record for his position with 43 dingers, while Darrell Evans had 41. Aaron was third on his own team with 40, while the Pirates Willie Stargell led the league with 44. In addition to his homers, Aaron also had 96 RBIs to go with a .301 average in just 396 at bats. The National League that year had twenty-eight players with 20 or more homers. Ironically, in the A.L., which hit two more homers than the National League, the leader was Reggie Jackson with 32, and just twenty-one players had 20 or more home runs. Obviously, there were a lot of players hitting between 10 and 20. Almost everyone apparently wanted to hit home runs now.

At the end of December that year, the United States Post Office gave Henry Aaron a plaque for receiving an incredible 930,000 pieces of mail. It was the most mail any U.S. citizen had gotten that year excluding politicians. And toward the end of the year, an interesting thing began to happen. Because there was so much publicity about the hate mail Aaron had received, he actually began getting more and more letters supporting him and encouraging him to continue his pursuit of the Babe's

Say Goodbye to Willie

It was almost fitting that as Henry Aaron approached what could be his greatest moment in baseball, the second of the two players who overshadowed him for so long retired. Willie Mays had seen his production begin to slip after the 1966 season. He continued playing with the Giants through 1971, when he hit just .271 with 18 homers and 61 RBIs at the age of forty. Instead of retiring then, he rejoined the Giants in 1972, but in May was traded to the New York Mets for a second-line pitcher named Charlie Williams and $50,000. He would finish his career where it began—in the Big Apple. Though he homered in his first game as a Met, the end was near. He would hit just eight home runs that year and in 1972 would only add six more to his ledger. Though he got to the World Series with the Mets in 1973, he was the proverbial shell of his former self. After the Series, he retired.

The Say Hey Kid left the game with a .302 lifetime average, 3,283 hits, 660 home runs, and 1,903 runs batted in. His home run total was third all-time behind Ruth and Aaron. It was almost as if Willie was yielding the stage to Hammerin' Hank as he left behind one of baseball's greatest careers. The Hall of Fame would invite him in five years later. Now, two-thirds of the trio that dominated their era was gone. Only Aaron was left to carry on and write his own legacy.

mark. Then, as the new season approached, the Braves began making plans for him to break the record, and it caused a bit of a stir.

Atlanta was scheduled to open the season with a three-game set at Cincinnati before returning home. Word was that the team planned to sit Aaron in the opening series so that he could hopefully tie and break the record in Atlanta. Not only did many sportswriters think this was a wrong move, but the commissioner's office also got involved. Finally, the Braves were ordered to play Hank in at least two of the games against the Reds. When the opener arrived, Cincy righthander Jack Billingham was on the mound and Henry Aaron was in the lineup.

Not one to waste any time, Aaron simply picked out one he liked and hit it over the left field wall for his first home run of the year in his very first at bat. More importantly, it was the

714th home run of his great career. He had now hit as many home runs as the great Babe Ruth, but he didn't get the record-breaker that day. Then Hank sat out the second game before he took the collar in game three against righty Clay Kirby. So the Braves came back to Atlanta and the team had their wish. Chances were good that Aaron would break the record in his home park. On April 8, 1974, the largest crowd in Braves history, 53,775 fans, jammed Atlanta Stadium in the hope of witnessing history. The Dodgers were in town and starting lefthander Al Downing.

When Hank came up in the first inning he drew a walk, prompting boos and catcalls from the packed house. Then he came up again in the fourth with the Dodgers leading, 3-1. There was a runner on first and Downing didn't want to walk him a second time. He tried to fool him with a low slider and, as he had done so often over the years, Aaron snapped those quick wrists and put the bat on the ball. He hit a high drive to deep left as the crowd collectively rose to their feet. They watched it as it cleared the fence and went into the Braves bullpen for home run number 715. As Hank circled the bases, a couple of fans ran out onto the field to accompany him around the sacks. Then his teammates mobbed him at the plate. Baseball had a new home run king!

Aaron's first thought after his momentous blast was that he was most "proud that my mother and my father were there." Asked if it was the best moment of his career, however, the man who was ever the winning ballplayer said, "The home run I hit in Milwaukee to clinch the pennant in 1957 was probably the greatest moment I had in baseball. Breaking Babe Ruth's record is probably number two."

But it was finally done. Whatever he accomplished the rest of his great career would be gravy. To show the state of the game then, by the time Hank came up for his third at bat of the night, many who were there at the beginning of the game had already left. They wanted to see a great moment and were now satisfied. His record-breaking home run was more important to them than the outcome of the game.

Henry Aaron would finish the 1973 season with 20 homers, giving him 733 for his career. He batted just .268 that year and many thought that, with the record in hand, he would simply retire. But like so many of the great players from that time, he loved the game and loved to be on a baseball field. After the season, he accepted a trade to the Milwaukee Brewers so he could finish his career in the city where it began. He would play two more years part-time, adding 22 additional homers to his total. But like Mays and Mantle before him, his final years weren't the real deal. He hit just .234 and .229, very un-Aaron like numbers, and retired following the 1976 season.

Henry Aaron left baseball with an envious record. Besides his 755 home runs, he also had more RBIs—2,297—than any other player in history. In addition, he had a .305 lifetime batting average and 3,771 hits, third on the all-time list today behind Pete Rose and Ty Cobb. There's little doubt that he was one of the greatest ever, and he followed his contemporaries—Mantle and Mays—into the Hall of Fame. With all his accomplishments, no one could ever accuse Henry Aaron of not "getting it." Asked in 1999 about the continued fascination with the home run and home run hitters, Aaron replied quickly, "A home run is the greatest thing in sports. The fans don't care about watching a no-hitter or a one-hitter, but they do care about a lot of offense. They want to see runs scored, people circling the bases, balls flying out of the ballpark. Anytime baseball is in trouble, they bring the home run back."

THE POWER LEVELS OFF

Big league hitters went over the 3,000 homer mark for only the fourth time in history in the 1973 season. The next year, of course, the big excitement was Henry Aaron's history-making home run. But once he broke the record the first week of the season, the excitement quickly died down and it was back to business as usual. There simply wasn't the kind of hype then that there would be today. Aaron was also just about the last of the group of home run swatters who had dominated the game for the past two decades. There were still a couple of older sluggers going at it. Willie McCovey continued on past 1976. Though on the downside, big "Stretch" was the last player from his era with a chance at 500 homers. He would eventually play until 1980 and finish with 521, the same number as Ted Williams.

The next generation of sluggers wasn't quite defined as yet. After hitting 47 in his second full season of 1969, Reggie Jackson of the A's had been consistent but not explosive, finishing between 23 and 36 homers a year. Third sacker Mike Schmidt of Philadelphia was just getting started but beginning to look like a potential high-octane slugger. There were plenty of players hitting between 15 and 25 each year, accounting for the overall rise in homers, but suddenly players in the 45-50 range seemed at a premium. And no player had hit 50 since Mays in 1965. The closest were Killebrew with 49 in 1969 and Pittsburgh's Willie Stargell with 48 in 1971.

Stargell, in fact, was an interesting case. He was a big left-handed hitter, extremely strong, and he could hit the ball a country mile. He was also a good hitter, topping the .300 mark on several occasions and hitting .282 for his career. Though he had two explosive years with 48 and 44 homers (1973), he also had off years where his batting average was down and his home run output was pretty low for a power hitter. Stargell had mid-career seasons of 20 (twice), 22, 24, and 25 home runs. Though he would finish his career with 475 home runs and eventually be elected into the Hall of Fame, he's got to be considered just a cut below the major sluggers of the era.

From 1974 to 1976 not a single big league slugger would reach the 40-homer mark. The American League leaders during those three seasons were Dick Allen with 32, Reggie Jackson and George Scott of Boston with 36, and Graig Nettles of the Yanks with 32. In the National, Mike Schmidt of the Phils began coming into his own, leading the senior circuit all three years with 36 and 38 twice. From 3,102 homers in 1973, however, big league hitters only produced 2,649 in 1974, 2,698 in

1975, and then 2,235 in 1976. The latter total was the lowest in the majors since 1968, the famed year of the pitcher.

Was the game changing again? Attendance seemed to be stuck in neutral, holding steady but not increasing. There were also a number of great achievements during these years that had nothing to do with slugging. In 1974, Lou Brock of the Cardinals broke Maury Wills record by stealing 118 bases. He was far-and-away the best, but four other National Leagues swiped 50 or more that same year. The advent of artificial turf had definitely brought back more of the running game from the past. That same year in the American League, Nolan Ryan of the California Angels fanned 367 hitters. What made his achievement even greater was that the year before Ryan had broken Sandy Koufax's mark by striking out 383 batters. His two-year whiff total was the greatest in baseball history. The American League that year had nine twenty-game winners. It may not have been another year of the pitcher, but A.L. hurlers were winning big and completing a ton of games. Five pitchers (Ferguson Jenkins, Gaylord Perry, Mickey Lolich, Ryan, and Luis Tiant) had twenty-five or more complete games. No wonder no American League team hit more than 135 home runs.

In 1975 and 1976, stolen base totals continued to climb. The 2,488 swiped in 1974 was the most since way back in 1916. The next year runners waltzed to the tune of 2,524, and in 1976 the total of 3,054 marked the first time big league thieves topped 3,000 since 1914. Yes, the running game was back. The pitchers also kept in tune. Ryan had 327 strikeouts in 1976, while three pitchers won 20 or more and another three won 19 in the American League. By that time, the Kansas City Royals were developing an outstanding speed team, taking advantage of the artificial turf, while the Oakland A's led the loop with 341 steals on natural grass.

At about this same time, the number of complete games was starting to go down. The Los Angeles Dodgers were the first team to break the longstanding tradition of four-man pitching rotations. In the mid-1970s, the Dodgers went to a five-man rotation, meaning that each pitcher in the rotation got about eight fewer starts a year. That would soon become the norm. There were also more relief pitchers beginning to make their presence felt. Traditionally, relief pitchers were not specialists. They were either veterans who could no longer make the starting rotation or youngsters trying to break into the rotation. Occasionally, there were some who strictly relieved, such as Joe Page and Luis Arroyo of the Yanks in the late 1940s and 1950s, Jim Konstanty of the Phils, and knuckleballer Hoyt Wilhelm of the Giants, who also started on occasion later in his career. But by the early- to mid-1970s, relievers like Sparky Lyle, Rollie Fingers, Rawley Eastwick, Darold Knowles, and others were beginning to have specific roles out of the pen.

The other big change during this time involved free agency. At the end of the 1975 season, the notion that Curt Flood had tried to make a reality in 1970 finally came to fruition. Pitchers Andy Messersmith and Dave McNally played out their contracts and asked to be declared free agents. This time the courts ruled in their favor and more players would soon follow suit, changing the makeup of the game once more. It wouldn't be long before player movement increased due to free agency. Fewer and fewer players would spend the bulk of their careers with one team, and ballclubs with the biggest checkbooks would begin offering larger and larger contracts to get free agents into the fold and improve their teams.

In the early 1970s, the Oakland A's had been baseball's dominant team, winning three consecutive World Series from 1972 to 1974. This was a balanced ballclub that had some long-ball bangers like Reggie Jackson and Sal Bando, but they also had speed with a couple of ace basestealers in Bert Campaneris and Bill North, as well as solid starting pitching with Vida Blue, Ken Holtzman, and Catfish Hunter. Add a bullpen that featured Rollie Fingers, and this was a well-balanced team that could beat you in a lot of different ways.

Taking over from the A's in the middle of the decade was the Cincinnati Reds. This was more of a hard-hitting team that acquired the nickname the Big Red Machine. They had home run

A Dramatic Homer

While the middle years of the 1970s saw a dropoff in home runs, there was one big blast that not only made the highlight films of the day, but also has continued to be shown over the years and is considered one of the most dramatic homers of all time. It happened on baseball's biggest stage, the 1975 World Series between the Cincinnati Reds and Boston Red Sox. The two teams battled evenly for four games. Boston had a team that featured two great rookies, outfielders Fred Lynn and Jim Rice. But Rice had a broken bone in his wrist and was out of the series. Still, the veteran Carl Yastrzemski, catcher Carlton Fisk, and outfielder Dwight Evans could also hit with authority. Cincy had the aforementioned Big Red Machine going for it. And when the Reds won game five, they were really in the driver's seat.

Game six was back at Fenway Park in Boston. A Fred Lynn homer in the first gave the Sox a 3-0 lead, but Cincy fought back and going to the bottom of the eighth had taken a 6-3 lead. It was close to being over. But Boston didn't quit. Bernie Carbo pinch hit a dramatic three-run homer to tie the game at six. That four-bagger would have been the big story if the Sox had pushed across another run to win. But they didn't and the game went into extra innings. Neither team was able to score in the tenth or eleventh, and it was still tied when Boston came to bat once more in the bottom of the twelfth inning.

Carlton Fisk was due to lead off against righthander Pat Darcy. Fred Lynn would follow and was standing alongside Fisk at the on-deck circle. Fisk later said he had a feeling and, turning to Lynn, said, "Fred, I'm going to hit one off the wall. Drive me in."

The wall, of course, was the fabled Green Monster at Fenway, high and imposing, but not far away. With the count 1-0, Fisk went after a fastball and hit it high and deep down the left field line.

He took a few steps toward first, then turned to watch the ball. The image is unforgettable. Fisk started jumping up and down and began waving both arms from left to right, over his head, as if he was trying to keep the ball from going foul. It hit the net attached on the fair side of the foul pole for a game-winning home run. The Boston catcher circled the bases as his jubilant teammates gathered at home plate to greet him. It was one of the most dramatic homers in World Series history. And although the Reds would win it all the following day, the sight of Fisk waving his arms to keep the ball fair continues to be seen in replays today, over and over again whenever great home runs are showcased.

hitters like Johnny Bench, Tony Perez, and George Foster. Second sacker Joe Morgan could do both—hit it out or get on and steal a base—and everything was set in motion by Pete Rose, whose will to win was as strong as his desire to get a hit every time he was up. The starting pitchers were never that dominant, but manager Sparky Anderson had a deep bullpen and was smart enough use it. The Reds won world championships in both 1975 and 1976, beating first the Boston Red Sox and then the rejuvenated New York Yankees.

But while the game obviously had a lot of talented and exciting players, these years were not defined by sluggers and home runs. There was no M & M Boys, no one challenging Roger Maris's record of 61 homers, no Henry Aaron methodically hitting home runs year after year. In fact, it's good to remember what the aforementioned Aaron said when asked about the fascination of the home run.

"Anytime baseball is in trouble, they bring the home run back."

8

Sluggers Juice Up the Game, 1977–1993

In a sense, the 1977 season was a pivotal one for Major League Baseball. The American League jumped ahead of the National by expanding again, adding two new teams, the Eastern Division Toronto Blue Jays and Western Division Seattle Mariners. Now there were fourteen teams in the American League and still twelve in the senior circuit. The National would hold the line until 1993, when they would finally add another pair of teams, the Colorado Rockies and Florida Marlins. The final expansion would come in 1998, when the Arizona Diamondbacks joined the National League and Tampa Bay Devil Rays came to the American. At the same time, the Milwaukee Brewers were shifted over to the National League giving baseball is current configuration of sixteen National League teams and fourteen in the American.

But as of 1977, it was the A.L. that took the first step. They gave Canada a second big league team and felt the time was right for a second try in Seattle. The franchises would be successful on both fronts. The game on the field was another thing. Despite the addition of the DH, home runs had dropped dramatically in 1976 after cresting three years earlier. Pitching was very strong and relief specialists were beginning to make their presence felt. Free agency was just beginning and one of the biggest acquisitions that year was the Yankees signing slugger Reggie Jackson. Oakland had traded Jackson to Baltimore the year before and after the season the slugging outfielder filed for free agency. The Yanks had rebounded to win the pennant in 1976, their first since 1964. New owner George Steinbrenner, who bought the team from CBS several years earlier, liked to win and was willing to spend in order to make that happen. He had

Another Walk-off Blast

Baseball got another wake-up call about the power of the home run during the 1976 American League Championship Series. The Yankees were playing the tough Kansas City Royals in what was still a best-of-five then. It was a hard-fought series that came down to a fifth and final game at Yankee Stadium. The New Yorkers led by a 4-3 score after just three and increased their lead to 6-3 after six innings. But just when it looked as if it was over, Kansas City's George Brett came up big. The A.L batting champ with a .333 average that year, Brett could also hit it out. He came up in the eighth with two on facing lefty reliever Grant Jackson. The southpaw-swinging Brett promptly deposited one into the right-field seats to tie the game.

But that soon became a secondary story. It was still tied in the bottom of the ninth. Relief ace Mark Littell was in the game for Kansas City as lefty swinging first baseman Chris Chambliss led off for the Yanks. Chambliss was a good hitter who had belted 17 homers during the year, but he wasn't considered a major slugger. On this day, however, he was. He picked out Littell's first pitch fastball and hit it deep to right center. As the fans jumped to their feet, the ball cleared the fence for a pennant-winning, walk-off home run. Chambliss couldn't even circle the bases. By the time he got to second, the fans were on the field and someone had literally swiped the bag, a real stolen base. When he reached third, he was engulfed by the joyous fans and he had to fight his way off the field. His teammates had to bring him back out to make sure he touched home plate.

It was the first Yankee pennant in twelve years and Chambliss's blast quickly became part of Yankees' lore, being shown over and over again on the team's TV station, and it's still shown today on the YES Network, the Yankees own station that often features franchise highlights. It was another home run not to be forgotten.

acquired pitcher Catfish Hunter in 1975 when a contractual error made the former Oakland righty a free agent. Now he added Jackson, and the once-mighty Bronx Bombers were the favorites once again.

What no one expected was the sudden resurgence in hitting, especially in the power department. Home runs in 1977 would leap to a new high as big league batters slammed 3,644 balls out of the park, an incredible increase of more than 1,400 homers from the season before. Yet no one questioned whether there had been any changes in the baseball. It seems as if the word was out among more players. Hit home runs and you make more money. More players than ever seemed capable of reaching the fences and they were swinging the bat in an obvious effort to put the ball in the seats.

The American League jumped by 891 home runs to a record 2,013, while the National clubbed 1,631, an increase of 518 over the previous season. This led to the new major league record 3,644, topping the previous mark set back in 1970. Not surprisingly, attendance figures reflected the return of the power parade. With two new teams, the American League drew 19,639,551 fans, including an average of 17,365 a game, up more than 2,000 fans from the year before and setting a new record. The National did even better, averaging a record 19,620 fans. The fact that an attendance record went hand in hand with a record number of homers could not have been lost on the lords of the game. Baseball needed some new sluggers who could attract the kind of attention Mays, Mantle, and Aaron had in the previous generation. They got their star, all right, and a few surprises as well.

For one thing, the game on the field was becoming a much more exciting one than the station-to-station game that characterized baseball from the 1930s right into the 1960s. Sure, there were plenty of great stars then and it was the real beginning of the home run era. There were also plenty of great moments to remember, but the game that was emerging in 1977 was more multidimensional. There were still many outstanding starting pitchers, now being joined by relievers who could come in and shut the door in the late innings. Despite the presence of more hitters who could put the ball in the seats, stolen base totals were at a level not seen since the dead ball era.

The game was being played in a variety of stadiums. Older parks, such as Wrigley and Fenway, were still in existence. Yankee Stadium has been renovated and reopened with a smaller capacity and closer fences. The cookie cutters, with their artificial turf, also changed the game and there were even a couple of domed stadiums that brought the game indoors. As the season progressed, twenty-eight-year-old George Foster of Cincinnati, who had never hit more than 29 homers in a season, was hitting them more frequently than any player in either league and threatening to become the first player in twelve years to top the 50-home run mark.

Foster would wind up with 52, also leading the National League with 149 RBIs while hitting a robust .320. It was an altogether great season. Foster was followed by Jeff Burroughs of Atlanta with 41, Greg Luzinski and Mike Schmidt of Philly with 39 and 38 respectively, and Steve Garvey of the Dodgers with 33. Though the league sported six twenty-game winners, there were also nine players with 100 or more RBIs. The N.L. as a whole batted .262, and the Dodgers, of all teams, hit a league best 191 homers, with Ron Cey, Reggie Smith, and Dusty Baker joining Garvey by hitting 30 or more. Remember the Koufax-Drysdale-Wills pitching and running Dodgers of the 1960s? Not anymore.

While the American League didn't have a single slugger reach the 40-homer mark, hitters still slammed nearly 400 more homers than the National. Jim Rice of Boston, fast becoming one of the game's top sluggers, led with 39. Graig Nettles of the Yanks and Bobby Bonds of the Angeles were next with 37, while George Scott of the Red Sox had 33 and Reggie Jackson, in his first year with the Yanks, smacked 32. What made the difference was that a record thirty-three hitters walloped 20 or more homers, compared to just twenty-one in the National League, and thirteen American League hitters drove in 100 or more runs. The league hit .266, perhaps helped by the young pitchers brought up to staff the two new teams. Kansas City had a team batting average of .299 while the Red Sox hit 213 home runs. Hitting nearly .300 as a team, the Royals also found time to swipe 170 bases and belt 146 homers. That was the kind of balanced game the good teams were playing.

But it was in the World Series that year when a single player again showed the baseball world just how a home run hitter could turn everyone on. The Yanks had beaten the Royals for a second straight year in a five-game ALCS, while in the National the Dodgers prevailed, topping the Phils in four games. Now the two old rivals would meet in the fall classic for the first time since 1963. While many eyes focused on the old rivalry and re-surfacing stories from the forties and fifties, when the Dodgers were still in Brooklyn, it was the newest Yankee who would take over center stage and put on a performance that no one would ever forget. Not surprisingly, it involved the home run.

Since hitting 47 home runs in 1969, Jackson had hit between 23 and 36 in the intervening years, only topping 100 RBIs once during that time. He was always a free swinger who struck out often, but he was also capable of generating great drama. In the 1971 All-Star Game at Tiger Stadium in Detroit, Jackson clubbed one of the longest homers ever seen in that old ball-park. The ball cleared all three decks in right center and the only thing that kept it from going out of the ballpark was that it hit a light tower positioned on the roof. Fans marveled at the young slugger's power. Yet with the Orioles in 1976, Reggie had hit just 27 homers and drove in 91 runs. But George Stein-brenner still signed him. There were problems immediately, when Reggie clashed with Yankee captain, Thurman Munson, claiming he was the straw that stirred the drink, and later when he battled with the team's combative manager, Billy Martin.

Still, he had a good season with the Yanks, hitting 32 homers and leading the team with 110 RBIs, all while finishing with a solid .286 batting average. Then it was time for the World Se-ries. The Yanks won the opener behind lefty Don Gullett, an-other free agent acquisition and a guy who had pitched well against them for Cincinnati in the Reds sweep the year before. The Dodgers tied it in game two, then the Yanks won the third game behind Mike Torrez. In the fourth, the Yanks took a com-manding 3-1 lead by beating L.A., 4-2, behind Ron Guidry. In that game, Reggie Jackson smacked a solo homer and also banged a double. The Dodgers won game five, 10-4, despite an-other home run from Reggie. Then came the sixth game and Jackson was about to etch his name firmly in home run history.

Mike Torrez started for the Yanks against the Dodgers' Burt

Hooton. In the first inning, Hooton walked Jackson on four pitches. When he came up again in the fourth, the Yanks were trailing, 3-2, with Munson on first. Jackson swung at Hooton's first pitch and hit a high drive into the right-field stands for a two-run homer, giving the Yanks a 4-3 lead. When Reggie came up again in the fifth, there was again a runner on first and reliever Elias Sosa on the mound. With the crowd chanting "RE-GGIE! REGGIE!" Jackson again went after the first pitch. This time he hit a blistering liner that carried into the lower right-field stands for his second two-run homer of game. His second homer increased the Yankee lead to 7-3.

Finally, Reggie came up again in the eighth. Now, knuckle-baller Charlie Hough was on the hill. Reggie got set, and with the crowd still chanting he once again went after the first pitch. He caught the knuckler and hit a huge drive to deep centerfield. It cleared the wall with room to spare, a mammoth home run and his third of the game. Reggie Jackson had hit three homers on three pitches against three different hurlers. The Yanks won the game, 8-4, taking the World Series in six. Reggie went 9-for-20 in the Series, a batting average of .450. He set a record by blasting five home runs, and his last three will never be forgotten. For his great play in the Series, something that would continue the remainder of his career, he would forever become known as *Mr. October*.

NEW BREED SLUGGERS

Now baseball was on the move. Home run totals might continue to fluctuate somewhat, but they wouldn't drop off. In fact, they would gradually rise. So would attendance figures as more and more people began enjoying their time at the ballpark. The product was exciting and the league still had many fine ballplayers. And over the next few years it became more obvious than ever that baseball was putting a premium on the home run. More players were hitting them and some probably wouldn't even have had a job in the majors in an earlier time. These were the swing-from-the-heels sluggers who didn't con-

Frank "Home Run" Franklin of the Philadelphia Athletics lives up to his moniker in this early photo. © Underwood & Underwood/CORBIS

Babe Ruth hit his first home run as a member of the Boston Red Sox, against—ironically—the New York Yankees. © Underwood & Underwood/CORBIS

Yankees power hitter Lou Gehrig eyes his arsenal. © Bettmann/CORBIS

Three sluggers pose in the 1950s: Joe Dimaggio, Mickey Mantle, and Ted Williams. © Bettmann/CORBIS

All-time home run leader Hank Aaron relaxes in the Atlanta Braves club-
house after clinching the National League Western Division in 1969.
© Bettmann/CORBIS

Roger Maris on October 1, 1961, the day he beat Ruth's record by one.
© Bettmann/CORBIS

St. Louis Cardinals' Mark McGwire watches his 65th home run of the year on October 3, 1999, the year he won the home run title. © Reuters/CORBIS

Barry Bonds celebrates after hitting his 70th home run of the season during the ninth inning against the Houston Astros on October 4, 2001.
© Reuters/CORBIS

cern themselves with batting average or how many times they struck out. In 1978, Jim Rice of the Red Sox had 46 and Foster hit 40 to lead their respective leagues. Then, a year later, two of the new-breed sluggers emerged. Gorman Thomas of the Milwaukee Brewers led the A.L with 45 and big Dave Kingman of the Cubs blasted 48 to lead the National League.

Both of these players were emblematic of the all-or-nothing slugger. Thomas was a 6'2", 210-pound righthanded hitter who came up with the Brewers in 1973. He didn't really become a regular until 1978 when he hit 32 home runs. But his batting averages leading up to that season were .187, .261, .179, and .198. The year he hit 32, he batted .246 and struck out 133 times. Then, in 1979, Thomas clubbed his 45 and drove home 123 runs in the process (outstanding numbers). But he only hit .244 and led the league with 175 strikeouts. Thomas knew his limitations as a ballplayer. He was a pretty good outfielder, but a bit reckless, and he once joked, "The fans come to see me strike out, hit a home run, or run into a fence. I try to accommodate them at least one way every game."

Thomas would hit 38 homers the following year and then tie for the league lead with 39 in 1982. His last big slugging year was with Seattle in 1985, when he hit 32 homers and drove home 87 runs, but hit just .215. A year later, after developing rotator cuff problems, Thomas hit 16 more home runs and retired. He finished his career with 268 homers and just a .225 batting average, one of the lowest in big league history for players with 2,500 or more at bats. He also struck out 1,339 times in just 4,677 at bats, one of the poorest ratios of all time. As a slugger, though, he did the job. His home run ratio was one in every 17.45 at bats. Reggie Jackson, who would retire with 563 homers, hit one in every 17.52 at bats. As a hitter, however, Gorman Thomas was definitely one-dimensional.

As for Dave Kingman, it was a similar story. Kingman was a huge man, standing 6'6" tall and weighing about 210 pounds. He was nicknamed "King Kong" Kingman for the mammoth home runs he used to hit. In fact, Kingman hit them so far that retired slugger Ralph Kiner once said that Kingman "can hit them out of any park—including Yellowstone." Like Thomas, Kingman never hit for a high average and struck out way too much. He also wasn't a good fielder and played for seven different teams, including the Giants twice, in a sixteen-year tenure. His 48 homers in 1979 was a career year. He also hit .288 that year, the best of his career. But when he retired after the 1986 season, his lifetime average was just .236, and he had fanned 1,816 times, which was fifth all-time back then.

But Dave Kingman also hit a total of 442 homers, finishing his career as pretty much a full-time designated hitter. Had Kingman managed another 58 homers, he would have undoubtedly become the first player with 500 homers *not* to make the Hall of Fame. Gorman Thomas and Dave Kingman may be the most overt example of the one-dimensional slugger. But in the late 1970s and 1980s, if you could hit the ball over the fence with regularity, there was a place in the game for you.

In 1980, Reggie Jackson and Ben Oglivie of Milwaukee had 41 each, and Mike Schmidt cemented his reputation as a great modern slugger by whacking 48 for the Phils. Schmidt, too, was emblematic of another type of modern slugger. He was definitely a run producer and slugger, a feared hitter who could take the ball out of any park. He didn't hit for a high average (.267 lifetime) and struck out 1,883 times, third on the all-time list when he retired after the 1989 season. But he also smashed 548 lifetime homers, passing the likes of Jimmie Foxx and Mickey Mantle, and was one of the great fielding third basemen ever. He would lead the league in homers eight times and in RBIs on four occasions, and he also led the Phils to a world championship in 1980. There was no question about him being a Hall of Famer, and because of his combined home run hitting and fielding ability, many have chosen him as best all-around third sacker of all-time.

The 1981 season was marred by yet another labor dispute between the players and owners. On June 12, the players went on strike, staying away for fifty days until the two sides reached an agreement. It was the longest strike in professional sports history to that time. The strike was settled on July 31, and the question became what to do with the season. It was decided that the four teams leading the division when the strike began would meet the division winners from the second half. By having this "split" season, a couple of teams with the best overall record were left out of the playoffs.

Mike Schmidt was again the game's top slugger, hitting 31 homers and driving in 91 runs in just 107 games. He definitely might have had a chance at 50 had the players not gone on strike. Over the next five years, Schmidt would continue as the National League's dominant slugger, winning home run titles with 40 in 1983, tying Dale Murphy with 36 in 1984, and whacking another 37 in 1987. Aside from Schmidt, there really wasn't another National League slugger who defined these years, though league attendance continued to rise, reaching a record 22,333,471 in 1986, an average of 23,048 a game.

The American League had a similar identity problem when it came to slugging. Four players had led the league with just 22 homers in the strike year of 1981. The following year, aging Reggie Jackson, now playing for the California Angels, hit 39, as did free-swinging Gorman Thomas. Jim Rice, arguably the most feared hitter of this period, hit 39 in 1983, while the unheralded Tony Armas had a career year with 43 in 1984. During the next two years, the leaders were Darrell Evans of Detroit with 40 and Jesse Barfield of the Blue Jays, also with 40.

Evans was another player emblematic of a very good home run hitter who is now largely forgotten. He played with four teams in his twenty-one-year career in which he had a lifetime average of just .248. He hit 40 or more homers twice and 30 or more twice. Yet he had nine seasons in which he didn't even reach 20. Still, he finished with 414 homers, more than Joe DiMaggio, Hank Greenberg, Johnny Mize, and Ralph Kiner—all remembered as outstanding sluggers and players who are in the Hall of Fame. He would even hit more than the aforementioned Jim Rice, who finished with 382 in a sixteen-year career. Yet Rice was considered by many as the dominant power hitter between 1977 and 1986, and still may make it into the Hall of Fame. As for Darrell Evans, he was a very serviceable major league player with the power to hit the ball out. Because he played for so long he wound up with more than 400 homers, something that probably would not have happened in an earlier time.

In 1986, baseball set yet another home run record—hitters blasting 3,813 balls into the seats with 2,290 being slammed in the American League (yet another record). While Toronto's Jesse Barfield was the only player to reach the 40 mark, there were ten players who hit 30 or more, and an almost incredible forty-one American League players who hit at least 20. So the number of players who could reach the seats with regularity was growing. What was almost equally amazing is that no single slugger had come along to dominate the game, to go over the 50 mark and maybe even challenge the 61 hit by Roger Maris a quarter of a century earlier.

And the names were changing. Among the players topping 30 homers were Don Baylor, Don Mattingly, Barfield, Rob Deer, Pete Incaviglia, Jose Canseco, Dave Kingman, Gary Gaetti, and Kirby Puckett. Joe Carter of Cleveland was the RBI champ with 121 to go with his 29 home runs. Canseco, who played for Oakland, was one of the game's imposing new sluggers. The 6'3", 185-pound Canseco was a native of Cuba, though his family came to the United States when he was very young. The 1986 season was his first full year and he responded with 33 home runs and 117 RBIs. But he also hit just .240 and struck out 175 times. Still, his potential to excite the fans was already evident, and he would figure prominently in the next generation of sluggers in more ways than one.

The National wasn't quite keeping pace. Only eighteen senior circuit hitters reached the 20 mark and just three went over 30. But there were some young sluggers also making their mark, players like Darryl Strawberry, Andre Dawson, Dave Parker, Eric Davis, Bob Horner, and Dale Murphy. The Mets would win the World Series that year in a memorable victory over the Boston Red Sox, but it was the American League that seemed to have the abundance of young sluggers. More were

The Pine Tar Home Run

One of the most famous home runs in baseball history didn't win a pennant, a World Series, or even set a record. But it set off a controversy that is remembered well by everyone who witnessed it or later saw it in numerous television replays. It happened on July 24, 1983, when the Kansas City Royals were playing the archrival New York Yankees at Yankee Stadium. The Royals were trailing, 4-3, in the top of the ninth when George Brett came up with a runner on to face ace Yankee reliever Rich "Goose" Gossage.

It was a classic confrontation, a great hitter against a great fastball pitcher. Brett was already a two-time batting champ, a guy who hit as high as .390 back in 1980 and had good home run power as well, though he really wasn't a slugger. Gossage threw high hard ones and was an intimidating presence. He had been a star reliever with the Yanks since 1978 and was having yet another fine season. Brett got set in his unusual stance, weight on the back foot, bat held back almost flat. He picked out a Gossage fastball and hit it right on the nose, a long, deep drive into the right-field seats for an apparent two-run homer, giving the Royals a 5-4 lead.

Brett circled the bases with a smile on his face as his teammates cheered. But as he crossed home plate, Yankee manager Billy Martin was out of the dugout and had grabbed hold of Brett's bat before the batboy could get it. He then began pointing something out to plate umpire Tim McClelland. It was apparent they were examining the bat, then measuring it against the 17-inch width of home plate. Suddenly, McClelland raised his right hand and called Brett out. Brett came out of the dugout like a madman, eyes as wide as saucers and screaming at the ump. He had to be restrained by his teammates.

In those days, all players didn't wear batting gloves. Instead, they wiped a dark, sticky substance called pine tar on their bats for a better grip. The rules stated that the pine tar could not come more than 18 inches up from the knob of the bat. Martin knew Brett used a lot of pine tar and waited for the right time to call him on it. The plate umpire agreed. The pine tar was more than 18 inches up on the bat, making the bat illegal. The home run didn't count. The argument raged until Brett was pulled from the field. "I can still see his bulging eyes and red face," McClelland would say later.

Not surprisingly, the Royals protested after the Yanks apparently won the game. The protest was upheld by League President Lee MacPhail, who said, "The umpires interpretation, while technically defensible, is not in accord with the intent or spirit of the rules and the rules do not provide that a hitter be called out for excessive use of pine tar. . . . Games should be won or lost on the playing field." The home run was reinstated and the game had to be continued from that point. It was finished twenty-five days later, and the Royals won, 5-4, on the strength of the Brett homer. Ever since then, *The Pine Tar Game* has meant only one thing to baseball fans. It was a one and only . . . another milestone built around a controversial home run.

just around the corner, and so was a year in which a lot of questions about the baseball would be raised once more.

DID THEY JUICE IT AGAIN?

Unlike the years from the 1950s to the 1970s, the best all-around players in baseball during the mid-1980s were not really sluggers. They were guys like George Brett, Kirby Puckett, and Don Mattingly who could hit for a high average, had home run power, and were also outstanding in the field. Mattingly wasn't a big man, and when he joined the Yankees in 1983, he was considered a good line-drive hitter, but not a player with a great deal of power. He hit .283 in just ninety-one games that year, getting just four homers in 279 at bats. A year later he was a regular, and he won the American League batting title with a .343 average, hit 23 homers, and drove home 110 runs.

That was the beginning of a six-year run in which Mattingly became known as the best player in baseball. He hit as high as .352 in 1986, and the year before had a high of 35 home runs and a league best 145 RBIs. Mattingly was a digger who worked on his swing to produce more power, and he reached a point where he could jack the ball out, maybe not on a par with the bigger sluggers of the game, but he had 30-home run power and always hit .300. He was also one of the best fielding first baseman the game had seen in years, and thus he acquired the nickname *Donnie Baseball*, as well as the reputation as the game's best.

He was just one of many players who went back to work in 1987 and started producing long-ball power that hadn't been seen before. As soon as the year began, the home runs began to fly. A 6'5", 215-pound rookie first baseman with the Oakland A's named Mark McGwire began blasting home runs like no rookie ever had before him. Andre Dawson, who had been a fine player with the Montreal Expos since 1976, but who had hit only 30 or more homers once and was coming off a 20-home run season in 1986, was traded to the Cubs and began blasting balls out of Wrigley Field in a way that reminded fans of Hack Wilson and Ernie Banks. In fact, more players than ever—especially in the American League—were slamming balls over the fences. The fans began responding and both leagues would see their attendance jump by more than two million fans to record levels.

The aforementioned Don Mattingly set a new record that year by hitting six grand slam home runs. They would be the only grand slams he would hit in his career, and they all came during 1987. Mattingly also tied a record set by Pittsburgh's Dale Long back in 1956 by hitting at least one home run in eight consecutive games. This one would be tied years later by Ken Griffey Jr., but it just shows again the way the ball was flying out of the park during that one campaign.

Was it all a coincidence? Was it a natural growth of the direction the game had taken? Or was it because major league hitters were just swinging for the fences in place of good situational hitting? Was everyone now enamored by the tape-measure home run? All the slugging, however, brought up yet another question, especially to the purists of the game who felt the playing field should always remain level. Once again people began asking about the baseball. Had it been intentionally juiced? The way the home runs were flying, there didn't seem to be any other explanation.

There certainly wasn't a dearth of pitching. Both leagues still had plenty of outstanding hurlers and some new, young stars as well. Young Dwight Gooden of the Mets had gone 24-4 in 1985, and a year later Roger Clemens of the Red Sox had an identical record. They were projected as future superstars. But even some of the very good pitchers would have trouble winning because the gopher ball was taking the game out of their hands. The American League actually seemed to have more star pitchers than the National in 1987, yet they were giving up more homers.

Many writers and observers thought it had to be the ball. There hadn't been an expansion team for a decade, so the league wasn't filled with young, inexperienced pitchers rushed up to fill a need. The ballparks also hadn't changed in years. They may not have had the huge dimensions of the early years of the game, but the smaller parks that would come in the 1990s were still just a plan on the drawing board. No, with all those homers riding high, it had to come back to the baseball.

Jim Deshaies, who went 11-6 for Houston in 26 starts that year, looked back at the 1987 season years later and could reach only one conclusion. "I don't know that major league baseball said that we want to order balls that are harder, tighter wound so that they will fly more and create more offense," Deshaies said, "but I wouldn't discount it, either. I would argue though that it might not have been the conspiracy everybody thought it was. There are some parameters under which these balls are supposed to be made and the specifications are that they are wound this tight. It may be, though, that in certain years they are pushed toward the top end of how tightly the balls are wound and therefore may fly a little better."

Baseball, as always, would deny that the balls were intentionally juiced. But by the end of the 1987 season, American League hitters had slammed 2,634 home runs and National League batters added 1,824 for a record 4,458 four baggers, an increase of 645 home runs over the record set in 1986. And, when you break it down into the individual stories, you see immediately that something had changed dramatically in 1987.

Rookie Mark McGwire of the Oakland A's wound up the season with 49 home runs, breaking the old rookie mark of 38, set originally by Wally Berger in 1930 and tied by Frank Robinson in 1956. McGwire didn't only break it, he blew it away. In the National, Andre Dawson also had 49 home runs, after hitting just 20 the year before. Runner-up in the American League was George Bell of Toronto with 47. Bell hit between 26 and 31 homers between 1984 and 1986, and he followed his MVP season of 1987 with only 24 in 1988. He would never hit more than 25 in a single season again. Dawson, too, would drop off dramatically the next year, finishing with just 24. McGwire would drop off to 32 in 1988, but he would be heard from again in a very big way.

Goodbye Mr. October

One slugger who didn't fully participate in the homer barrage of 1987 was Reggie Jackson. At the age of forty-one, Reggie was winding down his career where it had started, in Oakland, having returned to his original team after spending five years with California. Reggie was a part-timer by then, having played in just 115 games. He still managed 15 more home runs to end his career with 563. As mentioned previously, Reggie was also emblematic of the new age slugger. He fanned 2,597 times, the most K's in big league history, and also set the record of 100 or more strikeouts in eighteen different seasons.

Striking out or hitting a mammoth home run, Reggie Jackson always produced excitement. He banged six home runs in league championship series and 10 more in five World Series appearances. His three homers on three pitches from three different pitchers in 1977 will never be forgotten, and his nickname, Mr. October, is still more than relevant today. Not surprisingly, Reginald Martinez Jackson is a member of the baseball Hall of Fame.

It's the lesser players whose numbers seem to raise the red flag of a juiced baseball. Of the 124 everyday players who had at least 300 at bats, 44 produced a season in which they hit a career high in home runs. Every team in the majors except Houston, the L.A. Dodgers, and San Diego had more home runs in 1987 than they had the season before. Then there were the young A.L. players who hit a lot of homers in 1987 and never came close to those totals again. They included the likes of Matt Nokes of Detroit (32), Mike Pagliarulo of the Yanks (32), Larry Sheets of Baltimore (31), Brook Jacoby of Cleveland (32), Ivan Calderone of the White Sox (28), and Wally Joyner of California (34). In all, 48 American League hitters had 20 or more home runs and 20 of them blasted 30 or more. In the National, the number was 26 hitting 20 or more, and eight blasting 30.

Then there were some real discrepancies. Dodger center-fielder John Shelby blasted 22 home runs in 508 at bats in 1987. For the rest of his 2,582 career at bats, he only hit another 48. Bob Dernier of the Cubs had eight homers in 188 at bats. In his other 2,284 big league at bats he had just 15 more. Even the light hitters blasted more home runs than ever before. Ozzie Virgil of Detroit slammed 27 home runs in 1987 and then hit just a total of 10 more over the next three seasons! And Wade Boggs, who won his fourth batting title in five years with a .363 average in 1987, and who was becoming one of the great pure hitters of his time, had a career-best 24 home runs. Boggs hit just eight homers the season before and would only hit five the following season when he would win yet another batting crown with a .366 average. He never hit more than 11 home runs in a single season the rest of his career. What do you think?

As for the pitchers, well, they suffered. Some twenty-one big league pitchers gave up 30 or more home runs during 1987. The year before only thirteen had yielded that many gopher balls. Big name pitchers giving up a lot of home runs included Bert Blyleven of the Twins (46), Jack Morris of the Tigers (39), Don Sutton of the Angels (38), Charlie Hough of the Rangers (36), and Bruce Hurst of the Red Sox (35). Nolan Ryan, now pitching for Houston, led the National League with a 2.76 earned run average and 270 strikeouts. Pretty good. But Ryan's record was just 8-16. Houston was one of the weaker hitting teams in the league that year, scoring the second fewest runs in the league. Ryan just didn't have the support.

Some people continued to feel that 1987 was simply an aberration, a year in which a lot of guys hit a lot of homers. Batting averages really weren't up. The National League hit .261, while the American, with the designated hitter, only batted .265. The runners were still moving around the bases. In fact, Vince Coleman of the St. Louis Cards stole 109 bases in 1987, a record third straight season in which he topped the 100-mark. Amid all this, the homers flew out of the park in record numbers, the only major difference from the seasons before. It really had to be more than just a fluke season. There had to be a reason and most speculators point to the baseball. If the ball is wound just a little bit tighter, making it just that much harder, it will jump off the bat and travel further. If anyone disputes that, all they have to do is look at the next season. Things changed in a hurry.

The only overt difference that year was a slight widening of the strike zone, but the sudden and very obvious drop in home runs suggests something else. From a record 4,458 home runs in 1987, the alleged sluggers were only able to pump 3,180 balls into the seats in 1988, a difference of 1,278 home runs. The sudden home run malaise affected both leagues. The American was down 733 four baggers and the National leaguers hit 545 fewer ball into the scats. Darryl Strawberry led the National League with 39, but only one other player, Glenn Davis of Houston, hit as many as 30. In the A.L., Oakland's Jose Canseco whacked 42, but only Fred McGriff of Toronto (34) and Mark McGwire of Oakland (32) were able to top the 30-mark. Remember, a year earlier, twenty American League hitters belted 30 or more.

Once again, such a radical change didn't make sense. Could it have been a repeat of the events from 1930 and 1931, when there was an admission that the ball was changed but the lords of the game suddenly saw the monster they had created—too much hitting that was leaving the pitchers shell-shocked. It might have been a similar situation. Home runs and attendance were both escalating, so why not create a few more home runs? Again, this was something that baseball would never admit, but the scenario was so similar to that earlier time. When seventy-four big league players can muscle out 20 or more homers in a single season, it might have become a bit much. Quality pitchers were giving up a slew of home runs. Maybe a third of those would normally have been outfield flies. But in 1987 they were clearing the fences. All it would take would be to adjust the machines that wind the baseballs. The difference between the two seasons was simply too striking to chalk up to coincidence.

The 1989 season saw home runs take yet another slight dip to 3,083, though attendance began sneaking upward again. The game was in another leveling-off period. Players were now beginning to earn much bigger money because of free agency and arbitration, and they were well on their way to becoming the same kind of celebrities as rock stars. With more people than ever going to the ballpark and watching on more and

A Pinch Hit Homer for the Ages

The 1988 World Series featured a meeting between the surprising Los Angeles Dodgers and the power-laden Oakland A's. The A's were considered big favorites. They had sluggers Jose Canseco and Mark McGwire, already tabbed the *Bash Brothers* by the media; two top starters in Dave Stewart and Bob Welsh; and a lights-out relief pitcher in Dennis Eckersley. The Eck, as he was called, had been a solid starter for years, then was converted into a reliever and was one of the first great "closers," a reliever who usually came in for the ninth inning and slammed the door.

Los Angeles was at another disadvantage because their team leader and MVP, Kirk Gibson, was badly injured. Gibby had a severely pulled left hamstring and strained ligaments in his right knee. He wasn't expected to play and the Dodgers would miss his bat and his leadership. In game one, the Dodgers took an early lead on a two-run homer by Mickey Hatcher. But Canseco showed his muscle with a grand slam in the second inning, and by the ninth the A's were still nursing a 4-3 lead behind Dave Stewart. When the Dodgers came up for their final at bat in the bottom on the inning, Dennis Eckersley was standing on the mound ready to go.

Eckersley retired the first two hitters, but then the third drew a rare walk. Manager Tommy Lasorda needed a pinch hitter but didn't expect the call he got. Kirk Gibson, who had been hitting off a batting tee under the stadium, called his manager and said he wanted to bat. Lasorda played a hunch and gave Gibby the okay. Gibson limped up to the plate as the fans cheered and hoped. But Eckerley, who always threw strikes, quickly got a pair of them on the slugger. And Gibson didn't look good taking a cut at one of them. Finally, however, the count ran full.

Then Eckersley delivered again and Gibson went after an outside slider. He hooked the ball toward the right-field seats and, amazingly, it carried into the stands for a game-winning, two-run homer. Gibson smiled as he limped around the bases, barely able to finish his home run trot, and television announcer Jack Buck voiced what many were thinking, "I can't believe what I just saw."

Neither could the A's. Gibson was so badly injured that he didn't appear for the rest of the series as the Dodgers upset the A's in five games. Later, he said that a scout had told him that Eckersley always threw a backdoor slider on a 3-2 count to a lefthander hitter. That's a pitch that appears as if it's going to be wide and breaks over the outside corner of the plate. Gibson was looking for it and said it was the only pitch he could have possibly hit. But his dramatic homer with such severe leg injuries was one of the most incredible ever and was later voted the greatest moment in Los Angeles sports history.

more cable television outlets, there was little doubt about baseball's continued growth. Fred McGriff was the American League home run champ with just 36, while the Giants' Kevin Mitchell had a career year with 47. But to draw another comparison with 1987, just twenty American League hitters and seventeen in the National managed 20 or more homers. Two years earlier seventy-four players had done it. And the leagues were filled with essentially the same players. Add to that the fact that only five players in each league reached 30, compared with twenty-eight players reaching that mark two years earlier, and it became even more obvious that there had to be a juiced baseball in 1987. Any other explanation didn't wash.

The 1989 World Series was an all Bay-area affair, with the Oakland A's meeting the San Francisco Giants. The A's won the first two, then just before game three in San Francisco on October 17, a devastating earthquake hit the area. The Series wasn't resumed until ten days later. In that game, the A's hit a record-tying five home runs to win, 13-7, and then finished their sweep the next day. It was a dramatic way to end a decade, but with what had happened in the final two years, everyone wondered what direction the game would take beginning in 1990. Would the home run continue to diminish, or would it come back again? No one then knew just what was in store for the game within the next ten years. But once again, it would evolve around players who could hit the baseball a country mile.

Maybe there was a hint in 1990. In the American League, a burly, twenty-six-year-old, designated hitter/first baseman named Cecil Fielder was traded from Toronto to Detroit. Fielder had been a part-timer for several years with the Jays, but with the Tigers he got to play every day and erupted with 51 home runs and 132 RBIs. The 6'3", 230-pound slugger was hitting long, high homers and became the first major leaguer since George Foster in 1977 to crack the 50-home run barrier. In the National League, young Ryne Sandberg, a second sacker with the Cubs, had his best year by banging 40. Homers went back up to 3,317, not a huge change considering the league had hit more home runs back in 1970, twenty years earlier. And there wasn't really a single dominant slugger, though the Bash Brothers, Canseco and McGwire, looked as if they could both be the real deal. Canseco showed it again in 1991 by tying with Fielder at 44 homers each. But in the National League, Howard Johnson of the Mets won it with 38. The senior circuit was also looking for new slugging blood.

Then, slowly, they began emerging. Juan Gonzalez of Texas won his first home run titles in 1992 and 1993, hitting 43 and 46 respectively. Gonzalez looked like a fine, all-around hitter with the ability to hit .300 while driving in a ton of runs. In the National, Fred McGriff won it again with just 35 in 1992, and then in 1993 a player began to really make his presence felt, and he would soon become one of the focal points of the game.

Barry Bonds began playing with the Pittsburgh Pirates in 1986 as a twenty-one-year-old. He was a 6'1", 185-pound left-handed hitter who choked up slightly on the bat, something rarely seen in the modern game. He was also the son of Bobby Bonds, who was a fine player in his own right from 1968 to 1981, winding up with 332 home runs. Young Barry didn't seem like a home run hitter at first, but he began getting better and better with each passing year. In 1990, he hit 33 home runs, drove in 114, and hit .292. His fine-all-around play in the outfield and on the bases combined to make him the league's Most Valuable Player. A year later he had 25 homers and 116 RBIs, and in 1992 had 34 homers and 103 runs batted in to go with a .311 batting average. That year he was the MVP once again and after the season became a free agent. He then signed with the San Francisco Giants for the 1993 season.

Playing on the West Coast, Bonds seemed better than ever. He won his first home run title by blasting 46 and added 123 RBIs with his .336 batting average. He led the league in homers and RBIs on base percentage, slugging percentage, and total bases. He was also fourth in the batting race. Not surprisingly, Bonds won his third Most Valuable Player Award in four years. Was he going to be the next dominant player in the game? He seemed well on the way.

At the same time, the game was thriving. Homers took another big leap in 1993 with big league batters hitting 4,030, a jump of nearly 1,000 home runs over the previous year. This time there was no talk of a juiced ball. Instead, there seemed to be more young sluggers coming into the game, guys who knew they would be paid to hit home runs and were constantly swinging for the downs. At the same time, baseball attendance flourished. A record 33,333,365 fans came to American League parks, an average of 29,395 a game, while 36,924,573 watched National League baseball, with 32,533 showing up on an average at every game, an increase of almost 8,000 a game from the year before. With new teams in Florida and Colorado, the senior circuit found a whole new group of fans.

It seemed as if the game was about to enter a new golden age. But in 1994, greed would get the better of everyone as the players and owners would go to war once again. This time, there would be a setback that threatened to reverse all the good things that had happened in 1993 and would leave baseball wondering how to resurrect the game. The answer would be the same as it was in 1920, after the sport was rocked by the Black Sox Scandal. Back then his name was Babe Ruth. This time it would be a whole group of Babe Ruth wannabes, and a number of them would prove to be the real deal and baseball's headline makers for the next decade.

9

Big Mac and Sammy Go Yard, Over and Over Again, 1994–1998

By 1994 baseball was riding the crest of a large wave of success. The game on the field was flourishing, new stars were coming aboard, new ballparks were springing up, and the home run hitters looked ready to begin dominating once again. After setting an all-time attendance record in 1993, there was no reason to think the trend wouldn't continue. Though ticket and concession prices were higher than ever, people seemed to enjoy a day or night at the ballpark and full houses were becoming more common. Teams now looked to top the 3,000,000 mark in attendance to deem the season a success, and that meant averaging more than 37,000 fans a game. A number of ballclubs were beginning to do just that.

Even longtime, established teams were beginning to rethink the venues in which they presented their product. In 1992, a new ballpark opened in Baltimore that would again change the look of the game. Oriole Park at Camden Yards replaced the old Memorial Coliseum. It was the first of the so-called "Retro" Parks, giving baseball a look of the past with a ballpark that had a distinctly individual appearance as well as all of the modern amenities. There would be no more cookie-cutter bowls constructed for major league baseball. The new parks were also totally fan friendly. They had plenty of "skyboxes" or luxury suites for which corporations paid a hefty price. These suites had comfortable seating behind glass, bars, private bathrooms, and all kinds of available food. But they were for the very wealthy and provided teams yet another way to increase revenue so they could pay the escalating player salaries.

Regular fans also enjoyed the new Orioles ballpark. The ambience was great. An old warehouse stood behind the right-field wall, helping to give the ballpark its retro look. Camden Yards had a capacity of 48,876. Most of the new parks would have capacities in the 40,000 to 50,000 range. No more carnivorous stadiums that could seat 75,000 or 80,000 fans. There were a variety of foods available, places where people could picnic, music, play areas for small children, and a great view of the field from everywhere. The Baltimore fans came flocking, and the new ballpark was a huge and immediate success.

Two years later, Jacobs Field opened in Cleveland, replacing old Municipal Stadium, a huge, cold place dubbed "the mistake by the lake." Jacobs was another retro park that the fans loved. A third retro stadium was the Ballpark at Arlington, the new home for the Texas Rangers. Those three were already in place when the 1994 season opened and would pave the way for a whole other group of parks to open within the next decade. Once the National League embraced the trend, the cookie cutters and their artificial turf would also almost disappear. Those who had complained that baseball had lost much of its character when places like the Polo Grounds, Ebbets Field, Crosley Field, Forbes Field, and Connie Mack Stadium disappeared were now getting some of that character back.

The game being played on the field was also changing. Two more teams had joined the National League, the Colorado Rockies and the Florida Marlins. In addition, the players were getting bigger and stronger, both the hitters and the pitchers. Many of the great sluggers of the past were from 5'10" to 6'1" tall and weighed anywhere from 175 to 200 pounds. Sure, there were bigger men like the Babe, Hank Greenberg, and Johnny Mize, but Mantle, Mays, and Aaron were certainly not huge and they had left an impressive legacy. Yet they looked nothing like Canseco, McGwire, or Frank Thomas, and there were other hitters who now stood 6'3" or taller and weighed 225 pounds or more. These guys could generate great bat speed, especially with the lighter, thin-handled bats of the day, and consequently put the ball in orbit. Many of them, however, were not the all-around players that so many of the earlier sluggers had been.

There was, however, one little cloud on the horizon of this bright baseball picture, a cloud that would become increasingly larger and more ominous as the season wore on. The players and owners were going at it again. The collective bargaining agreement had not yet been renewed, and the players were already talking about a strike, one that could come during the second half of the season. Many remembered the strike of 1981, when the players stayed out for fifty days and a strange "split" season had to be put in effect to salvage the playoffs. Could that happen again? Or could it be even worse? That was a question yet to be answered.

A year earlier, in 1993, big league batters had slammed 4,030 home runs, only the second time in history that more than 4,000 baseballs had left the yard. The other season, of course, was the suspected juiced-ball year of 1987. Yet in April of 1994, the hitters were already putting on a show. When the month ended, big league batters had sent 210 more balls flying into the stands for home runs than they had the previous April. It looked as if everyone was on a record home run pace and, once again, people were pointing fingers in the usual direction—the Rawlings Sporting Goods Company—the people who made the baseballs. Had the balls been juiced once more?

One veteran baseball man who thought they were was Sparky Anderson. Sparky was managing the Detroit Tigers in 1994, but he had seen plenty of sluggers in his time, especially when he managed the Cincinnati Reds Big Red Machine. "I wasn't convinced earlier," Sparky said, "but I am now. Soon [Rawlings is] going to have to make a statement that they souped up the ball."

Some felt the reason was the continued dilution of pitching due to the increasing number of teams. "Whenever you expand the league, you decrease the quality of the pitching," said a longtime coach. Others felt the umpires were not giving the pitchers calls just off the outside corners, thus compressing the strike zone. One who felt that way was former pitcher and current Rangers pitching coach Claude Osteen. He felt pitchers were throwing too many fastballs through the center of the plate, allowing the hitters to get set and drive the ball. He called these homers "giveaways" and said there were more of them because pitchers weren't getting the calls on the corners.

Then there were some who simply felt the players were getting better, that they were bigger, stronger, quicker, and had the advantage of better nutrition and improved training methods, including the proper use of weight and strength training. In addition to that, modern technology allowed players and coaches to study their batting techniques and swing via tapes made from all angles, and then make the necessary adjustments. Hitters could also get tapes of the various pitchers and see how they worked the hitters before facing them. All this, supposedly, worked to the advantage of the hitter.

But if all that was true, why was it that only the home run hitter was taking advantage? If batters had this tremendous advantage, why weren't there any .400 hitters, or a bunch of guys coming in between .350 and .380 each year, as they had done in the early days of the game? Most seasons you simply didn't have that outside of a few pure, old-fashioned hitters like Rod Carew, Wade Boggs, and Tony Gwynn. And why were the guys hitting all the homers, getting the "giveaways," still striking out a host of times and many of them hitting in the .260's? No, it wasn't *hitting* that was taking a giant leap, it was *home run* hitting. And when that happened, it always seems to go back to the baseball.

A spokesman for Rawlings said that since the company became the supplier for the majors in 1977, they had been making the baseballs in the same way every year and were using the same materials. Each ball was supposedly weighed and measured so that it fell within the specifications, and samples from each batch were then tested for what they called "hitability." If any balls were found to have more "juice," they were supposedly rejected.

At the same time, a physicist from a well-known independent laboratory compared the balls being used in 1994 with some balls from 1987. He said they took the baseballs and bounced them from a height of 24 feet, dropping them onto concrete, and measuring how high they bounced. His conclusion was that "the ball today doesn't bounce any more than the ball from 1987."

What's wrong with this picture? When they performed the test didn't they remember what happened in 1987? That was the year big league hitters erupted for a record 4,458 home runs amidst all kinds of speculation that the ball was juiced. If they compared the ball from 1994 with the ball from 1987 and they were exactly the same, wouldn't it stand to reason that if one was juiced, then the other was juiced as well? Why didn't they compare the 1994 ball with some from 1988 when home runs plummeted to 3,180? That would have made more sense. Maybe someone didn't want anyone to reach any definite conclusions about the ball and was content to let the hitters swing away and watch the results.

By the All-Star break, a number of hitters looked as if they were on the way to career years. Not only were the home run hitters belting the ball all over the lot, but a number of others were sporting batting averages much higher than they ever had before . . . or ever would again. This could be construed as more evidence that the ball wasn't quite the same. But there was still something clouding this pretty picture. The labor dispute between the two sides wasn't anywhere close to being settled. Finally, the players set a strike date of August 11, telling the owners that if a settlement wasn't reached, they would walk, and they didn't mean by taking ball four. A late-season strike in August could be devastating. If the two sides couldn't settle quickly, the end of the season as well as the playoffs and World Series could be in jeopardy.

Despite all the hitting, there was a great deal of animosity due to the labor dispute. Kevin Kennedy, who was managing the Texas Rangers that year, described the atmosphere as "ugly" right from the start of spring training. There was little joy in most of the locker rooms around the league. While players were tearing the hide off the ball, they weren't doing it with smiles on their faces. Everyone seemed to know what was coming. Unfortunately, neither side was bluffing, nor were they willing to budge. Sure enough, after the games of August 11, the players struck, making it the thirteenth work stoppage since the players and owners started battling each other for the bucks. Only this time it wasn't settled, and before long the worst-case scenario came sharply into focus. In early September, it was announced that the remainder of the season had been canceled. There would be no chance of a new home run record and, more importantly, no playoffs and no World Series. Baseball had come to a halt.

Most teams lost in the neighborhood of forty-eight games. The Montreal Expos had the Majors best record at 74-40, while the Yanks were 70-43 and the Braves 68-46 when the strike hit. Now none of that mattered. The individual records, of course, would count, but with players missing out on nearly fifty games, everything was incomplete. Had the season gone on to its conclusion, there would have undoubtedly been some great numbers put on the board. As it was, big league hitters slammed 3,306 home runs, more than they had hit in the full seasons of 1988 and 1989, just a few short years earlier. Had the season not ended early, several players might have gone over the 50 mark and even come close to challenging the all-time record of 61.

Third baseman Matt Williams of the Giants was in the midst of a career year. He had 43 home runs when the season came to a halt. Right behind him was young Jeff Bagwell of the Astros with 39. Barry Bonds had 37 and Fred McGriff checked in with 34. In the A.L., twenty-five-year-old Ken Griffey Jr. of the Mariners led the way with 40. Big Frank Thomas of the White Sox was next with 38, while the Indians Albert Belle had 36. All of those players had a chance to hit 50, while Williams, Griffey, Bagwell, Thomas, Bonds, and maybe even Belle might have approached 60 had the season continued.

A look at the batting leaders also showed the way the hitters were dominating when the strike was called. Paul O'Neill of the Yanks was the American League batting champion with a .359

average. O'Neill was a very good hitter, but he would retire with a .288 lifetime average and would never hit higher than .324 again. Belle was next at .357. His high in all other seasons would be .328. Frank Thomas of the White Sox was next with a .353 mark, while Kenny Lofton of the Indians was fourth with a .349 average. Lofton's next best effort would be .333.

Thomas is an interesting case. Known as *The Big Hurt*, Thomas stands 6′5″ and weighs in the neighborhood of 255 pounds. A former football player, he was on his way to becoming a very good all-around hitter by 1994. He was fully capable of blasting more than 40 homers, driving in 140 runs, while still maintaining a high batting average. While his .353 in 1994 was a career high, it wasn't an aberration like some of the others. Thomas would also have batting averages of .349 and .347 in subsequent years. He had a great batting eye and was also among the leaders in walks. It would only be later in his career that he would admit that his job was to hit home runs and he wasn't as worried about a high batting average as he was in earlier times. For a number of years, however, he did it all as a hitter and slugger, a throwback to an earlier time. At the end of the 2004 season, the thirty-six-year-old Thomas had 436 home runs and a .308 lifetime batting average.

In the National League, the great Tony Gwynn was on his way to possibly making history. When the season ended, Gwynn had a .394 batting average. Three more hits and he would have been at .400, the first player to reach that level since Ted Williams in .401. A great pure hitter, Gwynn didn't worry about homers, but he would hit .372, .370, and .368 in other years and would win eight National League batting crowns. Gwynn would eventually retire with a .338 lifetime mark and more than 3,000 hits, so he was a guy capable of a run at .400. It's just interesting that he came the closest in 1994, a season in which he hit 22 points higher than in other seasons.

Bagwell of Houston batted .368 to go with his 39 homers. He would continue to be a top slugger and very good hitter, a guy with 446 home runs and a .297 lifetime batting average at the end of the 2004 season, potential Hall of Fame numbers.

But while he was a good hitter, Bagwell hit .320 in 1993, then topped out at .368, and never hit higher than .315 after that. It's further evidence that something was done in 1994 to allow the hitters to flourish in every way.

One player who didn't need extra help was the American League home run champ, Ken Griffey Jr. The son of Ken Griffey Sr., a fine ballplayer in his own right, Junior came up to the Mariners as a twenty-year-old in 1989, and he arrived with the advanced notices that said he would be the game's next great superstar. A 6'3", 205-pound speedster, Griffey Jr. could do it all. He had a Willie Mays type of ability in centerfield, could hit for average, and began to show more power with each passing year. As a rookie, he had just 16 homers, following up with 22 in each of his next two years and 27 in 1992. A year later he erupted for 45 and was on his way to topping that when the 1994 season ended. Griffey Jr. was a lefthanded hitter with a long, sweet swing. He was more in keeping with some of the game's older sluggers as opposed to the big muscular modern home run banger, and he would be heard from even more over the next few seasons.

So the cast of characters was beginning to fall into place for a home run barrage unprecedented in the long history of the game. But first things first. Baseball had still not settled its labor dispute. It lingered throughout the off-season, and when spring training for 1995 rolled around, the players were still out. But the lords of the game were not about to cancel another season. They announced that, if necessary, they would begin the season with replacement players—minor leaguers, guys from the independent league, players who were not part of the union—and each team immediately began assembling teams with largely unknown names and lesser talents. The tactic worked. The strike was finally settled, but the returning players would need more time to get ready. By the time everyone had rounded into shape, the belated spring training has cost each team 18 games. That made 1995 into a 144-game season.

THE POST-STRIKE HOME RUN PARADE

The strike of 1994 definitely hurt the game. For some years now, players salaries had been escalating into the stratosphere to the point where even mediocre players were beginning to get million-dollar contracts. Fans had to pay higher and higher prices to come to the ballpark. Even the cost of a hot dog and soda were inflated, yet people continued to come, setting new all-time attendance record in 1993. The game might have set another new record in 1994, though the crowds began tailing off once the strike date was announced. The strike itself did sour a great number of fans. Apparently, people were simply getting tired of millionaire ballplayers arguing with billionaire owners to see who would be able to put another couple of million in their pockets.

Kevin Kennedy, who had moved from the Rangers to manage the Boston Red Sox in 1995, said that many longtime Red Sox fans were sending boxes of valuable memorabilia to his office in Fenway Park—pennants, autographed baseballs, pictures of their longtime heroes—and saying they didn't want it anymore, that they were finished with baseball. There had certainly been strikes and lockouts before, but this one caused the cancellation of the playoffs and World Series, and that was difficult for many fans to swallow. Kennedy said he and Red Sox officials tried their best to return the memorabilia to its rightful owners, but the fact that it was sent to the ballpark in the first place showed the depth of many longtime fans disgust.

Further proof was in the attendance. It would take an entire decade to reach prestrike levels again. The greatest decline was in 1995, the year after the strike. Average attendance in the National League would drop from 32,139 a game in 1994 to just 24,936 the following season. In the American it went from 30,367 down to 25,108. That's a significant change. Was there a remedy? You just have to remember the words of Henry Aaron. Hammerin' Hank said, "Anytime baseball is in trouble, they bring the home run back."

The home run was more than back before the strike, and once the game returned to the field, there was no reason not to encourage the continued long-ball barrage. There was almost more drama associated with the home run now, a kind of theatric that wasn't there in older times. When Mantle, Maris, Mays, or Aaron hit one—as did most players of that generation—they would start to run as soon as they hit it, and once the ball was in the seats, they would finish trotting around the bases. Mantle, in fact, always ran with his head down, saying he didn't want to give the pitcher or his opponents the impression he was showing them up. It started to change with guys like Reggie Jackson who, when he hit a home run, would often stand and admire the ball before trotting around the bases. Now, almost all players who really tagged one would admire their handiwork before beginning to run around the bases.

In the old days, someone posing like that would pay the price the next time up. Imagine a player admiring a home run with Bob Gibson or Don Drysdale on the mound? The next time up, the ball would be lodged squarely in his ear. But the knockdown or purpose pitch had been taken out of the modern game to a great degree, so the home run hitters could pretty much have a field day watching their drives clear the fences, and the fans seemed to enjoy it.

During the next three years, 1995–1997, the trend continued. More and more players were hitting more and more home runs. There were still great pitchers, and the baserunners continued to steal. But it was the hitters who kept bringing more offense to the game as almost everyone was swinging for the fences, which weren't as distant as they had been years ago. Ballparks all had similar dimensions now. All the new parks were about 330 feet down the lines and 405 feet to center, give or take 10 to 15 feet here and there. Some of the older parks had their fences moved in, and there were no more 460-feet centerfield walls daring players to hit the ball over it.

Though 1995 was shortened by eighteen games at the outset to let the striking players get back in shape, the hitters still slammed 4,081 homers. A year later, they drove the total up to

4,962, and in 1997 had 4,640. Now, the 4,000 barrier had been cracked and it just seemed a matter of time until big league batters began putting 5,000 or more homers into the seats. In 1995, Albert Belle slammed 50 home runs, making him the first player to hit that number since Cecil Fielder five years earlier. Only three other players—Dante Bichette of Colorado, who led the National League, and American Leaguers Jay Buhner and Frank Thomas—hit 40. But there were a lot of guys over 30 and plenty more over 20.

Then in 1996 it really exploded. Back to a full, 162-game season, major league hitters came within 38 home runs of hitting a combined 5,000 circuit shots. Eight players in both leagues would hit at least 40 home runs with two checking in with 50 or more. The leader was Oakland's Mark McGwire, who had been quiet for a number of years due to injuries. McGwire played in just 74 games in 1993 and 1994, then began to rebound in 1995 when he hit 39 homers in just 104 games. That year, he had more homers than singles (35) and hit the most homers ever for a player with so few at bats. In 1996, the big guy was still limited to 130 games and 423 at bats, yet he cracked 52, the most since George Foster hit that number in 1977. He also set a record that year by hitting one home run every 8.13 at bats. People began to wonder what McGwire could do if he were able to stay healthy for the entire season.

The other player hitting 50 home runs was a complete surprise. Brady Anderson was the Baltimore Orioles centerfielder and leadoff hitter. He was a solid, all-around player in his ninth season with the Orioles and a guy who had never hit more than 21 homers in a single season. Suddenly, Anderson erupted for 50, including a record 12 leading off a game. Ironically, though he remained a fine player for the remainder of his career, he never hit more than 24 homers in a season after 1996. Looking back, Anderson's achievement in 1996 made some people begin to wonder about players who were suddenly hitting so many homers and, years later, when the fingers began pointing toward the use of performance-enhancing drugs, Anderson found himself being asked how a guy who never hit more than 21 homers before could suddenly hit 50.

"Because I only hit 50 home runs once, it was, in fact, an aberration," he said. "However, it was not a fluke. Nothing can be considered a fluke that takes six months to accomplish. Rather it was a culmination of all my athleticism and baseball skills and years of training peaking simultaneously. This was my athletic opus."

"I know what I accomplished, am proud of it, and know that it was done with integrity," he continued. "It was 26 more home runs than I hit in any other season, but that's just one more home run per week, just one more good swing. That is the data that simultaneously comforted me and haunted me, the small difference between greatness and mediocrity."

Cal Ripken Jr., a teammate of Anderson's, remembers him as a player obsessed with physical fitness and nutrition, and one who worked out obsessively. "Now protein mixes are an acceptable part of everyone's diet," said Ripken. "Brady always had a much more advanced concept of cross-training and his diet. He was just ahead of the curve."

Ripken also said that Anderson's swing that year was totally locked in. "He had good swings every at bat," said Ripken. "Bearing witness to it all year, he was a marvel to watch. I don't remember him ever being in a slump. Brady always had a fly-ball swing, which he was criticized for as a leadoff hitter, but that year he was right on the ball."

Maybe Anderson did have a once-in-a-lifetime season. If so, he picked a good year because so many other players were hitting homers. Though a fuss wasn't made about the ball this year, there still had to be questions. In the A.L., Ken Griffey Jr. had 49 homers, Albert Belle had 48, Juan Gonzalez bashed 47, while Jay Buhner and Mo Vaughn each had 44, and Frank Thomas also had 40. In the National, big Andres Galarraga lead with 47, while Bonds and Gary Sheffield each had 42. Catcher Todd Hundley of the Mets had a career year with 41, while four players—Ellis Burks, Ken Caminiti, Vinny Castilla, and Sammy Sosa—had 40 each.

There was one team that definitely had an unfair advantage in the homer hunt of the era. Sluggers wearing the uniform of the Colorado Rockies and hitting at Coors Field had the advantage of the thin air of the mile-high city. The ball definitely carried further there. Galarraga and Castilla had a combined 87 homers for the Rockies in 1996, and a year later were joined by Larry Walker, who led the league with 49 home runs. Galarraga would check in with 41 and Castilla with 40 once again.

But the Rockies hitters weren't the big story in 1997. Rather it was the slugging of two particular players that caught the eye of the baseball world. Ken Griffey Jr., a player with perhaps the sweetest swing in the game, erupted for 56 home runs to lead the American League. He had 12 more than runner-up Tino Martinez of the Yanks, who had a career year with 44. In the National, the leader was the aforementioned Larry Walker with 49. But there was a player who had more homers than both, yet didn't lead either league. That's because the Oakland A's decided they had to rebuild, acquire more pitching, and because slugger Mark McGwire was going to be a free agent at the end of the year, they decided to trade him. After hitting 34 home runs that had him running neck in neck for the A.L. lead with Griffey, McGwire was dealt to the St. Louis Cardinals in July.

Having to make the adjustment to a new team, new league, and new pitchers, McGwire hit just one home run his first ten days with the Cards. But after that he began launching them again, just as he had in the A.L. On September 16, he walloped a big, 517-foot homer in St. Louis, and the next day slammed his 53rd home run of the year, the most since Maris hit 61 back in 1961. McGwire would finish the year by hitting 24 home runs with the Cards. His total with both teams was 58. So while he didn't win a league home run title, he had hit the same number of homers as Jimmy Foxx in 1932 and Hank Greenberg in 1938. Only Ruth and Maris had hit more. And to put a cap on the season, the Seattle Mariners set a new team record by hitting 264 home runs, breaking the record of 257 set just the season before by the Baltimore Orioles. But even the slugging of

Remembering Albert Belle, for Better or Worse

Albert Belle has to be one of the most enigmatic sluggers of the modern era. During his twelve-year career, Belle had a number of run-ins with fans and reporters, acquiring a reputation as a surly individual and sometime trouble-maker. His teammates knew that he played hard every game. He was just one of those guys who wanted to do his job and be left alone. Yet Albert Belle, who had a nine-year run that was as good as any, may wind up one of those players largely forgotten. Beginning in 1992, his second full season in the majors, he hit 34, 38, 36, 50, 48, 30, 49, 37, and 23 home runs. In each of those seasons, including the strike-shortened 1994, he drove him more than 100 runs, including a career best 152 in 1998. He didn't lead the league that year, but in three other seasons he did.

Belle was also a .295 lifetime hitter who had seasons in which he hit .357, .328, .317, and .311. In the 2000 season, Belle still managed 23 homers and 103 RBIs, yet it would prove to be his last. An increasingly painful arthritic hip would force him into premature retirement at the age of twenty-four. Albert Belle never played again. In twelve seasons he hit 381 homers. Had he averaged, say, 30 homers for another four years, he would have entered the 500 home run club and definitely merited consideration for the Hall of Fame. Now that will probably never happen, but for most of the 1990s, Albert Belle was as good as any slugger in the game.

McGwire, Griffey, and the Mariners didn't prepare the baseball world for what was going to happen in 1998.

When the 1998 season began, there were two questions involving the home run. How many homers would major league batters hit? Would they finally top the 5,000 mark? And, secondly, what about Mark McGwire? Like so many of the modern sluggers, McGwire seemed bigger and stronger than he was as a rookie in 1987, when he set a record by blasting 49 homers. By hitting 58 with two teams in 1997, the big first sacker showed he could do it in either league. He was also hitting home runs with more frequency over the past three seasons than any player in baseball history. Now, the question was simple. How high could he go? Would he be the player to break the single-season home run record that had stood for thirty-seven years? Amazingly, Maris now held the record longer than the Babe. When Roger hit his 61 in 1961, it had been thirty-four years since Ruth has blasted his 60 in 1927. Who would have thought, especially in an age when so many more home runs were being hit, that the record Maris set would have lasted this long?

Once the new season started it became obvious immediately that the home run barrage was not about to stop or even slow down. If anything, it was increasing once again. By the end of April, all eyes were on two players. Not surprisingly, one was McGwire, who already had 11 home runs. The other was Ken Griffey Jr., who had also slammed 11 for the Mariners. They had become the focal point of the home run chase, even though there were many others capable of hitting their way toward 61. There was still Albert Belle and Jose Canseco (in a comeback year). Juan Gonzalez had proved himself capable of hitting a ton of homers, and young players like Manny Ramirez of Cleveland and Alex Rodriguez of Seattle were also making noise as American League sluggers.

The National didn't seem to have as many candidates. Guys like Larry Walker, Andrew Galarraga, Vinny Castilla, Barry Bonds, and Jeff Bagwell could hit a lot of homers, but no one considered them threats to the single-season record. If anyone was going to break it, most felt it would be the mammoth McGwire or the smooth swinging Griffey. And the way the two of them had started the season, that analysis seemed right on target.

McGwire looked as if he simply wasn't going to slow down. The big guy got red hot from May 12 to May 25, slamming an unbelievable 12 homers to run his total to 25. When May came to an end, McGwire already had 27 four-baggers. After just two months, the guy was almost halfway to 61. Griffey was next with 19, eight homers behind but still looking strong. Then, as the season swung into June, another player began to make his home run presence felt. Sammy Sosa of the Cubs hit a pair of home runs on June 1. Then he hit another two days later, and still another two days after that, on June 5. When he homered on the sixth, seventh, and eighth, Sosa had not only homered in four straight games, but he had run his total to 20 for the season, coming within nine of McGwire, who now had 29. Yet at this point, no one considered Sosa a serious threat to big Mac.

Sammy Sosa was born in the Dominican Republic in 1968. When he came to the Texas Rangers in 1989 at the age of twenty, he was a skinny kid and a raw talent. After appearing in just twenty-five games for the Rangers and hitting one home run in 84 at bats, he was shipped to the White Sox, ending the season with a .257 batting average and just four home runs in 183 at bats. He was traded to the Cubs in 1992 and hit only eight homers in 262 at bats that year. At that point, no one expected Sosa to be a major home run hitter, or even a star. But Sammy persevered and in 1993, with a chance to play every day, had a breakout season with 33 home runs and 93 RBIs. Coming into 1998, Sosa was well on his way to becoming an outstanding player. He had seasons of 33, 25, 36, 40, and 36 homers and was coming off three straight 100-RBI seasons. So he could hit it out. What no one expected, still, was the explosion that would ultimately occur in 1998.

By June 21, Sosa had already hit 17 home runs for the month and 30 for the season. He was just three behind McGwire. Sammy would wind up with 20 home runs in June, breaking the long-standing record of 18 homers in a month set years before by Rudy York. He also had 33 homers for the season, tying him with Griffey and putting both sluggers just four behind McGwire. Suddenly, there were three players with a very good chance of breaking Roger Maris's record of 61.

When the Cubs went to Kaufman Stadium in Kansas City for an interleague game at the end of June, the fans came out early just to watch Sammy take batting practice, a custom that had usually been reserved for Mark McGwire. Sosa obliged by hitting several mammoth shots into the far reaches of the stands as the fans roared. It was further proof that the modern fan loved nothing better than to see the baseball hit as far as possible.

McGwire got the same treatment and, on occasion, when he would skip batting practice, the fans would actually boo him.

As for Sosa, he felt that big Mac was the game's premier home run slugger. "Mark McGwire is in a different world," he said. "He's my idol. He's the man. No matter what people say [about competing with Mark], he's still my idol. I have a lot of respect for that guy. He's the guy everybody is looking for. . . . I have to continue to be the best player I can be."

At the All-Star break, it was Ken Griffey Jr. who won the annual home run hitting contest, and then all three players went into the second half of the season with a shot at the record. It was becoming more interesting by the day and the fans were jumping on board. A lot of other players were hitting a lot of home runs, but the big story of 1998 was fast becoming McGwire, Griffey, and the surprising Sammy Sosa. By the end of July it was apparent that the chase was for real. McGwire was still leading with 45 home runs, but Sosa with 42 and Griffey with 41 were both hot on his trail.

During the dog days of August, when bats sometimes begin to feel heavy, the three sluggers carried on. Then, the one who began to falter a bit was Griffey. The two National League stars kept hitting them. On August 18, Sosa hit number 47 to pull even with McGwire. Both were ahead of the Maris pace and the media was really picking up on the story. But then something else began happening as well, something that was a bit unusual for the modern-day athlete. Both Sosa and McGwire were complete gentleman who genuinely liked each other and were pulling for each other to succeed. They embraced the chase rather than making it a competition. There was no sense of me-first about it, and absolutely no arrogance or boastfulness from either player. For that reason, their chase of the record became one of the feel-good stories in sport.

In one series, when the Cubs and Cards met, Sosa approached McGwire, who was doing his stretching exercises. McGwire suddenly barked, "Get away! Get away!" The reporters quickly looked over, hoping maybe this was the controversial story they were looking for. Suddenly, McGwire jumped to his feet with a huge grin on his face and the two sluggers hugged. Sosa also had a habit when he hit a home run of tapping his chest over his heart then putting his two fingers to his lips, as if blowing a kiss. Asked about it, he said it was simply a gesture to his mother back in the Dominican Republic. So there was nothing to jump on except baseball. These were nice guys.

By the end of August the chase had become national news. It was talked about everywhere, a home run race that was generating the same kind of publicity as the M & M Boys race in 1961. In fact, with all the cable outlets and sports talk shows, the media hype was even greater. And when each slugger finished the month of August with 55 home runs, it began to look as if both would pass Roger Maris, barring an unforeseen slump or injury in the final month of the season. In fact, both sluggers were now within one home run of Hack Wilson's National League record of 36, set an incredible sixty-eight years earlier in the hitting-happy season of 1930. McGwire had already set a home run record. He had become the first player ever to hit 50 or more home runs in three consecutive seasons. So the home run records were already starting to fall.

McGwire showed quickly that he wasn't about to make people wait in suspense. He hit four homers in the first two games in September, breaking Wilson's record and running his total to 59, putting him within a homer of Ruth, two of Maris, and three away from setting a new mark. Sosa also hit one on September 2, his 56th, as the home run chase now began dominating the regular newscasts as well as the sports reports. It was *the* big story of the season. But unlike Maris, who had such a difficult time dealing with the media attention, both sluggers seemed to enjoy the spotlight, refused to be dragged into any kind of controversy, and made sure the only pressure was on the field.

When Sosa hit his 57th homer on September 4, someone pointed out that Sammy had hit 48 home runs in his last eighty-eight games, an average of more than one homer every two games. If he had done that all year, he would have been on a pace to hit some 89 home runs. On September 5, McGwire blasted his 60th home run of the season, becoming just the third player in history to hit that mark. On the same day, Sammy Sosa whacked his 58th, staying right behind the big guy. Now the two would go head-to-head in a two-game series at Busch Stadium in St. Louis.

The excitement in St. Louis was electric and both sluggers continued to root for each other. McGwire went so far as to say, "Wouldn't it be great if we just ended up tied?" How often do you hear something like that from a professional athlete? "I'm a fan of the game as well as a player," McGwire continued. "[Sammy] is having an absolutely magical year and, you know, I root him on just like everyone else."

On September 7, hitting against Cubs' righthander Mike Morgan, McGwire blasted his 61st home run into the left-field stands. He had tied Roger Maris. Sosa stood in right field and applauded. Then the next night, with five of Roger Maris's six children in the stands, McGwire did it. Batting against Steve Trachsel in the fourth inning, McGwire hit a low line drive that just cleared the wall at the 341-foot mark. One of the shortest home runs he had ever hit was perhaps the biggest of his life, his 62nd home run of the season. When he crossed the plate, he lifted his son, Matt, into the air. He then pointed to the Maris family, tapped his heart, and pointed to the sky. Sammy Sosa then came running in from right field and the two sluggers hugged each other warmly.

The game was stopped as McGwire spoke to the crowd briefly, then looked out toward right field and said, "Sammy Sosa, you're unbelievable!"

It was a story that put the two sluggers and the game of baseball on the front pages. The home run had created one of the game's greatest moments, a story with no negatives. Two great sluggers had just taken the home run to another level and they weren't finished yet. It was only September 8. There were still some three weeks remaining in the season. Both Babe Ruth and Roger Maris had set their records in the last game of the year. McGwire had another eighteen games to extend the record, and

Sammy Sosa had that same amount of time to still try to catch him.

On September 11, Sosa slammed his 59th homer of the year at Wrigley Field, and then a day later, he belted number 60 off a pitcher named Valerio De Los Santos of the Brewers. It was yet another home run milestone. It marked the first time that two players had hit 60 or more in a single season, and Sammy Sosa had become the fourth player in history with 60 or more home runs. With McGwire holding at 62, there was still a home run race to be decided. Everyone was speculating on just how high the two stars would push each other. So even with the record broken, interest in the two players and their home runs remained sky-high.

Then on September 13, Sosa proved he was on another of his patented tears. He hit not one but two titanic, 480-foot homers at Wrigley that gave him 62 for the year and brought him even with McGwire once more. After the game, Sosa sent a message to his friend that read, "Mark, you know I love you. It's been unbelievable. I wish you could be here with me today. I know you are watching me and I know you have the same feeling for me as I have for you in my heart."

So the upbeat, feel-good story continued. By mid-September, the forgotten man in the race, Ken Griffey, also became part of 1998's home run history. He went over the 50-homer mark, blasting his 52nd on September 15. It marked the first time that three players were over 50 home runs in a single season. Maybe they should change the name of the sport from baseball to home run ball? The back-and-forth continued. After McGwire belted his 63rd, Sosa tied him again, blasting a grand slam and running his major league best RBI total to 154. He was putting together an incredible season.

McGwire got the next two, but Sosa tied him again on September 23, hitting his 64th and 65th in the same game. The way it was going was almost uncanny. Sosa hit his 66th against Jose Lima of Houston, taking the lead from McGwire for just the second time all year. Wouldn't it be ironic if Mark McGwire, who had been the first to break Roger Maris's record, wouldn't even wind up the home run champ. But Sosa's lead lasted just 45 minutes. Then word came from St. Louis that Mark McGwire had hit 66th against the Montreal Expos.

There were just two games left when Mark McGwire put on his final show. He blasted two home runs in each contest to finish the year with the incredible total of 70. Sosa failed to hit another and wound up with 66, but the two players had put together the greatest one-two home run show in the history of the game. They were a big part of a record 5,064 home runs hit by major leaguers in 1998. Griffey would lead the American League with 56. He had plenty of company. Albert Belle just missed getting 50 and finished with 49. Jose Canseco had 46, Juan Gonzalez and Manny Ramirez had 45 each, Rafael Palmeiro finished with 43, while young Alex Rodriguez had 42, Mo Vaughn 40, and Carlos Delgado 38.

In the National, San Diego's Greg Vaughn, who had hit just 18 homers in 120 games the season before, blasted 50 by season's end, extending the record to four players with 50 or more home runs. Then came Vinny Castilla with 46 and Andres Galarraga with 44. The home run parade was in full swing, but Mark McGwire and Sammy Sosa had made it a special, season-long event.

McGwire had a great all-around year. In addition to his 70 homers, he had a .299 batting average and 147 RBIs. He had played in 155 games, staying healthy, had walked 162 times, and fanned on 155 occasions. His slugging percentage of .752 was one of the best of all-time. Sammy Sosa also had a tremendous all-around season. In 159 games, he had 198 hits and a .308 batting average. His 66 home runs helped him to a league best 158 runs batted in. Incredibly, the free-swinging Sosa walked just 73 times and struck out on 171 occasions. His slugging average was .647. Yet, after the season, it was Sammy Sosa who was named the National League's Most Valuable Player.

It was a season to remember. Baseball was turning into a home run derby and, sparked by the record-setting race between Mark McGwire and Sammy Sosa, everyone became caught up in it and loved it. The game wasn't just relegated to the sports page. It was front-page news, the top-of-the-hour story, and the sport had some great new heroes. Attendance in both leagues was again moving upward. It hadn't yet reached prestrike levels, but if these big sluggers could continue to belt homer after homer, who knows where it might go? Many felt that a guy like Mark McGwire might well reach 80 or more homers, especially if there was a Sammy Sosa to push him.

Though no one could know it then, somewhere on the distant horizon the storm clouds were beginning to gather, and in the center of the storm would once again be the fans favorite baseball moment—the home run.

10

Bonds Raises the Bar amid a Growing Home Run Controversy, 1999–2004

There was one slight blemish during the great home run chase in 1998, one that was soon swept under the rug but would certainly be resurrected in the years to come. It happened innocently enough during the season when a group of reporters gathered around Mark McGwire's locker after a game against the New York Mets at Shea Stadium. While the reporters were questioning big Mac, an Associated Press writer noticed a bottle sitting in McGwire's locker. When the reporter asked about it, McGwire said it contained a supplement called androstenedione. Suddenly, some eyebrows were raised.

Androstendione is a natural chemical found in the body that produces the hormone testosterone. Taken as a supplement, it can boost testosterone levels. According to experts, it can help build muscle and also help a person recover from injury. When it was discovered in McGwire's locker, it was not a banned substance in major league baseball, though it was already banned in both the Olympics and the National Football League. Muscle-building enhancers called anabolic steroids were already illegal and couldn't be used. Andro, as it was commonly called, has been described as a steroid precursor, though some doctors would describe it as a steroid. McGwire told reporters that he took the supplement to try to avoid the injuries that had cost him a large number of games several years earlier.

Other ballplayers came quickly to his defense, saying this was not an illegal substance and that McGwire's privacy was being invaded. Reporters and other people had no right to question him about a substance that was perfectly legal. Others pointed to the fact that, as a rookie, McGwire was listed in the baseball encyclopedia as weighing 215 pounds. In 1998, some felt he weighed closer to 250 pounds and, as one player said, the bat seemed like a toothpick in his hands. A few people even wondered if his record-setting 70 home runs were the result of taking a supplement that could help make him stronger. But the story soon died and a year or so later McGwire would say that he was no longer taking the substance.

So when the 1999 season began, baseball simply expected more home runs and wondered whether McGwire, Sosa, or another slugger would top the record. Ironically, the best team during this period was the New York Yankees. Under Joe Torre, the Yanks would win four World Series between 1996 and 2000. The New Yorkers had a fine team with outstanding pitching, a great bullpen, and winning ballplayers. What they didn't have—as they always did in the past—was a couple of big sluggers feasting on the short-field porch at Yankee Stadium. First sacker Tino Martinez had 44 home runs in 1997, the one year the Yanks didn't win, but even he was usually a 25–30 home run guy. So the team that brought the home run to baseball via Ruth and Gehrig was winning big without a Sosa, McGwire, Bonds, or Griffey.

The New Yorkers would win again in 1999 and 2000 without a huge banger, but the sluggers around both leagues would continue to do what was expected of them and, sure enough, up came the red flags about the baseball again. In 1999 another record was set. Big league hitters slammed 5,528 home runs, topping the previous year by nearly 500. The big guys did their usual. McGwire and Sosa once again proved the best of the best, hitting 65 and 63 respectively, and thus both becoming the only players in history to hit 60 or more home runs twice. Other than that, there was the usual group in the 40s. In the National, Greg Vaughn had 45 after his season of 50 in 1998, young Chipper Jones of the Braves also hit 45, while Bagwell had 42, as did another young slugging star, Vladimir Guerrero of the Montreal Expos. Catcher Mike Piazza of the Mets had 40.

In the American, Griffey was the leader again, this time with 48. Right behind was Rafael Palmeiro with 47, Carlos Delgado and Manny Ramirez with 44, and Shawn Green of the Blue Jays with 42, the same number hit by Alex Rodriguez of Seattle. Those numbers reflected the leaders in other years, but not when the league as a whole hit so many. No, the record-setting numbers were helped by many hitters in the 15-25 range, hitters not considered sluggers. One big league manager said he was tired of seeing mediocre hitters reach for an outside fast ball, hit it to the opposite field, then watch it go into the stands for a home run. That was something you didn't see years earlier.

With Mark McGwire and Sammy Sosa both topping Roger Maris's old record two years in a row, there was little doubt that a new home run era was overtaking all of baseball. There was a time when middle infielders—shortstops and second basemen—were usually smaller men and hitters without much power. Now there were players like Alex Rodriguez, Nomar Garciaparra, Jeff Kent, Miguel Tejada, and Derek Jeter all displaying hard-hitting power. Rodriguez was one of the top home run hitters in the league and would only get better. Just about everyone was hitting them out. The singles hitter was now the rare commodity in the way the slugger once was, and when the 2000 season began, there were so many homers leaving the ballpark in the opening month of the season that even the least skeptical followers of the game began raising eyebrows.

It started early. By April 26, the St. Louis Cardinals had already hit 50 home runs, setting an all-time record by any team for the first month of the season, breaking the record of 49 set by the 1997 Cleveland Indians. That wasn't all. On one day in April, big league hitters set another mark by blasting 57 home runs. Over a ten-game stretch at the Skydome in Toronto, hitters combined to produce 180 runs, an average of 18 runs a game. In the first two series there against the Mariners and Angels, the three teams scored 142 runs on 84 extra base hits and 33 home runs. All that in just seven games. And by the end of April, big league hitters had slammed out a record 931 home runs, some 140 more home runs than had been hit the previous

Numbers Hanger or Hall of Famer

A player who has kind of snuck up on everyone to become a major modern-day slugger is Rafael Palmeiro. Raffy has spent most of his long career shuttling between Texas and Baltimore and is probably the quietest and least-known member of the exclusive 500 home run club. Palmeiro has always played in the shadow of other first sackers and has never had the good fortune to be on a championship team. In his early years, he wasn't even considered a home run hitter. During his first two full seasons with Texas in 1988 and 1989, he hit just eight home runs. A year later he had 14. Then he began to mature. Not a big man at 6 feet and 188 pounds, Palmeiro has developed a sweet swing and is a deadly fastball hitter.

Still, he didn't reach the 40 home run mark until 1998, when he hit 43 at the age of thirty-four. After that, he became one of baseball's most reliable home run hitters, getting 47 twice and driving in more than 100 runs nine years in a row. Back in Baltimore in 2004 and approaching his fortieth birthday, Raffy had started to slow down a bit. He finished with just 23 homers and 88 RBIs. But for his career, he now has 551 home runs and 1,775 RBIs to go with a very solid .289 batting average. He's also won three gold gloves for his play at first base and has hit over .300 in six different seasons.

Yet because he has played so much of his career in the shadow of others, Palmeiro has been called a "numbers hanger" by some. In other words, he's just an average ballplayer who racks up good stats each year. But you can't be just a numbers hanger and have lifetime statistics like he does. He's been one of the most unheralded home run hitters of his time, an extremely reliable and consistent player who cannot be ignored when it comes time to vote for his induction in the Hall of Fame. He fully deserves to be there.

April. For the first time, fans were beginning to look twice. Was this really the way baseball was supposed to be played?

"Of course we have concerns," said Baseball Commissioner Bud Selig. "We always have concerns. But at this stage we're just sitting back and monitoring. Let's just see how this plays out."

Some were more outspoken, such as Braves star pitcher Tom Glavine. "I don't like it," Glavine said, referring to all the home runs. "I think it's taken away a lot from the game. I feel like what Mac and Sammy did two years ago should be a once-in-a-lifetime kind of thing. I'm not so sure it's going to be. I think it's definitely tarnished the image or the excitement associated with the home run. It's one thing for the legitimate home run hitters to be going out there and doing it, but it's everybody else that makes you kind of wonder what the heck is going on."

What Glavine was saying, in effect, is that when something is supposed to be special, it ceases to be that way when everyone is doing it. Others agreed, especially the pitchers. Another fine veteran hurler, Kevin Brown, said, "It's not a good time for pitchers, there's no doubt. There are a lot of ways to get hurt out there, the way the ball is flying."

Tony Muser, the Kansas City manager, put it this way: "The poor pitchers go home at night and turn on ESPN and there's 28 minutes of balls reaching the seats. The mindset of the game today is try to pound the other team into oblivion and win 12-11, and say, 'Man, what a ballgame!'"

There was still more. Houston had built a new ballpark to replace the old indoor Astrodome. Enron Field, as it was called at first (it's now Minute Maid Park), had produced an average of 3.83 home runs in the first twelve games played there. At the old Astrodome, the average was 1.54 home runs for the entire 1999 season. Most of the new ballparks were certainly hitter friendly. By late May, each game was producing an average of 2.58 home runs, ahead of the record 2.28 home runs hit in 1999. If the sluggers and quasi sluggers kept up the pace, there would be more than 6,200 homers hit in 2000. The first inclination was to point a finger at the baseball. Was it juiced? Liz Daus, a spokesperson for the manufacturer Rawlings, said no.

"They've made [the baseballs] in the same place with the same materials and the same way since we shifted production to our Costa Rica plant ten years ago," she said.

Many of the guys who were hitting more home runs than ever claimed it was the result of good, old-fashioned hard work. They were all using weight and strength training, getting bigger and stronger, and swinging the lighter, thin-handled bats harder than ever. The pitchers didn't have the same luxury. Lifting weights or working on Nautilus machines didn't add 5 miles per hour to their fastballs. Pitcher Dwight Gooden, who had to serve a sixty-day drug suspension in late 1994 and, because of the strike, didn't return until 1995, said he noticed the hitters were differently when he came back.

"It seemed like it happened all in one year," Gooden said. "After I came back I noticed right away that everyone looked huge. And all of them were swinging much harder, as well."

No one disputed the fact that the big sluggers made the big salaries. That was given as another reason for so many players swinging for the fences. "No one is embarrassed to strike out anymore," Cubs' general manager Ed Lynch said. "A lot of hitters will gladly exchange three strikeouts in a game if, in the fourth at-bat, they've hit a home run. That's how arbitration and free agency have changed the game."

So the theories abounded and the home runs continued. Many players and pitchers felt it was the ball. A former player and coach, Joe Nossek, said he found a ball in the batting practice bin at Comiskey Park that still had a needle sticking out of it. He felt it came from the machine that stitches the cover on the ball. "They sew 'em so tight, they can't even get the needle out," he said.

Several pitchers said that the seams on the ball seemed fractionally lower than in previous seasons, making it more difficult to get movement and throw breaking balls. Remember 1930? That was the year the seams were almost flat or even recessed. Cubs' pitcher Kerry Wood, on a rehab assignment in the triple-A Pacific Coast League, felt he developed a blister because the seams on the minor league ball were higher than the ball being used in the majors. Hall of Fame pitcher Jim Palmer agreed with others that the rash of homers was producing a game he didn't like.

"The endless home runs on the game highlights are silly," he said, "since there is little action in a home run besides seeing the ball fly over the fence."

Yet Devil Rays general manager, Chuck LeMar, had his own theory about why the home run had become the one thing most fans wanted to see—more than a nifty double play, a diving catch, or a one-hit, 15-strikeout pitching gem.

"[Hitting a home run] is the one thing most of us can't do," LaMar said. "Most of us have played the game, and most of us could field a ball, or throw to a base, or pitch. We weren't good enough to make the major leagues, but we did it. But what we couldn't do is hit a ball as far as Jose Canseco or Mark Mc-Gwire can."

Canseco echoed this sentiment when he said, "People love home runs. Not just home runs, but long home runs. The kind you don't think, 'Is it out?' They like the kind you think, 'How far is it out?' The kind where [a hitter] can just stand and watch. It's power. It's strength. It's the complete domination of a baseball."

And what of Mark McGwire? What was he doing for an encore in 2000? By the end of the 1999 season, big Mac had 522 home runs. His 65 home runs that year allowed him to pass Mel Ott (511), Eddie Mathews and Ernie Banks (512), and finally Ted Williams and Willie McCovey (521). When McGwire blasted his 20th home run of the season the last week of May, he was once again the major league leader. Even more amazing was the frequency of his home runs. In 1998, when he hit his 70th, McGwire set a record by hitting one home run every 7.3 at bats. By contrast, all-time leader Henry Aaron hit one every 16.4 at bats, while the Babe held the all-time mark with a home run every 11.8 at bats. After hitting his first 18 homers of the season, McGwire was blasting one out of the park every 5.7 times he came to the plate. Many were already speculating that even at an advanced baseball age, McGwire could well past Aaron's 755 before he was through.

The one thing that was rarely, if ever, mentioned was the possibility of something else. Dwight Gooden has said that so many players were now bigger, more sculpted, "huge," as he observed. Yet the blame for the home run barrage was always the baseball, the smaller parks, the shrinking strike zone, and pitchers who no longer wanted to come inside for fear of a brawl erupting. Despite the fact that Mark McGwire had a questionable—though legal—

supplement in his locker back in 1998, there was little or no speculation about players using other supplements, the kind that build muscle mass—illegal anabolic steroids.

Yet the home runs kept flying. On a Sunday in May, big league players set a record by hitting six grand slam homers in one day. J. T. Snow of the Giants, Brian Hunter of Philadelphia, Jason Giambi of Oakland, Adrian Beltre and Shawn Green of the Dodgers, and Anaheim's Garret Anderson all connected with the bases loaded that day. To most, the most culpable reason was still the baseball. To quiet its critics, Major League Baseball commissioned Jim Sherwood, a mechanical engineering professor at the University of Massachusett's Lowell campus, to test the baseball to see if it fell within rulebook specifications.

As it turned out, baseballs from 1998 and 1999 were tested, along with those from the 2000 season. The result was that the balls were not found to be "juiced," But the balls were said to be very close to "too lively" by Major League standards.

"The balls today are at the upper end of the spectrum," announced Sandy Alderson, the commissioner's executive vice president of baseball operations, after meeting with Jim Sherwood. "There is a range of specifications the ball has to fall within. There is a consistency within that range among the balls we've seen from the last three years. We're looking to see if we can find balls to test from further back."

That wouldn't be easy because temperature and humidity, where and how they are stored, can affect the ball after several years. The conclusion was that the ball has been about the same for the past three years, at the upper end of the spectrum, but no one could say how it was before that. The past three years, of course, had produced more home runs than at any time in the history of the game. So it seemed that the ball was at least a part of the equation.

As the hitters continued to bang the ball all over the lot, more people began to complain that there were simply too many homers. It wasn't only the pitchers complaining, it was the sportscasters and fans, people who appreciated the purity of the game and would be just as happy to watch Roger Clemens throw a two-hit shutout as to witness a team belt six home runs and score 12 times. And, for the first time, there were starting to be some references to "steroid-like substances," such as the androstenedione that Mark McGwire had used. There was a call for baseball to ban any substances that caused unnatural muscle growth. McGwire, as mentioned previously, said he had stopped using the substance during the 1999 season.

The home run parade continued for the entire season, though the pace slowed somewhat in the second half, making some wonder if maybe the baseball had been toned down. The other big thing that was missing the second half of 2000 was Mark McGwire. Patella tendinitis in his knee relegated him to the bench for much of the finals months. He would wind up playing just eighty-nine games and, after his fast start that made some think he would break his own record, finished with just 32 home runs and 73 RBIs. But that didn't stop the rest of the league from setting more records.

Major League hitters slammed out 5,693 homers, some 165 more than the season before. National League batters also set a mark, with 3,005 home runs, more than both leagues had hit combined back in 1978. There were no individual records set, though Sammy Sosa had 50 home runs to lead the majors. Barry Bonds had 49 and Jeff Bagwell had 47 with Vladimir Guerrero hitting 44. So the National League had familiar names at the top. In the American, big Troy Glaus of the Angels emerged as a star with 47 homers. Jason Giambi of Oakland had 43, as did Frank Thomas. Tony Batista of Toronto had a career year with 41, joined by Carlos Delgado, David Justice (who split time between the Indians and Yankees), and Alex Rodriguez.

It wasn't so much that the names were the same or that no one hit 60 or more. It was the sheer numbers. A year earlier, in 1999, there were sixty-four players hitting 25 or more home runs and thirteen hitting 40 or more. There were times, not that long ago, when the league leader didn't even reach 40. Go back to 1992 and Fred McGriff of San Diego led the N.L. with just 35. Ironically, three years before that, in 1989, McGriff also led the A.L. for Toronto with 36. Fast forward to the 2000 season and forty-six players, twenty-three in each league, hit 30 or more home runs. With those kinds of numbers, how could a guy with 25 or 30 homers be called a slugger, or even a home run hitter. The definition had changed. Players were making more money than ever, the fans were coming back, the Yanks were World Champs again, and all seemed right with the baseball world. No one seemed anxious to change what was happening, let alone look for a reason.

BONDS RAISES THE BAR

At the beginning of the 2001 season, Barry Bonds was roughly three months from his thirty-seventh birthday on July 24. He was coming off a season in which he hit 49 home runs, drove home 106 runs, and had a slugging percentage of .688. He was a three-time MVP in his early years, but now seemed even better with age. Though a top home run hitter, he still choked up slightly on the bat. Yet he had great batting technique from the left side of the plate and a discerning eye. He was one of the few sluggers in modern times who walked more than he struck out. A selective hitter, Bonds didn't go after bad pitches and when he got one he liked, he hit it hard. He also had 494 career homers. So he was just six away from joining the elite 500 home run club. He also had 471 stolen bases, something that had been a lost commodity among modern sluggers. Had his career ended suddenly after the 2000 season, he would still be a Hall of Fame caliber player

Bonds was also a much bigger man than he was at the outset of his career. During his days with the Pirates, he was listed at 6'1", 185 pounds. Now his weight was said to be about 228. Even though he choked up on the bat, he could still hit the ball as far as anyone. The season, however, started slowly for him. He hit his first homer off Woody Williams of San Diego on April 2, and then didn't hit another for ten days. But when he homered off the Padres Adam Eaton on April 12, it was the first of four straight games in which he would hit one. By the end of

April, Bonds had 11 homers, a solid month, but not something to get overly excited about. After all, this was the age of home runs, so what he was doing didn't look like anything too special.

Then, in May, Bonds picked up the pace. He went on a tear and slammed 17 home runs to finish the month with 28. When he hit his 30th on June 4, he had reached that number faster than any player in history, even McGwire in 1998. And he wasn't stopping. On July 12, Barry Bonds hit his 40th home run of the season off Paul Abbott of Seattle in an interleague game. No player in history had reached 40 faster. It was time for the All-Star break, and now Barry Bonds was writing a story that many didn't think would be written again, at least not so soon.

When he came out on the other side of the break and promptly belted two homers off the Rockies' Mike Hampton on July 18, then finished the month with 45, it was apparent he was going to take a shot at McGwire's three-year-old record of 70 home runs. There were plenty of other guys hitting home runs, though not quite at the pace of a year earlier. Sammy Sosa, in fact, was having another outstanding year and chasing Bonds, but wasn't close enough to make it the kind of race he had given McGwire in 1998. In fact, though the record chase was beginning in earnest, there was not the same level of excitement that had arisen spontaneously three years earlier when McGwire and Sosa began chasing each other as well as the record.

There were a number of reasons the story didn't elicit the same widespread response. For one thing, Barry Bonds did not have the outgoing personality of Sosa and was not as genial with the fans and media. He already had a reputation as a sometimes moody, sometimes surly individual who was never that popular. Because it wasn't a two-man race, as it had been with Sammy and big Mac—two players who genuinely liked each other—there was nothing of the feel-good story that had overtaken the entire sports world in 1998. And, finally, maybe with so many players hitting so many homers, and so many records starting to fall, Bonds's chase simply didn't generate the same kind of excitement with the fans. In other words, hitting a ton of homers was becoming old hat.

But none of that could stop Barry Bonds. A mentally strong player with great concentration, he simply remained in the groove. Home run number 50 came on August 11, and on September 6, he belted his 60th of the season off Albie Lopez of Arizona. He had reached both of those milestones faster than any other player, as well. Now he was taking dead aim at Mark McGwire and the single-season record. Obviously, Bonds's chase was on all the sports stations, and now creeping into the news reports. What he was doing certainly couldn't be ignored, but it still wasn't like the McGwire/Sosa chase in terms of fan interest and overall media hype.

Bonds, however, wasn't wasting any time. On September 9, he belted three homers against the Colorado Rockies, but after that didn't hit one for eleven days. Then he connected off Wade Miller of the Astros for number 64, and three days later hit another pair off Jason Middlebrook of San Diego. He was now at 66, tying Sosa for the second-best total ever, and he still had another two weeks to break McGwire's mark. A day later he walloped number 67, then hit numbers 68 and 69 in back-to-back games on September 28th and 29th. Five days later, on October 4, the Giants were playing in Houston. Bonds led off the ninth inning against lefty reliever Wilfredo Rodriguez. But southpaws didn't bother the lefty-swinging Bonds. He dug in and waited for his pitch.

When he got the fastball he wanted, he crushed it. The ball traveled an estimated 480 feet. Like so many of Barry Bonds home runs, there was simply no doubt. He trotted around the bases with a smile on his face, knowing he had tied Mark McGwire and still had three games left to set a new mark.

"When [Wilfredo Rodriguez] threw the first pitch, I just was 'Wow!'" Barry said, afterward. "It's really rare when you see left-handers that throw harder than Billy Wagner or Randy Johnson. He doesn't throw as hard as them, but he's not that far off. When he threw the first pitch, I was like, 'Whoa, this guy throws harder than it looked when he was warming up.'"

But no pitcher could sneak a fastball past Bonds. He used a very light bat and generated tremendous bat speed. With his great eye, which enabled him to pick the ball up perhaps faster than any player in the game, he could turn on anyone. In a season when the expansionist Arizona Diamondbacks were the surprise team in baseball, led by their great one-two punch of Randy Johnson and Curt Schilling, Barry Bonds was taking over center stage. And he wasted no time in putting his own personal stamp on home run history.

The very next day, the Giants came home to Pac Bell to meet the L.A. Dodgers. Righthander Chan Ho Park was on the mound and in the first inning Bonds came up with two outs and none on. He went after a 1-0 pitch and sent the ball some 440 feet into McCovey Cove, the body of water beyond the right field stands named after former Giants slugger Willie McCovey. It was home run number 71, a new record, and he did it just three years after Mark McGwire set a standard that many people thought would never be broken. Not one to rest on his laurels, Bonds came up again leading off the third, and this time crushed a 1-1 pitch off Park for number 72. Again, the home fans went wild, and then the next day he played to another packed house and gave them yet another encore, belting number 73 off righty Dennis Springer for his final home run of the season.

What a year it had been. Not only had Bonds set an incredible home run record, adding 137 RBIs and a .328 batting average to his resume, but he set several other records as well. By hitting 73 home runs, Bonds has raised his career total from 494 to 567 in one season. That enabled him to surpass ten members of the 500 home run club—Eddie Murray, Mel Ott, Eddie Mathews, Ernie Banks, Ted Williams, Willie McCovey, Jimmie Foxx, Mickey Mantle, Mike Schmidt, and Reggie Jackson. He now trailed only Harmon Killebrew (573), Mark McGwire (583), Frank Robinson (586), Willie Mays (660), Babe Ruth (714), and Henry Aaron (755) on the all-time list.

And that still wasn't all. Bonds also became the oldest player ever at thirty-seven to lead either league in home runs, as well as the oldest player to ever hit 50, 60, and 70 home runs. He broke the Babe's record for walks in a season with 177, had the best on-base percentage (.515) in the National League since John McGraw's .547 way back in 1900, and also broke Ruth's single-season slugging percentage mark of .847 by putting together an incredible slugging mark of .863. And that still wasn't all. By hitting 73 home runs in 476 official at bats, Bonds set yet another record of hitting one home run every 6.52 times he stepped in and swung the bat. That's how incredible his season had been. Needless to say, Bonds would also win a record fourth Most Valuable Player Award after the season.

While Barry Bonds was the BIG home run story in 2001, he wasn't the only one. Sammy Sosa finished the year with 64 home runs, making him the only player in baseball history to hit 60 or more three different times. In third place was Luis Gonzalez of the Diamondbacks with 57, and he became another poster boy for the argument about a juiced baseball. Shawn Green of the Dodgers and Todd Helton of the Rockies were next at 49, while big Richie Sexson of the Brewers had 45 and Phil Nevin of the Padres slammed 41. New names were joining the party every year. In the American League, young Alex Rodriguez had his first 50-plus season with 52, while Jim Thome of Cleveland rapped 49. Rafael Palmeiro whacked 47, Troy Glaus and Manny Ramirez had 41, while Carlos Delgado slammed 39 and Jason Giambi hit 38. Total homers were at 5,458, just 135 fewer than the record set in 2000.

Getting back to Luis Gonzalez, he's another example of a good player who suddenly emerged as a top slugger. In his first full season of 1991 with Houston, Gonzalez hit 13 homers and drove in 69 runs while hitting .254. During the next three seasons he hit just 10, 15, and 8. Gonzalez split the 1995 season between Houston and the Cubs, hitting 13 homers. The next season, playing in the friendly confines of Wrigley Field he hit just 15. Then he returned to Houston for a year, hit 10 homers and, in 1998, spent a year in Detroit. During that homer happy season, he began to emerge with 23. Moving to Arizona in 1999, Gonzalez hit 26 homers and had his first 100-RBI season

Say Goodbye to Big Mac

One name was conspicuously missing from the great home run chase of 2001. Mark McGwire was the guy making the big home run news in 1998, 1999, and the early months of the 2000 season, when balls were flying out of stadiums at record pace and McGwire was hitting one every 5.7 at bats. But big Mac took a seat for most of the second half of the 2000 campaign with a case of patella tendinitis in his knee. He wound up playing in just eighty-nine games and hitting 32 home runs. He then had surgery during the off-season, fully expecting to return to full strength in 2001.

It didn't happen. The knee began barking again and McGwire was once more reduced to being a part-time player. He would get in just ninety-seven games and hit 29 more home runs in 299 at bats. Even worse was that he had just 19 addition hits besides his home runs for an anemic .187 batting average. When the Cardinals offered him a two-year, $30 million contract extension, big Mac thought it over and said no thanks. He took the other option. He decided to retire.

So after 2001, big Mac was gone, retiring with 583 home runs and with the memory of the feel-good season of 1998 and his many prodigious home runs. He also left with a record of hitting one home run every 10.6 at bats, besting the Babe's previous standard of one every 11.8 times up. Though he would virtually disappear from the game, take up golf, and refuse requests for interviews, McGwire's name would surface many times over the next few seasons as the specter of illegal steroid use settled over the game. Reporters would again write about the bottle of andro found in his locker in 1998, which he said he took to avoid injuries, and how he stopped taking it a year later only to see his body break down. But there's no denying his ability to hit long and frequent home runs, and play a major part in the home run revolution of the late 1990s. His 583 homers, and his 70 in 1998, will definitely get him a ticket into the Hall of Fame when he becomes eligible in 2006.

with 111, hitting .336 along the way. The next season he was at 31 homers and 114 RBIs and a .311 average. At the age of thirty-three, he was emerging as a home run hitter. But 57? That's what he did in 2001, adding 142 RBIs and a .325 average.

During the next two seasons, Luis Gonzalez would go back to hitting 28 and 26 homers and still driving in 100 runs. He had obviously become a very good hitter, but the fact that his home run numbers and slugging coincided with the seasons in which home run hitters topped the 5,000 mark can only lead to more speculation about the game and the baseball. Gonzalez, with his thin, wiry build, was never mentioned when speculation about performance-enhancing drugs became rampant, but in 2001 he produced a season that ranks with the greatest slugging performances of all time.

THE SUSPICIONS DEEPEN

The 2002 season saw a slight decrease in home runs to 5,059, just 399 fewer than 2001. But when big leaguers repeatedly slam more than 5,000 balls into the seats, it pretty much means that everyone is hitting them. Barry Bonds, at the age of thirty-eight, continued to be the most feared hitter in the game, to the point where pitchers were walking him more and more, giving him intentional passes, and trying to get him to bite at bad pitches. He wouldn't hit 73 home runs again, but in 2002 he did hit 46 despite a record 198 walks, and this time he also led the majors with a career best .370 batting average. In addition, he had a .799 slugging average, second best of his long career, so there was no slip in his play, especially with the bat. Bonds finished the season with 613 home runs. Only Willie Mays, the Babe, and Hank Aaron had ever hit more.

The Giants won the National League West that year and, in the playoffs, Bonds finally got the final monkey off his back. He had never hit well in the postseason, including three appearances with Pittsburgh and two with the Giants in 1997 and 2000. In fact, he had just a single home run in 97 at bats. But in 2002, he hit three in the Giants victory over the Braves in the division series, then one more in the team's win over St. Louis in the NLCS, and finally he hit four homers while batting .471 in a seven-game loss to the Anaheim Angels in the World Series. Though his team had lost, he set a post-season record by hitting eight home runs.

Sammy Sosa also continued his ride toward the Hall of Fame

with a league best 49 home runs in 2002, failing to reach 50 homers or more for a fifth consecutive season by just one. Bonds was next at 46, while Houston's Lance Berkman had 42, as did Shawn Green of the Dodgers. In the American League, Alex Rodriguez, who had signed a whopping, ten-year, $250 million contract with the Texas Rangers in 2001, led the American League with his best season, hitting 57 homers while driving home 142 runs. A-Rod had become one of the best, all-around players in the game. Jim Thome of Cleveland also joined the ever-increasing 50-home run club by blasting 52, while old reliable Rafael Palmeiro had 43 and Jason Giambi, who had signed a free-agent contract with the Yankees, hit 41.

By now, however, people had stopped counting. While all tests continued to say the ball was not juiced, many big league pitchers said it was *different*. One veteran pitcher said that you no longer could get the feeling you wanted on the ball by rubbing it up in your hands. The ball, a number of them said, seemed slicker, almost slippery. Others claimed the stitches were often inconsistent, some being wider than others, some very thin. And many pitchers said that beginning in 2000, the ball had a slickness to it that wasn't there before.

There were certainly big league pitchers who dominated and excelled during this time, guys like Roger Clemens, Randy Johnson, Greg Maddux, Curt Schilling, Pedro Martinez, Andy Pettitte, Tom Glavine, and others. Plus there were some great closers like Mariano Rivera, Troy Percival, and Eric Gagne, guys who could come in for the ninth inning and shut the door. More pitchers were using the split-finger fastball, which was first perfected by reliever Bruce Sutter, giving them a weapon pitchers from an earlier time didn't have. League batting averages, while somewhat higher, hadn't reached the stars the way home run totals had. So the biggest difference in the game of the twenty-first century continued to be the huge number of home runs.

Looking at the size of the players and the number of hitters who had gotten so much larger in body since they first came into the league, there was an almost inescapable conclusion being reached by many in and around the game. The reason for the proliferation of home runs wasn't so much that the ball was juiced, rather it was the players who were now juiced. More and more people pointed to illegal performance-enhancing drugs, such as anabolic steroids, as the culprit.

Baseball was not the only sport where there were problems with performance-enhancing substances. They had become an issue in international track-and-field competition, and certainly football was not without the problem, where size and strength were so important for success. It was becoming quite apparent that some players were using these substances. The question was, how many and which ones? At the time, Major League Baseball did not have a very strong testing policy. Random testing for any drugs had always been opposed by the Players Union. But when two former players—Jose Canseco and Ken Caminiti—came out publically and admitted that they has used steroids in their playing days, and then implied there were many others also using them, the screws were tightening. Many called for more testing and much harsher penalties for offenders.

In effect, the use of anabolic steroids and other performance-enhancing substances really equals cheating. In addition, these substances have potentially dangerous side effects that can hurt the user in later life. By taking these substances, a poor or average hitter will not suddenly become a good hitter or home run king. However, steroids do increase muscle mass and can give a hitter more bat speed. Increased bat speed, by its very nature, will allow the ball to travel further. The downside is that increased muscle mass puts more pressure on ligaments and tendons, which do not strengthen, and can lead to more injuries, especially pulls and tears.

Another thing that steroids do is shorten recovery time. They allow an athlete to work out very hard, then do it again without waiting the usual time for his body to rejuvenate. This can benefit the aging athlete who normally would need more days off and would wear down much faster than when he was young. In addition, the use of performance enhancers will simply give a player the confidence and belief that he can conquer the world. Mets outfielder Cliff Floyd addressed this very point.

"I've never taken the stuff, but talking to guys who have, they get a lot of extra confidence," Floyd said. "They think, 'When I hit the ball, it will go farther than when I hit it before.' They have this different attitude, like they're invincible, and they're just going to crush it. I think that's the real edge."

By 2003 it was pretty much of a foregone conclusion that the use of performance-enhancing drugs had permeated the sport. Home run totals would move up again, to 5,207, though no player would reach 50 for the first time since 1996. The one player who probably could have wasn't being pitched to as often. Barry Bonds continued his late-career assault on the record books by hitting another 45 home runs, giving him 658, putting him just two behind his godfather, Willie Mays. Bonds played in 130 games and was walked 148 times, so he had just 390 official at bats. He still managed a .341 batting average and .749 slugging percentage, which led to his third consecutive Most Valuable Player Award and a record sixth overall.

The league leaders in 2003 included Jim Thome, now with the Phils, who hit 47 to lead the National League. Bonds and Richie Sexson had 45, while the Braves Javy Lopez and young Albert Pujols of the Cards had 43 each. Sammy Sosa was still good enough to belt 40, while three players, Jeff Bagwell, Jim Edmonds, and Gary Sheffield, all had 39. In the American, A-Rod led again with 47, Carlos Delgado and Frank Thomas had 42 each, while Jason Giambi smacked 41. Veteran Rafael Palmeiro was still solid enough to hit 38, and second sacker Alfonso Soriano of the Yankees also had 38.

Soriano was an example of still yet another modern home run hitter. At 6'1", 180-pounds, he was very thin but muscular and wiry, and he generated great bat speed. The native of the Dominican Republic was just a natural hitter capable of producing home run power. More players like Soriano were maturing in the new game, swinging the light bats, many of which were now made from maple instead of the traditional ash, supposedly a more dense wood, and they were learning early how to get leverage and bat speed, and hit the ball a long way. With players like this coming into the majors each year, home run totals will probably stay high. Whether sluggers will ever hit 65, 70, or 75 home runs again remains to be seen.

The use of steroids had generated into a full-scale scandal by 2003. Every player who had become bigger over the years was subject to speculation. A guy like Frank Thomas, who was naturally big to begin with, as well as other clean players, called for more testing. They wanted a level playing field. After all, the big hitters still got the big contracts, and if a guy's numbers were inflated by the use of drugs, he could well get to the money first.

The story really began to reach the critical stage after the 2003 season. Major League Baseball announced in November that 5 to 7 percent of the drug tests collected during the past season were positive for steroids. That meant, by agreement, that testing could increase in 2004. A number of world-class athletes, including baseball's Barry Bonds, Gary Sheffield, and Jason Giambi, were also subpoenaed by a federal grand jury investigating the Bay Area Laboratory Co-Operative, or BALCO, a company that manufactured dietary supplements and had been suspected of supplying performance-enhancing drugs to a number of athletes.

"I think BALCO is the tip of the iceberg," said Steven Ungerleider, a sports psychologist who had written a book about the state-sponsored doping system in the former East Germany. "I think there are probably a dozen labs working with athletes and chemists to figure out designer drugs and not get caught."

It was already widely known that the majority of young athletes were willing to take a substance that would enable them to excel, to get a multimillion dollar contract, even though the evidence showed it may harm them or even shorten their lives. For young athletes, old age is an eternity away, and they just think of the money and glory that have come to be associated with modern sports. Taking drugs to enhance performance is a risk many seem willing to take.

At the beginning of the 2004 baseball season, however, a number of returning players looked noticeably smaller, and the media speculated that they had become alarmed and perhaps stopped taking the banned substances. With two random tests now allowed during the season, players simply didn't want to be caught. Meanwhile, some of baseball's all-time great sluggers were starting to speak their minds about the steroid controversy. Not surprisingly, one of them was none other than Mr. October, Reggie Jackson.

"Somebody definitely is guilty of taking steroids," Jackson said, just before spring training. "You can't be breaking records hitting 200 home runs in three or four seasons. The greatest hitters in the history of the game didn't do that."

"Henry Aaron never hit 50 in a season, so you're going to tell me that you're a greater hitter than Henry Aaron," Jackson continued. "Bonds hit 73 in 2001, and he would have hit 100 if they would have pitched to him. I mean, come on, now. There is no way you can outperform Aaron and Ruth and Mays at that level. There is a reason why the greatest players of all time have 500. Then there is that group that is above 550. There is a reason for that. Guys played nineteen, twenty, twenty-five years. They had 9,000 to 10,000 at bats, and it was the same for everybody."

"Now, all of a sudden, you're hitting 50 when you're forty."

The implication certainly was a reference to Bonds, who was doing things that no player over the age of thirty-five had ever done before. Not surprisingly, someone sought out Henry Aaron to ask his opinion. Aaron was never as outspoken as Reggie Jackson, and at age seventy Aaron was one of baseball's great elder statesmen as well as its home run champ. Asked specifically about what would happen if Bonds was proven to have used steroids, Aaron answered carefully.

"I'll let the public judge for themselves," he said. "I'm just hoping and praying nothing comes up. I admire Barry Bonds. Steroids or no steroids, he would have had a Hall of Fame career. At one time I thought Ken Griffey Jr. had the best chance to break my record, but injuries have hounded him. Barry

Bonds has done everything—hit home runs, steal bases, hit for average. He's practically carried his ball club on his back."

What Aaron said was true. Bonds was truly a great ball-player even before his late surge of home runs. But at this point in his career, only time would tell if anything could be proved. In fact, the steroid situation was a dilemma for baseball. If, for example, it was shown that a certain player had used steroids, could they really prove he had used them three or four seasons earlier when he might have had a career year or set a record? That would be extremely difficult. Baseball certainly couldn't put an asterisk alongside a home run record with the note that said, *possibly aided by performance-enhancing drugs.*

In 2004, the performance-enhancing cloud was heavier than ever. Before the season even began, some of baseball's top sluggers, including Barry Bonds, had to deny repeatedly that they were using steroids. Bonds's longtime friend and personal trainer, Greg Anderson, had been implicated in the BALCO scandal, and that made more people look twice at baseball's top home run hitter. Bonds was still dealing with the death of his father, Bobby, which occurred during the 2003 season. Now, when he came to camp, everyone was asking about his size, how he had changed from a 185-pound rookie to maybe a 230-pounder now.

"I'm about 225, maybe heavier," Bonds said. "People in my gym in San Francisco—where I go five days a week, from a couple of weeks after the season to spring training—say they wish they could tell the media how hard I work in the gym. I tell them, 'Don't worry about it, I'm a big boy.' I'll just let my bat do all the talking."

No one doubted Bonds's work ethic or work habits. Like so many contemporary players in their late thirties, he worked extra hard to stay in shape and keep his game at a high level. Players from an earlier time were often on the downside by their mid-thirties. In today's game, there were more players than ever keeping their skills at a high level for a longer time. But there was also little doubt that steroids could help a player stay stronger and work out more. Mario J. Vassalo, a former semi-

Injuries Slow Junior

When Ken Griffey Jr. hit 16 home runs as a twenty-year-old rookie in 1989, he was heralded as baseball's next great superstar. Soon, Junior was living up to that label. From 1993 through 2000, with the exception of an injury which shortened 1995, Griffey hit 45, 40, 49, 56, 56, 48, and 40 home runs. He was also a .300 hitter and the best centerfielder in baseball. Traded to his hometown Cincinnati Reds in 2000, Junior had 40 homers and 118 RBIs in his first National League season. At the age of thirty-one, he had already hit 438 home runs. If he could average 40 home runs a year for another eight seasons, he would have 758 home runs, and even Henry Aaron said he thought Junior had the best chance of breaking his all-time home run record.

But beginning in 2001, Junior had his career sabotaged by injury, and most of the injuries were simply the result of playing hard—diving for balls in the outfield, climbing the wall to make a catch, running as hard as he could on the bases. From 2001 through the 2004 season, Junior played in 111, 70, 53, and 83 games, hitting a total of just 63 home runs. He managed to hit number 500 and 501 in 2004 before a torn hamstring ended his season. But without the injuries, Griffey undoubtedly would have been over 600 and counting. That's how good he's been. To avoid further leg injuries, he may have to start playing some first base in 2005. He'll be thirty-six years old at the start of the new season, and hopefully his sweet swing will produce many more homers before he's done. But by losing the better part of five seasons (including 1995) to injury, Ken Griffey Jr. probably lost his opportunity to be at least one of the top three sluggers of all time.

pro football player who once used steroids, had since become a lead researcher at a Central Michigan University study of the addictive effects of steroids. He described their use this way.

"From my own personal experience," he said, "and thirty-six of the thirty-eight guys I interviewed said the same thing: once you start taking steroids, within the first three days, it's a different life you're leading. You feel invincible, on top of the world. Within two weeks, you feel your workouts change. You used to do an hour and a half and get tired. You can change to two hours a day and feel ready to go back to work and do the same thing again. And the pump you get, you don't want to lose it."

Some of steroid's side effects described by the experts were truly frightening. Vassallo said that some athletes experienced a personality change—"'roid rage," as it sometimes called. He said he never had any rages, but "I was just more on edge over little things." He said that a person on steroids "already had a short fuse, [the steroids] enhanced it." Men could also experience shrinking of the testicles, though they return to normal size once the person stops using steroids. Impotence was another side effect. Long-term use could result in raised cholesterol levels and elevated blood pressure, which create the risk of heart attack and stroke. The liver can also malfunction and adolescents taking steroids can stop growing because the growth plates in the bones close permanently. But because the most devastating side effects may not show up for years, young athletes simply did not think in those terms.

Others were also jumping on the bandwagon. Senator John McCain was one of the most vocal members of Congress addressing the question of performance-enhancing drugs.

"Sports organizations that allow athletes to cheat through weak drug testing regimes are aiding and abetting cheaters," Senator McCain said. "Each of you, and particularly major league baseball, has a legitimacy problem. As your athletes get bigger and stronger, the credibility of your product in the eyes of the public gets weaker."

So the pressure was increasing on baseball and its players when the 2004 seasoned opened. Ironically, no one took off on a home run pace that would threaten any records. The big stories that year were the Yankees–Red Sox rivalry and the continued excellence of Barry Bonds. The Yanks had made a deal with Texas to acquire Alex Rodriguez, called by many the best overall player in the game. They did this after the Sox failed to close a deal for A-Rod a few months earlier. Rodriguez, an all-star shortstop, agreed to switch to third base so he could play alongside the Yanks all-star shortstop and captain, Derek Jeter. The Sox had acquired righthander Curt Schilling, one of the best big-game pitchers in the league, and a guy who had starred for Arizona against the Yanks in the 2001 World Series. There was no love lost between the two ballclubs and whenever they met it was tantamount to war.

As for Bonds, he was starting the season with 658 home runs, just two homers away from Willie Mays's 660 and third place on the all-time list. He hit his 659th the first week of the season at Houston, and now everyone waited for the next one. Willie Mays, who had played in the same outfield with Bonds's father, wanted to be there and came to every game, traveling first to Houston and then to San Diego. Now they were back in San Francisco to face Milwaukee. When he came to bat in the fifth inning to face the Brewers' Matt Kinney, Bonds hadn't hit a homer in 24 at bats. He worked the count to 3-1, then turned on an inside fastball and hit a long drive over the right-field stands and into McCovey Cove for home run number 660.

"It is great to be home," Bonds said, after his homer helped the Giants win, 7-5. "This is the best feeling, right now, the icing on the cake. It was like a weight lifted off of my shoulders."

The very next night, Bonds pulled ahead of the Say Hey Kid, blasting the 661st home run of his career in the seventh inning. This one was on a 1-2 slider from reliever Ben Ford, and it sailed some 448 feet into McCovey Cove. In the five year history of the Giants ballpark, now known as SBC Park, 29 of the 38 home runs that have landed in the Cove were hit by Barry Bonds. After the game, Bonds paid tribute to his godfather.

"It's Willie, it's just Willie," he said. "It's all about keeping it in the family. I still feel like he's the greatest player of all time."

The pressure of passing Mays gone, Bonds preceded to have another great year. In fact, as he approached his fortieth birthday in July, he was being treated as no hitter ever had in the history of the game. The reason was simple. Opposing teams were in total fear of him when he came to the plate. They were walking him repeatedly, giving him more intentional walks than any player ever before him. He was walked intentionally in all kinds of situations, including with the bases empty and with the bases full. A manager would rather walk him with the sacks loaded and concede one run rather than risk him clearing the bases with one swing of the bat. Kevin Kennedy, the former manager of the Texas Rangers and Boston Red Sox, and now a baseball analyst, perhaps put it into the clearest perspective when he said:

"Barry Bonds is the only player in the game who changes the way you manage from the very first inning."

It was a season in which the shadow cast by the steroid scandal would not go away, and a season in which Barry Bonds continued his run to greatness. On Friday, September 17, the Giants were hosting the Padres at SBC field. His first time up, pitcher Jake Peavy hit him in the back. He came up again in the fourth, and Peavy's first pitch was on the outside corner for a strike. Peavy put the next pitch outside as well, but this time Bonds went out and got it. This one he didn't pull. Rather he hit a sharp, rising liner toward left. Left fielder Ryan Klesko raced to the wall, leaped, but couldn't get it. It just made the seats for Bonds 42nd home run of the year. More importantly, it was the 700th of his career, allowing him to reach a milestone that only Babe Ruth and Henry Aaron had reached before him.

When the year ended, Bonds had 45 home runs and 703 lifetime. He also put together a truly amazing season. He won the National League batting title with a .362 average and drove in 101 runs to go with his 45 homers. And he did it in just 373 official at bats. Opposing pitchers walked him a record 232 times, with more than 100 of them being intentional. Because of all the walks, he had an incredible on-base percentage of .609 and a slugging average of .812. There was little doubt that at the age of forty, he was still the most dangerous offensive force in the game.

Despite the continuing steroid controversy, big league hitters still slammed 5,451 home runs, the fourth highest total in history and the biggest number since 2001. The major league leader was the Dodgers' Adrian Beltre, a twenty-five-year-old who had a breakout year with 48 homers. Big Adam Dunn of Cincinnati, another twenty-five-year-old, looked as if he might be from the Dave Kingman school of home run hitting. Dunn had 46 four baggers while striking out 195 times and hitting just .266. Albert Pujols of St. Louis also had 46, and after Bonds's 45, Jim Edmonds of St. Louis and Jim Thome of Philadelphia had 42 each.

In the American, Manny Ramirez of Boston led with 43, while the only others to reach 40 were Paul Konerko of Chicago and David Ortiz of Boston with 41 each. Vladimir Guerrero, now playing for the Angels, would be the MVP with 39 homers as just a part of a great all-around year. To no one's surprise, the National League's Most Valuable Player for a fourth straight year and record seventh time overall was Barry Bonds. And when the Boston Red Sox capped an unbelievable season by overcoming the Yankees in the ALCS after being down three games to none, then went on to sweep the Cardinals for their first World Series triumph in eighty-six years, baseball was back on top. The sport set a new attendance record, completely rebounding from the disastrous strike of 1994 and having its most successful season.

Most of the talk during and after 2004 was about Barry Bonds. Speculation about steroid use was part of it, but his great achievements after the age of thirty-five was another. There was little doubt that Bonds was baseball's greatest all-around hitter from the age of thirty-five to forty. From 1999, the year he turned thirty-five, through the 2004 season, Barry Bonds hit 292 home runs. As mentioned earlier, many of baseball's earlier stars faded sooner. By way of comparison, let's look at the number of home runs some of baseball's other great sluggers would have had if they had been able to belt 292 after the age of thirty-five.

Henry Aaron, the all-time leader at 755, was also very good in his later years. Hammerin' Hank hit 245 home runs after he turned thirty-five. Had it been 292, he would have finished with 802 home runs. The Babe, for his high-living and sometimes destructive lifestyle, was such a talent that he still hit 198 homers after the age of thirty-five. Had he been able to do what Bonds has done, the Babe would have finished with 808 four baggers instead of 714. Willie Mays had 155 homers after the age of thirty-five. Make it 292 and the Say Hey Kid would have fin-

Albert Pujols, the Next Great Slugger

Tied for second in the 2004 home run race with 46 was Albert Pujols of the St. Louis Cardinals. Pujols was just twenty-four years old and already in his fourth full season. What he has accomplished so far is worth special mention. A 6′3″, 210-pound first baseman from the Dominican Republic, Pujols joined the Cards in 2001, won a starting job immediately, and proceeded to become the National League Rookie of the Year. He hit 37 home runs that year, drove in 130 runs, and had a batting average of .329. That was just for starters.

The next year, this strong, right-handed hitter had 34 homers, 127 RBIs, and a .314 average. In year three, 2003, Pujols collected 212 hits, whacked 43 homers, drove home 124 runs, while leading the league in hitting with a .359 average. And in the Cardinals pennant-winning season of 2004, he had 46 homers, 123 RBIs, and a .331 batting average. He also struck out a career low 52 times, showing a great and selective batting eye. In his first four seasons, Albert Pujols not only has 160 home runs, but he has also hit over .300, scored more than 100 runs each year, and has driven home more than 100, the only player in baseball history to accomplish that.

Pujols just seems to be a natural. He has never been mentioned in the steroid speculation and continues to get better and better. Right now, he not only looks to be baseball's next great slugger, but he also is a great all-around hitter in the tradition of Ruth and Gehrig, and the great ones who have come between.

ished his career with 797 home runs. The great Frank Robinson hit 136 after the age of thirty-five to finish with 586. But had he walloped 292, he would have had 742 home runs to his credit.

Harmon Killebrew, who had 573 homers, hit just 86 after turning thirty-five. Had the Killer been able to duplicate Bonds, he would have hit 779 home runs in his lifetime. Mark McGuire turned thirty-five at the tail end of the 1998 season, when he hit his epic 70 home runs. Not counting that season, big Mac would hit 126 more before his retirement to make 583. Had he hit 292 like Bonds, McGwire would have finished with 749 home runs.

The two greatest sluggers who faltered at the earliest ages

were Mickey Mantle and Jimmie Foxx. Mantle, because of high-living and injuries, managed just 40 homers once he reached the age of thirty-five. Had the Mick been able to hit 292 and add them to his 536, his final total would have been 788 home runs. Then there is the case of Foxx. Old Double-X was definitely a great slugger, a guy who had 500 home runs by the time he was thirty-three years old. That is when his hard-drinking ways began to get the better of him. Amazingly, Jimmie Foxx hit only seven home runs after he reached the age of thirty-five. Had he been able to do what Barry Bonds has done, he would be the all-time home run champ with an incredible 819 four bag blasts!

Of course, these numbers will soon change because Barry Bonds is not yet done. He indicated after the 2004 season that he would probably play at least two more years. If he can keep close to his pace of the last few seasons, that should be enough to allow him to take over the top spot from Aaron. So stayed tuned.

WHAT'S NEXT?

There are a lot of veteran baseball people writers, former players, and managers—who feel that while home run totals will stay high, it may be a long time, if ever, before someone ascends to the 60-70 home run level again. The two factors that could prevent this are the baseballs and increased pressure to rid the game of performance-enhancing substances. Though baseball has steadfastly denied it, there have been several seasons in which the huge and sudden increase in home run totals almost has to point to the baseball. It happened in 1977. There were 2,235 homers hit the year before and 2,956 homers hit the year after. But in 1977, 3,644 baseballs left the yard.

Ten years later it happened again. In 1986, hitters banged out 3,813 home runs. Two years later they hit just 3,180. But in-between, during the 1987 season, a record 4,458 home runs left major league ballparks. After the strike of 1994, baseball attendance dropped dramatically. In 1995, just 4,081 homers were hit in a season eighteen games shorter than usual. But a year later, in 1996, a new record of 4,962 home runs were hit, and two years later, when McGwire and Sosa captivated the baseball world, major league hitters topped 5,000 for the first time. At that point, many feel there was a confluence of factors—a period when the juiced baseball met the juiced player.

Now, the questions about steroids may finally be answered. Shortly after the 2004 season ended, a story broke in the *San Francisco Chronicle* when the newspaper published what they said was leaked testimony from the BALCO hearings. In that testimony, New York Yankees slugger Jason Giambi purportedly told the grand jury that he had injected himself with human growth hormone in 2003 and had used steroids for at least three seasons. Ironically, Giambi had an illness and injury-filled 2004 season, a season in which he looked markedly thinner than in past years. That wasn't all.

It was also reported that both Barry Bonds and the Yanks' Gary Sheffield told the grand jury they had used substances called "the clear" and "the cream," which they had obtained from BALCO. Both players said they didn't know these substances contained steroids, but that they thought they were nutritional supplements. Those admissions were greeted with some skepticism by many who feel professional athletes, more than anyone, know what they are putting into and using on their bodies. The admissions erased any doubts that many ballplayers had been or were using performance-enhancing substances.

Baseball responded quickly. Commissioner Bud Selig and the Players Union got together on a new, tougher testing program that would allow many more random tests both during and after the season, with increased penalties, starting with a ten-day suspension without pay for first-time offenders. It has apparently finally reached a point where baseball officials as well as the players seem bent on cleaning up the sport and leveling the playing field.

How will this affect the records that have been set since 1998 as well as the players who raised the home run bar to places most thought it would never go? Obviously, there cannot be another asterisk. The records will stand for the simple reason that it is almost impossible to prove with absolute certainty which players were doing what and when. It will simply be a matter of public perception. Are Mark McGwire, Sammy Sosa, and Barry Bonds greater sluggers than Henry Aaron, Babe Ruth, or Willie Mays? That's your call. Don't forget, Mark McGwire hit 49 home runs as a rookie in 1987, and Barry Bonds was a Hall of Fame caliber player long before he reached the age of thirty-five and began slamming homers all over the lot.

One thing is certain. The home run is here to stay. Fans loved it back in 1920 when the Babe showed everyone just how far a baseball could be hit and how often he could put it in the seats. There has always been a special fascination with the big slugger, the guy who is challenging a record or hitting tape-measure shots and is a threat to scald the baseball every time he comes to the plate. What do today's highlight films usually show?—an electrifying slam dunk, a 75-yard touchdown pass, or a 500-foot home run. It's the kind of world we live in and young players now arriving in the game know that the money is on the end of a 35 or 40 home run season.

Sure, there will still be players like Ichiro Suzuki of the Mariners, who broke an eighty-four-year-old record by slamming out 262 hits in 2004. And there will be pitchers like Roger Clemens and Randy Johnson, who keep winning big into their forties, and relievers like Mariano Rivera and Eric Gagne, who can close the door on everyone. But there will also be young players like Alfonso Soriano, Mark Teixeira, and Albert Pujols who come along with the innate ability to hit the ball into the seats. They don't need doctored baseballs or performance-enhancing substances to do it. The difference is they may only do it forty-five times a year instead of sixty-five times.

Let's face it. There is something in baseball now that will probably never change. Nothing gets fans more excited than seeing their favorite slugger come up with the game on the line in the late innings and proceed to hit one high and deep to the far reaches of the stadium as the announcer screams, "IT'S OUTTA HERE!"

Appendix 1: The Top Fifty Single Season Home Run Hitters

Player and Team	Year	Homers
1. Barry Bonds, San Francisco	2001	73
2. Mark McGwire, St. Louis	1998	70
3. Sammy Sosa, Chicago Cubs	1998	66
4. Mark McGwire, St. Louis	1999	65
5. Sammy Sosa, Chicago Cubs	2001	64
6. Sammy Sosa, Chicago Cubs	1999	63
7. Roger Maris, New York Yankees	1961	61
8. Babe Ruth, New York Yankees	1927	60
9. Babe Ruth, New York Yankees	1921	59
10. Mark McGwire, Oakland/St. Louis	1997	58
11. Hank Greenberg, Detroit	1938	58
12. Jimmie Foxx, Philadelphia A's	1932	58
13. Alex Rodriguez, Texas	2002	57
14. Luis Gonzalez, Arizona	2001	57
15. Ken Griffey Jr., Seattle	1998	56
16. Ken Griffey Jr., Seattle	1997	56
17. Hack Wilson, Chicago Cubs	1930	56
18. Mickey Mantle, New York Yankees	1961	54
19. Ralph Kiner, Pittsburgh	1949	54
20. Babe Ruth, New York Yankees	1928	54
21. Babe Ruth, New York Yankees	1920	54
22. Jim Thome, Cleveland	2002	52
23. Alex Rodriguez, Texas	2001	52
24. Mark McGwire, Oakland	1996	52
25. George Foster, Cincinnati	1977	52
26. Willie Mays, San Francisco	1965	52
27. Mickey Mantle, New York Yankees	1956	52
28. Cecil Fielder, Detroit	1990	51

29. Willie Mays, New York Giants	1955	51
30. Ralph Kiner, Pittsburgh	1947	51
31. Johnny Mize, New York Giants	1947	51
32. Sammy Sosa, Chicago Cubs	2000	50
33. Greg Vaughn, San Diego	1998	50
34. Brady Anderson, Baltimore	1996	50
35. Albert Belle, Cleveland	1995	50
36. Jimmie Foxx, Boston	1938	50
37. Sammy Sosa, Chicago Cubs	2002	49
38. Barry Bonds, San Francisco	2000	49
39. Albert Belle, Chicago White Sox	1998	49
40. Larry Walker, Colorado	1997	49
41. Mark McGwire, Oakland	1987	49
42. Andre Dawson, Chicago Cubs	1987	49
43. Harmon Killebrew, Minnesota	1969	49
44. Frank Robinson, Baltimore	1969	49
45. Harmon Killebrew, Minnesota	1964	49
46. Willie Mays, San Francisco	1962	49
47. Ted Kluszewski, Cincinnati	1954	49
48. Lou Gehrig, New York Yankees	1936	49
49. Lou Gehrig, New York Yankees	1934	49
50. Babe Ruth, New York Yankees	1930	49

Appendix 2: The Top Fifty Lifetime Home Run Hitters through 2004

Player	Years	Homers
1. Henry Aaron	1954–1976	755
2. Babe Ruth	1914–1935	714
3. Barry Bonds	1986–present	703
4. Willie Mays	1951–1973	660
5. Frank Robinson	1956–1976	586
6. Mark McGwire	1987–2001	583
7. Sammy Sosa	1989–present	574
8. Harmon Killebrew	1954–1975	573
9. Reggie Jackson	1967–1987	563
10. Rafael Palmeiro	1986–present	551
11. Mike Schmidt	1972–1989	548
12. Mickey Mantle	1951–1968	536
13. Jimmie Foxx	1925–1945	534
14. Willie McCovey	1959–1980	521
15. Ted Williams	1939–1960	521
16. Ernie Banks	1953–1971	512
17. Eddie Mathews	1952–1968	512
18. Mel Ott	1926–1947	511
19. Eddie Murray	1977–1997	504
20. Ken Griffey Jr.	1989–present	501
21. Lou Gehrig	1923–1939	493
22. Fred McGriff	1986–present	493
23. Stan Musial	1941–1963	475
24. Willie Stargell	1962–1982	475
25. Dave Winfield	1973–1995	465
26. Jose Canseco	1985–2001	462
27. Carl Yastrzemski	1961–1983	452
28. Jeff Bagwell	1991–present	446

29. Dave Kingman	1971–1986	442
30. Andre Dawson	1976–1996	438
31. Frank Thomas	1990–present	436
32. Juan Gonzalez	1989–present	434
33. Cal Ripken Jr.	1981–2001	431
34. Billy Williams	1959–1976	426
35. Jim Thome	1991–present	423
36. Gary Sheffield	1988–present	415
37. Darrell Evans	1969–1989	414
38. Duke Snider	1947–1964	407
39. Andres Galarraga	1985–present	399
40. Al Kaline	1953–1974	399
41. Dale Murphy	1976–1993	398
42. Joe Carter	1983–1998	396
43. Graig Nettles	1967–1988	390
44. Manny Ramirez	1993–present	390
45. Johnny Bench	1967–1983	389
46. Dwight Evans	1972–1991	385
47. Harold Baines	1980–2001	384
48. Frank Howard	1958–1973	382
49. Jim Rice	1974–1989	382
50. Albert Belle	1989–2000	381
50. Alex Rodriguez	1994–present	381

Index of Names